- 3 -

YOUR
TEENAGER
IS NOT
CRAZY

YOUR TEENAGER IS NOT CRAZY

UNDERSTANDING YOUR TEEN'S BRAIN CAN MAKE YOU A BETTER PARENT

DR. JERAMY AND JERUSHA CLARK

BakerBooks

a division of Baker Publishing Group
Grand Rapids, Michigan

Published by Baker Books
a division of Baker Publishing Group
PO Box 6287, Grand Rapids, MI 49516–6287
www.bakerbooks.com

Printed in the United States of America

Library of Congress Cataloging-in-Publication Data is on file at the Library of Congress, Washington, DC.

ISBN 9780801018763

16 17 18 19 20 21 22   7 6 5 4 3 2 1

To our precious teenage daughters,

Jocelyn Alexandra,
creator of fabulous fan fiction, gorgeous dress designs, and incredible artwork. The moment you entered the world you changed our lives forever and for better. PS: Though we would miss you like crazy, you'd be a great companion for The Doctor.

Jasmine Alyssa,
amazing gymnast, fantastic spa proprietor, and mastermind behind the "Bubble Theory." "Teenagers are like bubbles. If you touch them too hard, they will pop. If the bubble pops, all their anger is let out on you. If you continue to guide the bubble and lead it in the right direction, out of harm's way, it will continue to bubble and grow."

Contents

Foreword

Your Teenager Is Not Crazy is the first book in the Christian market to so thoughtfully integrate the latest in neuroscience with God's timeless truth. It is a landmark book that will help parents make sense out of the changes happening in their teens as they mature. What is so wonderful about *Your Teenager Is Not Crazy* is that it is born out of the Clarks' years of daily ministry and a passion to help teenagers, including their own, grow deeper in Christ while learning to live healthy lives—body, soul, and spirit. Jeramy and Jerusha help parents understand that they cannot separate adolescent brain development from soul development. If the brain of a teen is not working right, their spiritual development will be hampered. What is exciting to me is the emphasis on helping parents understand the remarkable uniqueness of their child's brain. What works to motivate one teen will not work to motivate another teen. Yet if you understand the uniqueness of how God has wired your teen and learn to work with that child as God created them, you can help them optimize and reach the potential God has wired into them. This book will help you do just that.

You will enjoy learning a great deal as you read through each chapter. *Your Teenager Is Not Crazy* will deepen your understanding of the inner world of your teen. An added benefit: it will help you make sense out of your own adolescent years! Tough issues like sexuality are addressed in an insightful manner that will help bring clarity to what can be a confusing and bewildering time for both parent and teen. As you read this book, you will become excited and passionate about the reality that God has uniquely wired your teen's brain for a relationship with Him. You'll also be excited and empowered by the practical strategies that Jeramy and Jerusha share.

Your Teenager Is Not Crazy is not only a book you'll *enjoy* reading; you'll actually want to buy it by the case to give to youth leaders, friends, and relatives! God will use it to help guide you through the exciting adolescent years of your teen's developing brain—which means your teen's developing soul. You will be grateful for the time you invest reading this groundbreaking book and the steps you take in implementing the insights and practical strategies.

Blessings!

Dr. Earl Henslin, PsyD,
author of *This Is Your Brain on Joy*
and *This Is Your Brain on Love*

Preface

If you ask parents to describe the teenage years, words like *crazy, confusing, frustrating, scary,* and *out of control* will likely crop up, as might—though perhaps less frequently—descriptors such as *exciting, adventurous,* and *exhilarating.* Research indicates that regardless of socioeconomic background, race, or location, parents of teens experience a relatively consistent set of emotions that leave many perplexed and exhausted.

Perform a similar exercise by inviting emerging adults to describe the years of their adolescence, and a fascinating trend emerges. The very same adjectives—describing the good, the bad, and the totally baffling—are used by those recently in the throes of their formative years to depict the tumult of their teenage lives.

A myriad of explanations has been set forth to decipher this perplexing phenomenon: adolescents seem out of their mind at some point, if not for the entirety of their teenage years. Vibrant one moment and sullenly apathetic the next, engaging in risky and impulsive behaviors one day and espousing profound reflections on life, relationships, and faith the next, teenagers confound parents, who wonder, *Who is this alien in my child's skin? Why did she stop smiling?*

Why is he angry all the time? What were they thinking? What in the world do I do?

One explanation—the one most prominent when we were teenagers—goes as follows: teenagers are a raging ball of hormones, and the best parents can do is buckle up, hang on for dear life, and pray that the entire roller coaster cart of their adolescent's life doesn't spontaneously jump off the track, explode, or get confiscated by federal authorities.

In this paradigm, hormones explained why guys were less mature than girls, why they seemed obsessed with some things and clueless about others, and why they did things like turn fire hoses on their biology teachers (not that Jeramy ever did that). This theory told parents of adolescent girls that hormones accounted for the outbursts of violent tears, the desire of their daughters to date the most ridiculous young men imaginable, and hours spent in the bathroom attempting to wrestle hair, makeup, and acne into submission.

According to the latest neurobiological research, however, hormones are only one piece of a much larger puzzle. The good news? You don't have to figure out how to predict your teenager's behavior based on biochemicals. Understanding basic physiological facts is important, but this book will enable you to see your teenager as more than an out-of-control hormoniac.

Another misconception popularized by the media is that teens experience a form of "temporary insanity" while their brains develop. Because their brains are immature, their behavior will be irresponsible. There's not much you can do but sigh deeply, try to be patient, and wait until your adolescent "grows up," hoping that no harm will come to your child (or other people!) because your teen is half-baked.

Radical neurological changes *do* occur during adolescence, and understanding them *is* crucial, but—as you might infer from the title of this book—what we now know about the brain doesn't support the notion that your teenager will be insane until further notice. Hear us loud and clear: your teenager is *not* crazy.

Furthermore, we cannot view adolescent brain development simply as a process of moving from immaturity to maturity. Indeed, because of the progressive remodeling of the brain during this period, the teen years can be an amazing season of cultivating creativity, self-awareness, and passion for the things that really matter.

If you're interested in navigating your child's adolescent years well, this book will equip you to understand the body, mind, and soul of teenagers. You'll also discover insights about yourself! Everyone benefits. So, if you're ready and willing, let's go!

Introduction

Some years ago, we discovered a leak in the foundation beneath our kitchen. It required the complete demolition of our countertop, sink, and a good deal of cabinetry. For weeks (which seemed like years), water to that area was cut off, meaning meals had to be prepared on makeshift surfaces and dishes had to be washed in a bathtub. As electrical wiring was reconfigured, the power was shut down. Remodeling is *not* easy.

Anyone who's spent time near a construction site—whether a large-scale project or an in-home remodel—recognizes factors common to all building or renovation: it's messy, it's time-consuming, and it always costs more than you think it should. Often an element of danger exists. Risks may be necessary. Mistakes are made—that's guaranteed. Frustrations abound. Relationships are strained. Why would anyone choose to suffer this?

Why? Because on the other side is a space more beautiful, more efficient, or more integrated. Knowing that what waits on the other side is not only new but also *really good* helps builders and remodelers everywhere get through tough days of sawing, sanding, wiring, and plumbing. Our amazing, renovated kitchen never could have magically appeared. The process had to be endured. In order for it not to drive us crazy, it also had to be embraced.

What if your body was a construction zone? Wouldn't you expect significant challenges? Wouldn't the goal be to emerge stronger and more resilient? Do you think you might be willing to endure a lot if you knew that something *great* was in store?

Now, imagine how you'd feel knowing your child's brain had to be progressively remodeled to develop a healthy adult mind. Along with the trials, wouldn't you be on the lookout for triumphs too? Wouldn't you feel more compassionate when your child was confused or frustrated by the project, especially if you knew the proverbial power was offline?

These aren't merely theoretical questions. Indeed, neurobiological studies show that every adolescent brain goes under construction between the ages of approximately twelve and twenty-four. *Hold on*, you may be thinking. *You're telling me that every teenage brain is being remodeled for more than a decade?*

Yes.

Until relatively recently, we couldn't see what went on inside the brains of live subjects (and let's be honest: it's a good thing no one tried!). Now, thanks to fMRIs (functional magnetic resonance imaging) and other forms of brain imaging, clinicians can evaluate the inner workings of the mind, observing that what we previously assumed about brain development formed a very incomplete picture.

For many years, scientists believed the human brain developed primarily between birth and age six. While it's true that the brain reaches over 90 percent of its *structural size* by the sixth year of a child's life, we now know that the brain undergoes dramatic and essential *internal development* in the years leading up to and throughout adolescence.

During childhood, the brain experiences explosive neurological growth. Much like a flourishing tree growing more branches, a child's brain establishes new connections and pathways as it matures. During the years prior to adolescence, millions of brain cells develop and begin to mature, enabling children to acquire knowledge at a wonderfully rapid rate. This explains in part why children learn certain skills so readily. Like "little sponges," they absorb all the world has to offer, stretching their brains in new ways every day.

The explosive growth of neurons during childhood slows as puberty approaches. Ultimately—somewhere between the ages of eleven (for girls) and twelve and a half (for boys)—the brain shifts course and begins to prune neurons, cutting back unused brain pathways. Pruning isn't the only radical change happening, however. Those neural highways that remain are strengthened in a process called myelination, during which a protective layering insulates neurons, improving the speed and efficiency of cognitive processing. Pruning and myelination continue throughout adolescence and result in what scientists describe as a wholesale, progressive remodeling of the brain.

Okay, you may be thinking. *That's neat, but what does this have to do with me?*

If you're the parent of a teenager, it has everything to do with you.

Do you want to know why teens do what they do? Do you want to communicate with your children in clear and compassionate ways? Many bizarre and baffling teenage behaviors become intelligible as we learn what's going on in the brain and how it impacts emotions and relationships, as well as how spiritual truths can revolutionize the experience of the teenage years for parents and children alike.

Teenagers Aren't Crazy; They're Just under Construction

Adolescents undergo a comprehensive remodeling of the brain, and—as noted earlier—messes and mistakes abound during renovation projects. At different points in the process, the plumbing or electricity may be offline. In a similar manner, portions of an adolescent's brain that are "under construction" may give the impression that your teenager is mentally "offline."

Here's one example: In early adolescence, neurons at the back of the brain are pruned. One of the first neural structures to undergo remodeling is the cerebellum, which directs—among other things—balance and coordination. Ever wonder why middle schoolers are so awkward? Knowing that the portion of your teenager's brain that coordinates balance is periodically "offline" while it's being remodeled can give you grace during your teen's awkward stages. As we'll see throughout this book, a basic understanding of your teen's brain also provides insights to help you parent well.

Let's start with two general and essential principles:

1. **Choices matter.** Teenage brain remodeling operates on a "use it or lose it" principle. The neural pathways your teen uses become stronger; those neglected are pruned away. Pioneering neuroscientist Dr. Jay Giedd sums it up this way: "If a teen is doing music or sports or academics, those are the cells and connections that will be hardwired. If they're lying on the couch or playing video games . . . those are the cells and connections that are going to survive."[1]

2. **Connections matter too.** In Dr. Giedd's words, "neurons that fire together, wire together." While the adolescent brain is being pruned and myelinated, it also becomes more interconnected and specialized. Somewhat akin to switching from dial-up internet to broadband, the brain increases its speed of transmission and ability to integrate information. Eventually, your teen's brain becomes a super-fast information highway. This is amazing! It's also limiting. In order to drive on a highway at eighty miles per hour, you have to sacrifice the option of changing direction whenever you want. Similarly, with fewer but faster neural pathways, adolescents' brains become progressively less open. They move toward specialization and integration.

Helping your teen learn to choose well is incredibly important. What your adolescent is exposed to will change him or her—dramatically. Choices determine what kind of connections and neural superhighways will exist.

In each chapter of this book we'll explore a common statement teenagers make in light of what's happening in an adolescent's brain and how that plays out in thoughts and emotions. Spiritual truths will equip us with understanding and for action. Each chapter closes with a practical tip and/or topic of discussion.

One word of caution: this book won't teach you how to control your teen's behavior. The only person you can control is yourself. People often say this, yet few actually work to change themselves, trusting that others will change as a result. Somehow, when it comes to our children, we think that applying the right formula will ensure that our home will be at peace.

This isn't a teenage behavior modification book. Instead, this book seeks to transform your understanding so that you can parent more effectively and compassionately. As you model growth and change, your teen *will* notice. Why? Because God has designed the world with this truth embedded at every level: everything is changed when you change.

Take Proverbs 15:1, for instance. "A gentle answer deflects anger, but harsh words make tempers flare" (NLT). When your teen is angry, you have a choice. You can answer calmly and kindly, or you can return wrath for wrath. You *can* choose how you respond, no matter how you feel. In chapter 8, "Why Are You Freaking Out?," we'll share astounding physical facts undergirding the spiritual truth that when you control your anger, everything changes.

This doesn't mean parents should excuse bad behavior "because of biology," or that responding with gentleness will reduce your authority or lessen the chances that your teenager will "get" what you're trying to communicate. Instead, God shows us that the best way to influence others is by being transformed ourselves.

Each chapter will demonstrate how God weaves his truth into our very biology. It's absolutely magnificent! There's so much to cover, so let's head right to the construction zone: the marvelous teenage brain.

1

You Don't Understand

"What are you talking about?"

The question came from the hall, where our fourteen-year-old had apparently been hovering, listening to us outline this book. Her head popped around the corner, and it struck me again: she looks *so grown up*. These days I (Jerusha) was constantly thinking—and too often for her liking, lamenting—that it was all happening too fast.

"We're talking about teens who feel their parents don't understand them."

As swiftly as it had appeared, her head vanished. A small scoffing sound escaped as she beelined toward her room.

Because verbal barbs—"You don't get it," "You wouldn't understand," "You have *no idea*, Mom" (insert an agonized adolescent sigh here)—had been aimed at me before, I wasn't so naïve as to believe she felt perfectly understood. Convincing myself this was about research, I followed her and asked, "Do your friends ever feel that way?"

The look she gave me spoke volumes: *Are you kidding me, Mom? I thought you were writing a book about this.*

"Uh, yeah. All of them."

I can't type the inflection she used, but the heavy drama with which she proclaimed this almost made me laugh. That, of course, would've spelled disaster, so I just muttered something like, "Hmm. I thought so," and returned to where Jeramy and the laptop waited.

All of them. Though teenage girls are prone to exaggeration, in this instance I believed her. The perceived understanding gap between teens and their parents is nearly universal. It crosses socioeconomic, ethnic, and gender barriers. At some point—and, for some, at *every* point—teens feel misunderstood.

Some parents try to ignore or dismiss this as adolescent foolishness ("Of course I understand! Do you think I was never a teenager?"). Becoming annoyed by it ("Well, how do you expect me to understand if you won't even talk to me?") or paralyzed because of it is easy. After all, frustration and fear are two of the most common emotions parents experience while raising adolescents.

Deciding to press into this, however, can propel you to action and effort. Let's start by investigating connections between this understanding gap and the radical changes happening in your teen's brain. As you read, we hope you'll develop compassion for your teen and discernment for parenting wisely.

Bio 101

Countless hours and billions of dollars are spent every year by parents trying to harness the potential of their child's early years. Providing the "right" toys, books, and opportunities becomes an obsession for some. Flash cards, reading programs, "smart" toys, and enrichment classes promise to make children more intelligent, better equipped for life, healthier, and happier.

Why do parents focus so much attention on the years between birth and three? Because we know—and the scientific evidence truly is profound—that a child's early years are incredibly important. We call them the "formative" years because what happens during this stage dramatically shapes a child's future.

In the not-so-distant past, scientists believed that the window of opportunity for significant influence closed as a child aged. Research over the last two decades demonstrates, however, that adolescence is a second period of radical neurological change and, as a result, powerful potential.

During the adolescent years, the progressive remodeling of the brain (the combined processes of *pruning* unused neural pathways and making the surviving ones more efficient through *myelination*) creates what scientists call heightened neuroplasticity.

The word *neuroplasticity* derives from a combination of *neuron*, the term used for the basic brain cell, and the word *plastic*, which means "able to be molded, sculpted, or modified." When we use the term *neuroplasticity*, we mean the brain's magnificent ability to re-organize and restructure itself by responding to learning and stimulus in the environment, forming new connections, pruning old ones, even recovering from injury and illness. The brain is incredibly malleable during the adolescent years. This is a time of amazing opportunity for you and your teenager!

Understanding your adolescent begins here: teens feel misunderstood because parents expect them to stay the same, but adolescence is all about *change*. If you can grasp that a remarkable and massive remodeling is going on in your teen's brain, you can develop greater compassion for the days of experimentation, exhilaration, and confusion. The process of parenting teens is one of constant and sometimes exhausting change. It seems nothing stays the same, and it's easier to assume "My job's almost done" when your kid hits the teen years than to believe you're called to gear up for a second period of incredible significance. Bridging the understanding gap starts with recognizing that your teenager's brain is highly impressionable.

Neural remodeling occurs in a relatively systematic way, from the back of the brain to the front. In practical terms, this means particular brain structures are under construction at different times and some for far longer than others. As these massive alterations occur, you can exercise patience and discernment. Though understanding your transforming teen is a challenge, it's not impossible.

After areas responsible for balance, coordination, and sensory processing, one of the first areas of the teenage brain to be pruned and myelinated is the emotional center of the brain, the *limbic system*. Teenagers feel high highs and low lows, in part, because the structures in their brains that control emotions undergo serious renovation. When your teen flips out, picture yourself putting on a hard hat. You and your adolescent are in a construction zone, so be aware and be cautious. Remember, something *really great* can come from remodeling.

Further complicating matters is the fact that while the emotional limbic system is highly aroused early in adolescence, the brain's control center—specifically the *prefrontal cortex*—matures last. The prefrontal cortex directs executive functions; its roles include forethought and planning, judgment, decision-making, and self-regulation. Kind of reads like a laundry list of what teens struggle with, doesn't it?

Consider for a moment: Do you imagine it might be difficult for teens to understand themselves if the emotional centers of their brains are active but their executive functioning is periodically offline (perhaps even off more than on)? Can this secure your compassion? We believe so.

Before reading this book, perhaps you caught glimpses of good judgment and wise decision-making in your teen. Maybe you figured he or she would be able to do better by trying harder. Bottom line, it's not that simple. Bridging the understanding gap will require more of you. There's fantastic news, though: because of your adolescent's neuroplasticity, all hope is not lost! The malleable adolescent brain can be shaped. Ready to find out how you can participate?

Psych 101

Here are some ways to help your adolescent through this period of radical remodeling.

- **Be "on-site."** The teenage years create fear and frustration in a lot of parents. It may feel simpler and safer to stay out of the way. Trouble is, you can have little—if any—influence from "off-site." Too often, after having been disconnected for some time, parents launch in, demanding change. It's easy to imagine how ineffective that can be. If you want to be part of shaping your teenager's brain, you've got to be consistently and courageously present.

- **Be observant.** A good subcontractor doesn't march onto a construction site and start barking orders. He walks the grounds, noting what's happened (or hasn't happened) and comparing his observations to the blueprint. In a similar manner—as a subcontractor in God's employ, helping shape your child's future—you should be a careful observer. Pay attention to your teen's words. Notice what makes her laugh, cry, or get angry. In short, be an observer of your teenager's inner life. You can detect a great deal by being a patient, on-site observer.

- **Ask, listen, and respect** (preferably in that order). Sometimes you simply won't understand. You can also humbly ask for help. When you ask, listen carefully. Do everything you can to keep from inserting your ideas, opinions, or suggestions. Trust that there will be time for that later. If communication is going well, ask follow-up questions to draw out your teen's thoughts and feelings. Finally, show respect for what your teen says by reiterating it, confirming you've heard and understand. Keep the conversation short and to the point; this is an especially effective communication tool with teens. Don't make every conversation into a lecture. Frequent, shorter conversations make a bigger impact on teens.

- **Remember.** This tip has two dynamics: One, remember what your teen tells you. Ask about it in a few days. Pray about it in the meantime, and let your teen know it's on your mind with a simple statement like, "I'm praying for you."

  Two, cultivate perspective. Remember your own teen days. You probably felt confused or overly emotional at times. More likely than not, you made some foolish decisions. If you think you caused no problems as an adolescent, ask your parents. They'll happily set you straight. Gaining perspective and remembering what your teen tells you shows great compassion; perspective also equips you to make good decisions.

- **Don't minimize;** *empathize.* If your daughter is crying in the bathroom because she's got a big zit on her forehead, please rethink the dismissive, "Get over it; everyone gets zits" comments. Your son's small stature, your daughter's friendship drama, any number of other issues: they *really matter* to your adolescent. The best way to show that you understand is by responding with affirming statements like, "I can see why that would be hard for you," "That must be frustrating," or even something as simple as, "Hmmm." The fastest way to perpetuate the understanding gap is to try to convince teenagers that feelings don't matter, that they should get past something, or that you've got the perfect way to fix the situation. Keep in mind that because adolescents often don't understand themselves, they can't imagine anyone else can understand them. You best demonstrate understanding not by solving the problem but by showing empathy. Recalling times when you've felt deeply (e.g., afraid, angry, rejected) and empathizing with your child is an incredibly powerful way to connect, and doing so helps integrate the emotional and logical portions of your teenager's brain.

Faith 101

Adolescence is a period of amazing neurological opportunity. And because God designed your teen with this remarkable neuroplasticity, the impact of the adolescent years on his or her spirit will be profound.

We appreciate how *The Message* renders Ephesians 5:16–17 and believe it speaks powerfully to parents of adolescents: "Watch your step. Use your head. Make the most of every chance you get. These

are desperate times! Don't live carelessly, unthinkingly. Make sure
you understand what the Master wants." These years are incredibly important. The Bible urges us not to
live carelessly, but this means more than simply "thinking before we
act." We must actively resist living with a survivalist mentality, just
"getting by," rushing from activity to activity without purpose or
intentionality. During this remarkable window of opportunity in the
teenage years, *make the most of every chance you get*.
J. B. Phillips translated Ephesians 5:16 as, "Make the best use of
your time, despite all the difficulties of these days." Undoubtedly,
there will be tremendous difficulties in these days. Make the best
use of your time.

Take a moment to consider what's hindering you from making
the most of the teen years. As one pastor puts it, "It's a waste of
time to think about strategies for parenting without first examining
ourselves."[1]

At the center of every struggle in life is misdirected worship. We
all worship something, and though many of us claim that we worship
God alone, we often spend our time and energy chasing other desires.
Longings for control, comfort, respect, appreciation, and success can
become idols that poison not only our parent-teen relationships but
also our relationship with God.

If your son's or daughter's lack of appreciation and respect for
"all you've done" becomes a point of bitterness in your heart, you
may have some thinking, forgiving, and reprioritizing to do. Ironically, you won't get respect or appreciation by making them the
goal of your parenting; developing godly character is a higher aim,
a God-focused (not parent-focused) one. Likewise, if you're expecting your child's behavior and accomplishments to make you feel
successful, pressure and trouble are brewing. If you're overly angry
at your teen for impinging on the order and peace of your home,
an idol of comfort may be at play. And if you're not able to let go,
trusting your teen to God, your idol of control will wound everyone,
yourself included.

Now is the time to pay close attention to your own heart and mind. The closer you are to God during the years you're parenting teenagers, the more the Holy Spirit can give you wisdom and insight, consolation and strength. You need those things, and you cannot manufacture them on your own.

The window of opportunity in your teen's brain and spirit is also an invitation to you: be transformed by the renewing of your mind. As Romans 12:2 commands, "Let God transform you into a new person by changing the way you think" (NLT). Don't waste these days, even the difficult ones. You and your teen can become stronger because of them.

Try It Today

As our daughters became teenagers, we weren't prepared to deal with our own conflicting emotions. We knew they'd have mood swings, but we didn't know we'd face such a sense of loss. Watching our girls transform during their adolescent years was amazing, but we also missed the snuggly kids they were seemingly moments ago.

Author Dr. Michael Bradley urges parents to press into this sense of loss. Indeed, failing to do so can lead to anger and resentment (*Who is this teenaged usurper of my "sweet girl" or my "little buddy"?*). Letting your teen change allows parts of his or her personality that you loved in childhood to resurface over time, stronger and more mature, better equipped to flourish in the adult world.[2]

Communication experts Adele Faber and Elaine Mazlish agree that grieving loss is an essential part of parenting adolescents. We encourage you to take some time within the next twenty-four hours to talk with a spouse or friend, journal, and/or pray about the following:

- **Loss of closeness.** Actively let go of the "Who is this hostile person? Where's the sweet kid who climbed up on my bed to talk every night?" type of thoughts.
- **Loss of "being needed."** It can hurt to hear, "You don't have to do that anymore, Dad. I can handle it."

- **Loss of confidence.** Asking, "Why did he do that? What is she becoming? Have I done something wrong?" or "Is there anything I can do?" will drag you under if you let it. You may feel like you don't know what you're doing. That's okay! Grieve the loss of confidence and gear up for a learning curve. God promises that you're not alone in this; he will strengthen you and help you; he will uphold you with his victorious right hand (see Isa. 41:10).

- **Loss of control.** We especially want to keep our kids from harm. Recycling "What if," "If only," or "Why?" thoughts can be agonizing!

- **Loss of ease.** The teenage years are anything but a "ho-hum" season of life. Grieving the loss of peace and ease actually helps you avoid fear, which tries to devour parents of teens.[3]

If you grieve these losses and equip yourself for the construction years, you'll be better prepared. Remember to keep your hard hat handy!

2

Leave Me Alone

"My daughter getting pregnant . . ."
  "My son getting addicted to drugs or alcohol . . ."
  "My teen getting depressed or ensnared by pornography . . ."
  "One of my children walking away from faith . . ."
  Over and over again, parents of teens confess fears like these to us.

What we usually *don't* hear is, "I'm afraid to let go of the control I once had over my child's life," yet this is a nearly universal—albeit often subconscious—parental concern. Despite daily evidence that we can't control our kids, many of us cling to the illusion that we can protect them from doing something foolish, something hurtful, something that will seriously damage their future opportunities. Our efforts to control life, however, are nothing more than a misconceived chasing after the wind.

As parents, it's difficult enough to let go of needing to be needed; it's exponentially more challenging to recognize that your adolescent is *daily* making a transition toward independence and unique identity. Moms and dads must learn (because it's not natural!) to step back and allow their teens to exercise self-regulation.

When I (Jeramy) decided to sport the most infamous of haircuts, the mullet, let's just say my dad wasn't pleased. Although we can laugh about this now, at the time it felt like a massive "who's in control" issue. Time after time I've counseled distraught parents lamenting their teen's choices. What do you do when your fifteen-year-old son wants to wear black fishnet gloves to school or your seventeen-year-old daughter tells you she no longer wants to attend college but plans to launch a fund-raising campaign so her band can tour? Do you rush to conclusions and clamp down? Do you take a laissez-faire approach? Do you mock him or manipulate her, trying to shame your adolescent into a "better choice"?

Too often, we operate on faulty assumptions about who's really in control of our teen's life. Sometimes we see our adolescent children as threats to our "good name." Many parents are convinced life would work better if teenagers just "got with the program," but what does forcing your agenda ultimately accomplish?

How you respond to your teen's desire to differentiate, his need to make independent choices, and her need to develop an identity apart from you will make a huge difference in the relationship you and your adolescent will enjoy or endure. You have a tremendous degree of choice in this matter, so let's dive into the biological, psychological, and spiritual dimensions of surrendering control and allowing your teen to mature.

Bio 101

As you now know, your teen's brain is undergoing massive and intense changes. That this is a physically exhausting process (and one the vast majority of teens aren't even aware is happening) should prompt us to extend grace when our teens "just want to be left alone." With so many new and confusing things going on inside and around a teen, needing time to process is completely understandable. Teens need room to become who they were meant to be.

Dr. Sheryl Feinstein, author of *Inside the Teenage Brain*, urges parents to remember, "Changes in the brain of the adolescent do not happen in isolation. It is during the teen years that a sense of identity is developed. . . . The search for identity is one of the most important jobs that teenagers have, and they pursue this mission with a vengeance. In order to discover an answer to this question ["Who am I?"], adolescents try on different hats. . . one morning parents wake up to a swing dancer and the next morning, a NASCAR freak."[1]

Do you believe that the search for identity is an important job for your teenager? If not, we implore you to reconsider. God designed the brain to develop self-awareness and personal accountability over time. Short-circuiting this process benefits no one and often leads to "identity crises" later in life, when adults realize they never decided for themselves what to believe and how to live it out. We needn't fear the search for identity, even if a teen "trying on" various preferences drives us crazy now and then.

Your teen's neural "hardware"—his or her capacity to evaluate life and make choices—is transforming. It's time to allow your adolescent to begin using this new hardware, even if there are some system glitches along the way. As the parent of an under-construction teen, you can exercise discernment, enabling your son or daughter to make an increasing number of choices in a variety of areas, with incrementally escalating responsibility. Frankly, it's easier to cling to control than to slowly, deliberately place it in your teenager's hands. This is hard work that takes diligence, grace, and above all, time. Sadly, many of us are too busy and too stressed to do the difficult work of letting go.

As your teen's brain is remodeled, he or she will approach the world in new ways. If you're hoping your teen won't rock the boat, you're likely to be disappointed (frequently!). Instead of going along with the status quo, your developing teen's brain wants to push the envelope, to discover novel and creative ways of being his or her own person. This means that when your teen says, "I don't want to . . . ," sometimes what he or she means is, "I don't want to do it *your* way."

Is it okay with you if your teenager decides to do things differently than you? We're not talking about choices between right and wrong, but rather teens discovering the unique ways God designed them. As your adolescent's brain becomes better equipped to think independently, "outside the box" thoughts and strategies will occur to him or her. Can you embrace this?

Of course, creative exploration and exerting independence can cause problems. As they search for meaning and identity, teens *can* become vulnerable to pressures from outside forces. They *can* drift and lose direction. Toddlers can also scrape their knees or even break bones when learning to walk, but we don't try to keep them crawling forever. As your teen matures, your job is to *guide*, not simply *guard*. As Dr. Jim Burns so brilliantly puts it, parents must move from "controlling to consulting and from micromanaging to mentoring"[2] if they wish to raise responsible adults who can make wise decisions.

Your teenager's under-construction brain is primed for learning. In order to capitalize on the profound opportunity presented by adolescent neuroplasticity, you must be willing to let your teen practice planning, make judgments, and exercise self-control. Certainly, their skills won't come out of the gate fully developed; indeed, their brain's CEO (the pre-frontal cortex) requires time and training to mature. It may be difficult not to swoop in and "fix" things in the early days, but resist this urge. We best nurture a teen's brain by releasing control gradually, allowing both the successes of great decisions as well as the bumps and bruises of bad choices to instruct.

Psych 101

Parents best equip their adolescents for adulthood when they deliberately give teens opportunities to exert control and show responsibility. Parents inhibit appropriate development when they hover and micromanage or, conversely, when they opt for a "hands off," permissive approach.

Autocratic parents who rigidly exert control through inflexible rules and mandated behavior raise teens who lack confidence when asked to solve problems. Since every choice has been made for them, these adolescents have no practice making their own decisions. Essential life skills that are necessary for independent adulthood haven't been encouraged, so these teens become followers rather than leaders. Adolescents who perceive that only a narrow, parent-determined path is acceptable either walk this tightrope with continual stress or rebel outright.

Another controlling approach has been identified by a variety of terms: "helicopter parent," "tiger mother," "stealth bomber dad." These parents hover around a child, clearing the path of any obstacles, focused on preventing failure and ensuring a "happily ever after." Trouble is, adult life is full of challenges that can't be whisked away by a parent. Adolescents with hovering parents lack the skills to make adjustments, persist through trials, and solve their own problems.

On the whole, today's college students have far fewer "life skills" than their counterparts from previous generations. Many didn't even fill out their own college applications. The cell phone becomes a digital umbilical cord, perpetuating dependence on parents to manage life and further delaying maturity. A nineteen-year-old who calls Mom, begging her to "convince" a professor to give an extension on the midterm project, is not capitalizing on the amazing potential of her remodeled brain, which can make decisions and exercise personal accountability.

On the opposite extreme, parents who raise teenagers in a laissez-faire environment—whether through overindulgence or neglect—leave teens with an excessive need for entertainment, a low tolerance for challenge, and a sparse application of logic. Permissive parents may wish to instill confidence and independence in their children, but instead they communicate that their pleasure and pursuits are more important than anything else. Ironically, both the indulged and the neglected child, rarely given guidance or limits, grow up feeling insecure; they lack decision-making skills and self-control because these traits were never modeled to nor instilled in them.

If you desire to raise a child who exerts appropriate self-awareness, self-control, and independence, offer structure while progressively equipping and empowering your adolescent. We affirm the counsel of Dr. Daniel Siegel: lend support while supporting separation.[3] Provide a warm, consistent, safe "base" from which your child can explore. Establish limits and stay firm in your resolve, giving your adolescent a sense of security and protective boundaries.

God created your teen to make choices and be accountable for them, and in the not-too-distant future, it will be up to him or her to live wisely or foolishly. Allowing your adolescent to practice the skills necessary for adulthood *while still in your home* is a tremendous gift. It takes more time, patience, grace, and discernment than simply controlling or checking out does, but such is the call of parenting a teen. It requires far more than most of us imagined it would.

Adolescent researcher Dr. Laurence Steinberg encourages parents to use "scaffolding," an approach that gives teens "slightly more responsibility or autonomy than they are used to—just enough so that they'll feel the benefits if they succeed but not suffer dire consequences should they fail."[4] Examples of scaffolding include extending your younger adolescent's curfew or allowing your older teenager to plan an activity. This gives adolescents practice in forethought and self-control (especially if a budget is necessary or the relationships involved cause emotions to run high), as well as the ability to enlist help when needed.

Here are a few additional ways to encourage teenagers to develop independence and personal identity:

- **Involve your teen in the process of making family rules.** Teens who live in rigid environments where everything is decided for them fail to develop self-regulation. You're not surrendering control *to* your teenager when you invite participation in family discussion; you are nurturing a developing brain and mind. Don't leave your teen with the choice between obediently toeing the line or acting like a lunatic to exert some level of control over life. Help your adolescent grow in the ability to negotiate, cooperate, plan well, and decide wisely by establishing a family process whereby rules are made and periodically evaluated. You also foster mutual respect and trust when you work toward agreement. According to Dr. Michael Bradley, "a good rules process advances your kid way down that road of consolidating his identity by forcing him to confront who he is now and how he wants to live his life."[5] An added benefit: the more your teen is involved in the process, the greater the buy-in to the decisions made.

- **Seize the opportunities presented by bad choices.** In their quest for freedom and independence, teens often make poor decisions. Expect this and choose—now—to approach these as opportunities, not inconveniences or personal defeats. If adolescents can learn the need to research better before making a purchase, the importance of owning their decisions, the downsides of acting impulsively, the upsides of delaying gratification, how essential it is to press on despite adversity, and the benefit of listening to others, then their bad decisions can lead to *really good* growth. Ironically, one of the worst things we can do as parents is try to prevent our kids from having to learn from their mistakes.

- **Take dabbling in stride.** Parents often fear that experimentation with certain preferences (music, after-school activities, appearance, etc.) will be "forever," but most adolescent expressions of independence aren't life defining. Be patient and gracious, letting go of noncritical issues (like hair color or style) so that you can focus on what's really important: moral development, spiritual formation, and strong relationships.

- **Keep your eyes on the prize.** The standard definition of adolescence includes two main components—separateness and self-assertion.[6] The ultimate "prize" of healthy adolescent development is launching an adult child equipped with self-awareness, a capacity to think independently, and the ability to responsibly live with and relate to others. Don't lose sight of these goals.

- **Sometimes actually leave them alone.** Teenagers sorting out their thoughts and emotions need some privacy. It's normal for adolescents to want alone time. When possible, give them space, ideally in a place they can "make their own."
- **Surrender your need to be right.** If you want to raise a thoughtful adult who can make wise decisions based on the information available to him or her, you must allow independent thinking to blossom in your home. Giving your teen freedom to express ideas and opinions is a great place to start, but this requires you to exercise discretion and patience. Again, this process may be difficult, but remember that your goal isn't to raise someone who simply recognizes you're right but rather to raise someone who can actively choose to do what's best.

Faith 101

How much control do you have over your teenager? How much control do you have over your own life?

In reality, we control very little in the world around us. Basically, we can regulate our thoughts and the choices that spring from our beliefs. That's it. Everything else is contingent, whether on another person's decisions or forces beyond human control. We cannot control our teenagers any more than we can control the barometric pressure. We may have more influence over an adolescent than over the weather, but influence is a privilege, not an entitlement.

Philippians 3:21 reveals that only God has "power that enables him to bring everything under his control." Can you bring everything under your control? Didn't think so. Neither can we.

God can. First Timothy 6:15 proclaims that God is "the blessed and only Sovereign" (ESV). Not only is he in control, but he's also *very good* ("blessed") at what he does.

You can choose to fight the One with authority to bring all things under his control, or you can join him in his perfect work. This choice makes all the difference in your parenting. Surrendering the control you never had over your teen's life is the only way to gain the influence you desperately need.

Take a few moments to open your Bible and read Psalm 139. Note the powerful way God describes his omnipresence. He knows *everything* about you. This marvelous truth applies to your teen too. You cannot control what your teen does, says, or thinks, but God knows. He never leaves or forsakes your adolescent. He truly *is* the blessed and only controller of all things.

Try It Today: Practice Saying Yes as Often as Possible

Parents of teens sometimes feel like "bad guys," always having to reign in exuberant adolescents who are bursting with energy and ideas. It's easy to get into a rut of saying no, simply because it's a lot less trouble than allowing teens to explore their creative drives and desires.

If, however, we want to raise independent and responsible adults, we must supplant our own need for comfort and release the fear that facing disappointment or failure will harm our adolescent.

We like Dr. Laurence Steinberg's advice on this point: "protect where you must, permit when you can. . . . In situations where your decision about an activity your child wants to engage in can easily go one way or the other, try to maximize your child's autonomy so long as doing so doesn't jeopardize his health, well-being, or future."[7]

Practice saying yes, not so that you can be your teen's best friend, but so that he or she can develop confidence in making independent decisions (which includes learning from mistakes!). While your adolescent is still at home, your developed prefrontal cortex can act as a safety net for his or her under-construction one. Your ability to influence is a tremendous gift, not to be squandered. Seize the opportunity by saying yes as often as you can and helping your teen learn from both successes and failures.

3

But *Why?*

By age eight, I (Jeramy) began looking for ways to make money, so when Mr. Baker offered me five dollars to mow his lawn, I jumped at the chance. After drafting my friend Eric into co-service, I set to work on the front yard. No problem. Then we walked around back.

Nothing could have prepared Eric and me for the sight before us. Mr. Baker had neglected to inform us that he hadn't picked up after his dogs in some time. Perhaps ever. I couldn't take a step without . . . well, I'll spare you the rest of the details.

Still eager to earn the five dollars, I started shoveling up the mess. To this day, I cannot remember when, or comprehend why, splattering the contents of my shovel on the Bakers' back wall seemed like a good idea. It never crossed my mind that Mr. Baker might be peeved. Eric and I laughed ourselves silly, decorating the wall with shovelful after shovelful. We mowed the lawn then went home. Simple as that. We ate our dinners in peace, blissfully unaware of the storm brewing next door.

Even when Mr. Baker called and asked my dad to send me over, it didn't occur to me that I might be in trouble. You can probably guess how the story unfolded from there. Needless to say, I was cleaning up for quite a while.

Fast-forward to Christmas Day about six years later. Picture my brother and me, both in our early teens, standing outside with our cousin Mikey, who was about as old as I had been during the fateful Baker yard fiasco.

Perhaps the holiday festivities bored Mikey; maybe he was trying to impress us. Whatever his thought process (or, more likely, lack thereof), Mikey opened the door to his neighbor's Jaguar and—I kid you not—began throwing fistfuls of mud into the impeccable interior.

My brother and I knew where this was headed. We made a few halfhearted suggestions—"Mikey, you better stop that"—but he kept laughing maniacally, now and then stopping to smear what he'd deposited on the dashboard. We didn't do what we knew we should: physically stop him. Observing Mikey in action had a surreal, hilarious quality to it.

Considering the mess Eric and I had made once upon a time, it's reasonable to question why I didn't join in. In part, I had "learned my lesson," but there was more going on than that. In the few short years between these episodes, I had begun to exercise one of the greatest gifts of adolescence: abstract reasoning.

Bio 101

Until approximately age eleven, children reason concretely, which means they think in "here and now," "what's right in front of me" terms. Facts interest small children more than ideas. When they ask, *Why?*, most kids are looking for a simple, causal explanation.

Things change with adolescence as a significant cognitive development occurs: the growth of abstract reasoning. With maturing neural pathways and higher-order thinking, adolescents begin to engage in what classical thinkers call "dialectic," the examination and discussion of opposing ideas in order to discover truth.

It's crucial that parents recognize and respect the development of abstract reasoning as an essential *process.* This in no way excuses bad behavior. It does, however, enable us to understand adolescents better, communicate with them compassionately, and use our knowledge of what's happening neurologically to build up, rather than undermine, our relationships.

When Eric and I made those foolish decisions in Mr. Baker's backyard, we thought concretely. We didn't reason sequentially or draw conclusions from the evidence at hand. We focused on how funny it was "here and now," not on why we shouldn't be doing what we were doing, what might happen, or how it would impact others.

By contrast, just a few years later, my brother and I reasoned in an abstract way, taking in the facts of the situation, weighing them against what we knew could and likely would happen, and processing it before making a decision. I wasn't a perfect abstract thinker; in fact, as I made my way toward adulthood, I did plenty of careless things. That day, however, as Mikey reveled in his muddy escapade, all the right brain systems were online. My dad, who—unlike my uncle—didn't have to pay to detail the Jag, was certainly grateful!

Abstract reasoning involves the ability to analyze information, detect patterns and relationships, and understand multiple dynamics and meanings. It also includes thinking creatively and solving problems on a complex level, with intangible and nonverbal dimensions.

Whereas children (i.e., concrete thinkers) look at things on a surface level and use facts to solve problems in a lateral and literal way, adolescents slowly move beyond specifics, reasoning in terms of generalizations, ideas, and deeper meanings.

For parents, this can be all at once wonderful and terrifying. With the advent of abstract reasoning comes an avalanche of questions, "Why?" being a favorite. When they've asked to stay out past their normal curfew and you've said no, most teens aren't satisfied with the answer, "Because I said so." They want to know (and usually argue with) your logic. Engaging in dialogue with a beginning abstract thinker can feel like torture. But we must move past the frustrations and inconveniences of our adolescents' journeys and see the beauty behind their developing reason. Without these new skills, our children won't become the men and women of character and conviction we want them to be.

When we begin to see adolescents moving toward a deeper understanding of the implications of ideas, actions, and their consequences, we often expect them to integrate these new capacities into their daily life—now! However, the development of abstract reasoning is a *process* that moves forward in fits and starts.

In his book *A Parent's Guide to Understanding Teenage Brains*, youth expert Mark Oestreicher observes, "You might rightly assume that young teenagers will more often be in concrete-land, and that older teenagers should have a decent working use of abstraction, but it's not that simple, unfortunately. . . . Teenagers shift in and out of it constantly in their long march to conquer it and make it useful. In the meantime, throughout the teenage years, kids are thinking concretely one moment and dabbling in abstraction the next."[1]

It's extraordinarily important that we allow adolescents to practice their abstract reasoning abilities, help teenagers hone these new skills, and exercise compassionate patience when they get mixed up and turned around. The consequences of a particular choice may seem obvious to you, but keep in mind that while "teenagers possess the ability to speculate . . . they're not very good at it." Oestreicher continues, "It's like a brand-new muscle that's just been added to their repertoire of thinking abilities—but it's a weak, flabby muscle that's never been used. Speculation takes practice and requires regular use before it's dependable and immediately available without intentionality."[2]

Your adolescent's brain is busy asking questions, sorting facts, comparing details, and practicing the newfound ability to draw generalizations and form ideas. Symbolism takes on new power. Exploring complex dimensions of justice, faith, and relationships becomes a passion for some teens. In terms of classical thinking, this stage is called dialectic because *dialogue* is a key component of developing abstract reasoning skills.

As parent to an adolescent, you are called to engage in this dialogue for the purpose of growing your teen's ability to perceive clearly, think deeply, and make sound judgments. As teens grow older, they will want to figure out problems and even teach you things. Be open to this important development, as willingness to learn from your adolescent can spark the fire of further growth in their cognition or quickly snuff it out.

Teenagers' abstract reasoning will impact how they see the world, how they interact with it, and how they view faith in God. On a primal and essential level, abstract reasoning leads teens to explore the whole of their identity.

Psych 101

The teenage years are fraught with the often-verbalized question "Why?," but they are also replete with unverbalized, abstract questions as well: Who am I? Who tells me who I am? Where do I want to go with my life? And how do I want to get there?

Sadly, many parents try to answer these questions for their children rather than journeying with their teens as the answers unfold. It's not easy to allow our adolescent children to explore their abstract reasoning any more than it is to let them find their identity, but we cannot overstate the futility of trying to skip this process.

On Monday, your teenager may express that he's bound and determined to be the next world champion ballroom dancer. The next day he may angrily tell you that "those dancer people" are losers. Trying to argue with this illogical shift is pointless. Addressing behavior (e.g., "Calling people losers is unacceptable") is important, but allowing for the trial and error of teenage reasoning is essential.

Here are a few tips for not only surviving but also thriving in the process:

- **Ask good questions.** What is it about that new music/way of dressing/type of book/group of friends that your adolescent finds important and attractive? Find out. Engage in dialogue as often as possible. Remember, the growth of abstract reasoning and the dialectic process (contrasting opposing ideas and drawing conclusions) are best done in active communication. Asking good questions involves stretching beyond those that can be answered with yes or no. Don't let an uncommunicative teenager run the show. Press for more gently, little by little. Even if they don't thank you for doing so, you're helping your teen significantly.

- **Refuse to take it personally.** Many parents see their teen's abstract reasoning as a personal assault (e.g., "He argues with everything I say, so why do I even bother?"). Other parents fear the "Why?" questions teens ask about faith will lead them astray (much more on this later), but please hear us loud and clear: you must not take this process personally. Not only will it devour you, it will derail your teen's development as well.

- **Expect it.** Be on the lookout for ways in which your teen will "try on" new ways of thinking, new ways of living, and new ways of expressing himself or herself. Don't react too quickly. An extreme statement made one moment may be tempered in the next. Patiently observe the process, engage in dialogue, and step in when it becomes clear that the teenager's health or welfare may be compromised. Use the discernment God gives you rather than reacting in fear.

- **Take deep breaths.** Don't dismiss this as simplistic! Taking a deep breath delivers fresh oxygen to brain cells, renewing your capacity to think clearly. Deliberately choosing to take a deep breath can also disrupt negative thought patterns, giving you a chance to change course. One breath can make a significant difference for you and your teen.

Faith 101

To an adult, abstract reasoning seems normal. Maybe you've forgotten, but you too had to *learn* it. You may be tempted to dismiss an adolescent's need to explore, thinking, *This is ridiculous. God is the one who tells us who we are, and we don't need to indulge teenagers in this "finding yourself" nonsense.* Such ideas are detrimental both to your parent-child relationship and to your adolescent's relationship with God. Identity formation through abstract reasoning is a process created by God, guided by his Holy Spirit, and directed for his glory. It's part of sanctification, knowing oneself, and knowing God, who fears no question and engages with every seeker. Indeed, when surrendered to God, both identity formation and abstract reasoning become key components of discipleship.

Adolescents raised in faith typically journey toward one of three ends:[3]

1. *Identity diffusion*: an adolescent never makes a commitment to a particular set of values and beliefs because the process has been disrupted or disallowed.
2. *Identity foreclosure*: a teen makes commitments to beliefs only as the result of force, typically by parents, but has little personal ownership.
3. *Identity achieved*: an adolescent chooses to be identified with Jesus.

As parents, we must not disallow the developmental process, nor stall it in order to make things safe and comfortable for ourselves. Instead, we can choose to engage abstract reasoning, helping our adolescent evaluate the claims of Christ regarding truth and identity. This is by no means easy, but it is worth every effort. In this, you help your teenager become a true disciple of Jesus. Harness the power of your adolescent's abstract thinking for discipleship.

We appreciate this simple definition: "Biblical discipleship is *look* and *live*."[4] Your teen can begin using abstract reasoning to follow Christ by looking at Christ and living as he did. Discipleship gives substance to the abstract, and as teens delve into the depths of their new abstract reasoning, they need to be discipled.

Let's apply this. Take, for example, the powerful command from Romans 6:11, "Consider yourselves to be dead to sin, but alive to God in Christ Jesus" (NASB). A concept like this is difficult for a child to decipher and apply. Your teen, however, has begun to reason abstractly. A teen can "consider" differently.

The word translated *consider* by the NASB can also be rendered *reckon*. This term is rich with connotation; it involves weighing an issue mathematically, puzzling over it in order to alter the course of an action or thought. A teenager can reckon in a way a child cannot, and upon this abstract reasoning, true faith is built.

In discipleship, helping our teen *look at* and *live out* the truth, an intangible concept—like considering oneself "dead to sin" and "alive to Christ"—becomes tangible. Discipling a teen means helping him or her connect the Word of God to daily life. You can be part of this amazing process.

As you may have noticed, however, this requires you to engage in the reckoning process. Before you continue with this book, ask yourself:

- Is your own identity solidly grounded in God's truth?
- Does your adolescent see you as a committed disciple of Christ?
- If not, what will you do about it?

Try It Today: Consider a Cross-Cultural Experience

In our combined three decades of youth ministry experience, we found that nothing formed teenagers' abstract thinking more dramatically than a well-executed cross-cultural experience. Being exposed to real people in real (often unthinkable) circumstances can change adolescents . . . forever. Mark Oestreicher describes it well:

> Due to the massive quantity and depth of the developmental changes occurring in their bodies and brains, teenagers are often rather narcissistic . . . but when they encounter people with real needs, especially in a different cultural context, the experience can knock them off-balance,

in a great way. They get a sense of themselves as part of a much larger story. They wonder why they have so much, while others have so little. They see, from outside of themselves, their own selfishness and materialism, and this messes with their priorities and values.[5]

With abstract reasoning comes the ability to empathize. Whereas sympathy involves feeling what *you* feel (in a cross-cultural context this may mean feeling "sorry" for people enduring horrible living conditions after a natural disaster), empathy draws on abstract reasoning to enter into another person's experience, to feel what *they* feel. A thoughtfully planned cross-cultural experience can teach empathy like nothing else can.

There are a myriad of ways to engage cross-culturally. You may decide to go with your church on an international building project or with a mission organization teaching English as a second language. You can think even more broadly about what "cross-cultural" means, however. Volunteering at an inner-city soup kitchen can be cross-cultural. You can find more ideas for cross-cultural experiences at Youth With a Mission's website (www.ywam.org).

4

I'm So Bored

None of my friends were home. There was nowhere to go that I hadn't been already and nothing on TV. I had zero interest in my mom's ten suggestions for what to do. I (Jeramy) was looking for something, anything really, that would be an adventure, but when you're a teenager and there's "nothing" to do, "no one" to do it with, and you're feeling profoundly bored, life hardly seems bearable.

Fast-forward about two and a half decades: my own kids are complaining that they're "*so bored*." At this point in my busy adult life, I haven't been bored since the early nineties, so I'll be frank: compassion for their adolescent boredom isn't always my strong suit.

"Bored?" I hear myself say. "Well, then I've got work for you to do."

"No thanks," they say, sighing deeply and slouching off in the direction of their "boring" bedrooms, where various electronic devices, art supplies, books, and neglected toys await. It's somewhat difficult to imagine that there's *nothing* for my girls to do.

Before we started research for this book, I got easily annoyed with my daughters' boredom. "I'm not your clown," I might say. "Figure something out."

I'm still not their clown, but my perspective on adolescent world-weariness has changed with my growing understanding of the teenage brain. On one level, simply remembering my own adolescence helps me enter into my daughters' world. But it's more than commiseration that's changed me. Jerusha and I have discovered some important facts about the "under-construction" teenage brain that help us—and we hope can help you—figure out what's behind the "I'm bored" complaints.

Bio 101

Study after study confirms that adolescents respond to pleasure and reward—indeed, even the anticipation of gratification—with greater sensitivity than either adults or children.[1] Neuroscientists attribute this to significant developmental changes occurring during adolescence in the brain's *reward system.*

Throughout this book, when we refer to the reward system, we mean the collection of brain structures involved in the experience and mediation of pleasure. When activated, these areas of the brain reinforce certain behaviors and deter us from others. For your son or daughter, everything from eating sweets to listening to ear-piercingly loud music to giving and receiving physical affection or playing video games can stimulate the brain's reward circuits, which includes the dopamine-rich neurons of the ventral tegmental area, the nucleus accumbens, and part of the prefrontal cortex. In order to better understand our teens, let's look briefly at each component of the reward system.

We previously discussed the importance of the prefrontal cortex, so you may recall its role in judgment, planning, forethought, and executive functioning. Remember, this portion of the brain is under construction for the entirety of adolescence. Also undergoing specialized and substantial alteration during adolescence are the nucleus accumbens (NAc) and the ventral tegmental area (VTA).

Each brain hemisphere has its own NAc, a small but mighty brain structure that plays an important role in the cognitive processing of pleasure, motivation, reinforcement learning, and the encoding of new motor programs. The NAc does this primarily by releasing dopamine, a neurotransmitter closely associated with pleasure.[2] The NAc's dopaminergic input originates mainly in the VTA, an area of the brain that also processes emotion and sends information to the prefrontal cortex for evaluation.

Think of it this way: the brain keeps score with dopamine. When something good happens, or a teen expects something good to happen, dopamine is released along the VTA-NAc pathway and is ultimately encoded by the prefrontal cortex: "I gotta do that again."

This "loop" created by rewarding stimuli (ice cream or hugging or defeating the next video game level), neurochemical response (dopamine release), and cognitive processing happens lightning fast in adults whose brains have developed the white matter "wiring" necessary for wise decision-making in the face of potential reward and/or risk. The story is a bit more complicated for adolescents.

You see, two major things happen in the teenage brain's reward system that can throw off the "scorekeeping." First, research suggests that adolescents have a lower baseline level of the feel-good neurochemical dopamine. Second, dopamine release in response to experience is higher during the teenage years.[3] Teens have less dopamine naturally, but when it's released, they feel its impact more powerfully. Wild, isn't it? According to UCLA's Dr. Daniel Siegel, this "can explain why teens may report a feeling of being 'bored' unless they are engaging in some stimulating and novel activities."[4]

What's behind your teen's boredom? A developing reward circuit that's thirsty for experience, preferably new and thrilling experience. Some clinicians call this sensation-seeking, others novelty-seeking. It amounts to basically the same thing: teens long for something different, something exciting, something that will raise that naturally lower dopamine level in their under-construction brains.

Does that mean you should become your child's cruise director, constantly providing exciting excursion options for them? Gasp! Do I have to become my daughters' clown after all?

By no means! Understanding the neurobiological realities can, however, secure our compassion for adolescents who want to explore, try new things, and experience higher highs. They're facing very real drives and desires. This knowledge can also enable us to help teens harness the power and potential of their push toward novelty.

Psych 101

Consider this: if your teenage son never tried anything new, he would never move out. If your adolescent daughter wasn't motivated by the hope of some pleasurable outcome, she wouldn't pursue higher education, a challenging career, or marriage and motherhood. Adolescents' drive for reward, and their sensitivity to it, are essential for the transition from dependence to independence. Because they push teens to learn in new ways, unique surroundings, and different social interactions, novelty- and sensation-seeking actually play a crucial role in your teen's acquisition of social, physical, and cognitive tools necessary for adult life. In other words, hidden within "I'm bored" is the seed of some amazing personal growth.

How can parents help in this process?

- **Fuel the fire of curiosity.** Remember the wise words widely attributed to satirist Dorothy Parker: "the cure for boredom is curiosity." We imagine some skeptical parents out there are shaking their heads. "But my son isn't curious about *anything!*" Don't be too sure. Maybe you just think what he's interested in isn't "worthwhile." Too often we want our kids to be interested only in things we consider "time well spent" or "valuable for the future," but curiosity doesn't always work that way. You may need to stretch your idea of what's worthy of spending time and money exploring. If your teen likes skateboarding, find a new skate park or a skate museum. Get a book or magazine about skateboarding. You may be surprised to discover that your adolescent is fascinated by baking, volcanoes, or gardening. Of course, not all activities are equally edifying, so discernment is required. We'd be leery of fueling the fire of a curiosity about horror films, for instance. The key is to harness curiosity and direct it positively. Your teen's drive toward novelty will emerge in some way. You cannot hold it back, but you can help direct its flow.

- **Allow for course correction.** As we encourage our adolescents to try new and different things, we must also keep in mind that experimentation doesn't equal lifelong commitment. Teens benefit from the freedom to try various activities, and your support makes a big difference, even if that means allowing your teen to stop something you value. It was very difficult for me (Jerusha) when our daughters no longer wanted to take piano lessons. Growing up, music was a huge part of my family's life, and I wanted the girls to be able to play instruments and sing with us. If I hadn't surrendered my desire and allowed the girls to pursue other interests, our older daughter may not have become an artist, nor would our younger daughter have discovered her passion for gymnastics. Not only is she growing physically skilled, she's also reading a biography of an Olympic gymnast, and the story of hard work and perseverance is one we're excited for her to focus on!

- **Don't think of this as a problem to be solved.** As far as you are able, resist the urge to "fix" your teen's boredom with work or the "same old" activities. Adolescents need enough down time to sort through what they're actually thinking and feeling, and sometimes feeling bored is precisely what launches them into exploring things that ultimately help them grow. Of course, teenage experimentation and the desire for fun can drive us crazy. That's a given. Buying into the misguided idea that the brain's natural and healthy push toward new and thrilling experiences should be tamed, however, is detrimental to all. The adolescent mind is full of tremendous power and potential. The development of creative expression shouldn't end as we grow older; indeed, adolescence should be a time of burgeoning curiosity and fulfillment.

- **Make spending time together an enjoyable priority.** It may surprise you to learn that teens identify "not having enough time together with their parents as one of their top problems."[5] The vast majority of teens also report that they think highly of their parents (roughly 86 percent say they do) and like being with them (approximately 77 percent agreed with the statement, "I enjoy spending time with my mother or father").[6] Why, then, do our teens so often complain when we want to have a family night or ask immediately, "Can I bring a friend?" when we plan to go somewhere? Part of the answer lies in the fact that parents want to do the same things over and over again. To help our teens harness the power and potential of this important season of life, we should expose them to new things, particularly things that expand their view of the world. This takes time and effort beyond "Let's have a Friday movie night." It may mean sacrificing financially in one area so you can take your kids to that concert or cultural event. It's worth it.

- **Enjoy the highs with your teen.** When dopamine is released in your son's or daughter's brain, a powerful sense of being alive surges through them. This is a wonderful feeling and one that many adults have forgotten. Trying something new with your adolescent may give you a rush like you haven't had in some time. Even more importantly, it will bond you together in significant ways.

Faith 101

Many teens experience the increased activity in their brain's reward systems as a longing they can't quite identify, a hunger they can't satisfy, a restlessness with the status quo. Under healthy circumstances, the physiological changes in your teenager's brain motivate them to engage in activities and with ideas that increase their zest for life, making them more open to change and willing to try new ways of doing things. Adolescents can be movers, shakers, and even world changers, ready to risk in ways adults feel averse to, captivated by things adults dismiss as irrelevant or too daring.

One way teenagers seek novelty is by pushing away from what they've known thus far. It's inherently rewarding for them and often terrifying for their parents. During adolescence, your son will process many thoughts, beliefs, perspectives, and intentions he's never had before; your daughter will have adventures of which you know very little, if anything at all. These realities can be frightening for involved, loving parents.

This is part of letting go and allowing God to make something new in your teen. He didn't create another you when he brought your adolescent into the world. God populates the world with the novel and unique in every birth! He also designed the brain to seek novelty during adolescence, when teens can still be protected by parental oversight but can also explore much of the world before stepping into adulthood. Don't squander this remarkable gift. Don't distrust it. Instead, wade into the churning waters of your child's heart and mind.

In the busyness of our daily lives, it's easy to get frustrated with teenage boredom or curiosity. Bottom line, we sometimes don't want to be bothered with it; it takes too much effort, and we can't figure out what they want anyway.

We must not settle for this. One of our chief purposes as parents is to cultivate our children's hearts—the place of deep intimacy with God and with others, engaged with the world God created. An adolescent's expanding desire for new and different things opens a window of tremendous spiritual potential. This is the time to explore new forms of worship, try different bands or Bible studies, or expose them to Christian visual artists or speakers. Do this with your child. Talk to him or her about it. The possibilities are powerful.

You draw out the heart of your teen when you refuse to allow the "same old, same old" to overtake their spiritual life (or your own). Five different times in Psalms and once in Isaiah, the Lord commands us to sing a *new* song (see Pss. 33:3; 96:1; 98:1; 144:9; 149:1; Isa. 42:10). God is not afraid of novelty; on the contrary, he desires it for and from us. We should engage with our children in the same way, drawing their heart from the deep waters within and nurturing the exciting potential.

Try It Today: Do Something New with Your Teen

Over the next twenty-four hours, try something new with your teen. Stop at that ethnic restaurant, bakery, or grocer that you've passed a hundred times and pick out a unique snack. Better yet, grab a sampler platter. Test the flavors with your teen, and have fun with it if one or both of you starts smoking at the ears or racing for a glass of water as a new blend of spices rockets across your taste buds.

Take your teen to a go-cart track after school. Try on a style of clothes you've never worn. Listen to a new genre of music. Your imagination sets the only limits. Don't throw in the towel if your son or daughter doesn't seem into this at first; your attitude makes a big difference, so stay positive and pray that great memories can be made.

5

That Could Be *Epic*

We called it the airplane field, and legends were made there.

Sprawling acres of abandoned and mostly demolished government housing, peppered with the crumbling concrete remains of foundations and roads, overgrown with weeds and covered with motorcycle-carved pathways, the airplane field was our adolescent playground.

I (Jeramy) can still hear the throaty, percussive idle of my Yamaha 125's two-stroke engine, its high-pitched pinging at full-throttle acceleration. I can almost smell the acrid mixture of oil-gas exhaust and feel the crisp bay air whipping across my teenaged cheeks.

One day, two popular kids from school wandered into our wonderful wasteland. As a ninth grader, I was far from an outcast, but I also wasn't as popular as these guys. I'll be honest: I wanted to impress them, so when they turned to the sand jump and asked, "Can you take that thing, or what?" I popped off, "Wait right here."

About twenty feet tall and leveled to a plateau on top, the sand jump was one of the bigger obstacles the airplane field offered. The popular kids moved to the side as I buzzed away, giving myself about the length of a football field to get the bike wide open, into sixth gear.

Engine screeching, dirt flying, wheels spinning, I launched—and that really is the only applicable word here—into the air as I hit the jump at full throttle. I will never forget looking down at those guys with their heads fully tilted back, staring slack-jawed at me flying through the air. As the bike began to descend, it hit me: I'm either gonna be epic or in the emergency room.

As the ground rushed up to meet me, the bike hit with such ferocity that it repeatedly bounced several feet in the air, trying to correct forces that the 125's poor suspension couldn't account for rapidly enough. Somehow, by the grace of God, I didn't wipe out. And for that moment, I was epic.

Bio 101

I (Jerusha) distinctly remember adults in my teenage years making comments like, "Teenagers think they're invincible. Wait until you're older; then you'll understand." This never quite made sense to me. When I tried to get my parents' Mazda up to 110 mph on the freeway coming home from prom at 4:30 a.m., I didn't think I couldn't die. The fact that I could made it *more exhilarating.*

Of course, I look back now and immediately think two things: one, I was a complete fool, and two, my kids probably are going to do something equally foolish someday. Lord, please preserve them!

For the adolescent brain under construction, the combination of novelty and risk is a tantalizing concoction, stimulating production and a powerful release of the pleasure neurochemical dopamine. As we read in the last chapter, lower baseline levels of dopamine in the adolescent brain lead teens to seek new and thrilling activities. At the same time, adolescents often add a lack of impulse control, and the chemical results can be the neural equivalent of a Fourth of July fireworks finale.

According to adolescent brain researchers, impulse control is among the last areas to mature in teenage brains.[1] It's part of the brain's *regulatory system*, serving to rein in full-throttle drives and desires, as well as coordinating with other brain structures to exercise sound judgment. As parents, when we hear about teenage antics, we often chalk up the behaviors to an invincibility complex and an underdeveloped neural "brake system." These things are important, but there's more going on.

As Jeramy took the sand jump and as Jerusha pushed the pedal to the metal all those years ago, a unique and significant cognitive dynamic came into play: *hyperrational thinking*. Many teenagers are prone to this thought process, which takes the strong emotional bias of adolescence, the drive for danger, a still-developing regulatory system, *and* a maturing prefrontal cortex, then rolls it into one fascinating (and, for parents, often infuriating) ball. (Note: Since some teens are risk averse, hyperrational thinking doesn't apply to every teen. Understanding it is crucial for every parent, however, because even if it doesn't readily impact your teen, it may play a role in your son's or daughter's friendship cluster.)

According to neuroscientist Dr. Daniel Siegel, with hyperrational thinking,

> We examine just the facts of a situation and don't see the big picture; we miss the setting or context in which those facts occur. . . . As adolescents we can place more weight on the calculated benefits of an action than on the potential risks of that action. Studies reveal that as teens we are often fully aware of risks, and even at times overestimate the chance of something bad happening; we simply put more weight on the exciting potential benefits of our actions.[2]

What does this mean for us as parents? In order to understand adolescents and help our teens develop the incredibly important regulatory system, we can keep a few things in mind:

- **Hyperrational thinking isn't void of reason or reflection.** Hyperrationality differs from pure impulsivity in this way. When teens engage in hyperrational thinking, they use a cognitive process that places far more weight on potentially positive results than possibly negative outcomes. In other words, though some parents mistakenly attribute adolescent behavior to a lack of thinking, the adolescent brain actually works very hard to calculate pros and cons. Hyperrationality causes the brain to amplify pros and downplay cons.

- **Hyperrational teens *are* aware of consequences.** Adults often try to "correct" hyperrational thinking with education, assuming that if adolescents knew the dangers, they wouldn't engage in certain behaviors. Studies show, however, that teens are *hardly ever* oblivious to the risks of potentially dangerous activities.[3] Indeed, the negative consequences are fully known, but the positive benefits of a situation—the thrill, the reward, the chance to *be epic*, if only for a moment—appear greater. For this reason, lecturing your teen about "what could have happened," isn't the best approach. Instead . . .

- **Focus on motivation more than on specific behavior.** It's easy to concentrate on the apparent craziness of hyperrational thinking, but we must resist this temptation. Of course we need to maintain our child's safety. But finding out what "pros" an adolescent was after, what drove him or her to engage in an activity, is equally important and in some cases far more important. Increased activity in neural circuits utilizing dopamine in your adolescent's brain makes the drive for reward incredibly strong. Determine what reward a teen is seeking, and you'll be better able to address hyperrational behaviors. By age sixteen and under good conditions (i.e., given time, free of pressure, and with adequate physical health), adolescents are capable of calculating the risks and benefits of particular behaviors as well as adults. If we assume teens just "can't control themselves," we miss the more complex story at play: teens *are* developing impulse control and don't have it down yet, but they are *also* displaying a stronger—sometimes carefully calculated—preference for immediate rewards.[4] Don't overplay the behavior and fail to figure out what's behind it.

• **Teach in ways that change.** If simple education about the potential risks of dopamine-producing activities worked, we should have a wise adolescent population. After all, the United States shells out hundreds of millions of dollars each year trying to convince adolescents that they're not invincible, most often through school-based programs warning them of the dangers of driving and texting, substance abuse, unprotected sex, and so on. Statistics show, however, that despite knowing about potential negative consequences, teens still engage in hyperrational thinking and related behaviors. When it comes down to it, information simply isn't enough. Instead of focusing our attention and resources on trying to transform teens with data, we need to change the circumstances under which they make decisions. Let's turn our attention to that now.

Psych 101

Both adults and adolescents make decisions within a social and emotional context. We never make judgments in a vacuum. Because a teenager's regulatory system and relationship system are under simultaneous remodeling, hyperrational thinking becomes activated when teens hang out together and even when teens believe their friends will find out what they've done. The desire to be epic plays a major role in some teens' choices and relationships.

In one study, adolescents and adults were asked to complete a simulated driving course. The goal: reach the end of the track as quickly as possible, thereby maximizing a monetary reward. At different points, the simulation forced participants to make rapid decisions regarding yellow lights. Running through the yellow light certainly increased the likelihood of a speedy finish, but it could also result in a crash, which meant significant delay. Each test subject performed the simulation in isolation and while observed by peers. While playing the game alone, adults and adolescents performed comparably. When the peer observation component was added, things got interesting.

According to the research, adolescents took a greater number of risks when they knew friends were watching. In addition,

regions of the brain associated with reward showed greater activation when the adolescents knew they were being observed by peers. These results suggest that the presence of peers does not impact the evaluation of the risk but rather heightens sensitivity in the brain to the potential upside of a risky decision. . . . If the presence of friends had been simply a distraction to the participant, then we would have seen an impact on the brain's executive function. But that is not what we have found.[5]

What the researchers did find was hyperrational thinking—teens weighing the potential positive outcomes more heavily in the presence of their peers than when alone. Even more fascinating is that teens took more risks when they *assumed* their peers were watching, though in fact they were playing in isolation.

Here's why this is significant for parents:

- **Circumstances count.** This study and numerous others demonstrate that a teen's capacity to exercise good judgment is directly impacted by context. Physical, social, and spiritual circumstances can strengthen or undermine your teen's decision-making and cognitive processing. Hyperrational thinking occurs more often in highly charged emotional or social situations. Judgment deteriorates when teens believe the rewards of an action—even a dangerous one—will outweigh the negative consequences, and this happens more readily when teens are upset, excited, or tired. Exhaustion and stress can interfere with prefrontal functioning (good judgment, forethought, and decision-making) at any age, but the tenuous, under-construction circuits of your teen's brain are more vulnerable. Bottom line, teens make better choices when they have enough sleep, good nutrition, and lower stress levels. Adolescents exercise better judgment when their peer groups reward one another for what's truly positive, not what could be epic. You can help teens discover fun, exciting, *and* healthy ways to get the dopamine release they crave. Desiring the dopamine rush is not the problem; getting it in unhealthy ways is. Don't mistake the two.

- **Reward your teen for self-control and good judgment.** Research shows that under positive circumstances, free of distractions and overly emotional reactions or social pressures, older adolescents are capable of self-control *when they know success will be rewarded.*[6] It's difficult for many adults to deal with anger, over-stimulation, or exhaustion, but for a teen, whose brain circuits are still under construction, it's exponentially more challenging. Show that you recognize this and reward your teen when he or she makes good decisions. Grant a special privilege (perhaps a later curfew for an event) when you've seen good judgment at play. Connect self-control and good decision-making with reward, and next time a hyperrational thought darts into your teen's mind, the potential pro of a reward from you may out-weigh other, competing drives and desires.

- **Engage surrogate prefrontal cortexes.** In other words, surround your teen with adults—coaches, pastors, mentors, friends of the family, or family members—who have fully-developed executive functioning. As we get older (and if we get wiser), we realize when we can do things on our own and when we need help. Your teen's brain needs support from those who know how to use their brains and do so even in charged situations.

- **Establish clear boundaries.** Having well-defined boundaries enables your teen to factor important details into the equation when hyperrational thoughts come. With teens, succinct and clear limits help tremendously. In setting boundaries, we encourage you to refrain from issuing threats, causing your hyperrational teen to calculate, for example, whether it's worth a month's grounding to disobey. Sometimes teens weigh the pun-ishment and decide—in a hyperrationally adolescent manner—that they'll take it. Instead, let your teen know that boundaries exist and will be enforced if needed. For some teens, specifying a consequence becomes a game of chicken that nobody wins.[7]

- **Let reality do the talking.** Whenever possible, let natural consequences teach your teen about hyperrational thinking so you can stay supportive. If you let the world teach your adolescent a lesson, you can stay "on their team." You might say, for example, "That's too bad about your gym teacher not allowing you to wear your fedora during PE. What would the world be like without these limitations?"

- **Promote neural integration.** As teens mature into adulthood, their brain systems will work with one another more efficiently and effectively. The area of the brain most impacted by hyperrational thinking—the prefrontal cortex—is one of the last areas to mature, but during the pruning and remodeling stage, it gets better at enlisting other brain regions to support its important work.

Brain fMRI scans of adults, children, and adolescents reveal that when engaged in self-control challenges, adolescents show less widespread neural activation than both their younger and older counterparts. Children have what clinicians call a "diffuse and scattershot pattern," while adult brains display highly coordinated activity across various brain systems, similar to the swift and efficient play of experienced athletes versus the "disorganized play of kids who know the basic rules but haven't yet figured out the intricacies of team play."[8]

Just as teamwork on the athletic field increases with practice and connection between players, brain integration occurs as nonneighboring brain regions make physical connections via white matter "wiring" (myelination). Remember, the process of myelination is, in many ways, the ultimate use it or lose it prospect. An adolescent's brain will continue to lay down the neural cables connecting various brain networks into his or her midtwenties, and adults can promote neural integration by exposing teens to experiences and equipping them with resources that build good decision-making skills and model wise judgment. Reading quality books, evaluating the behavior and judgments—both good and bad—on display in film and television, and discussing news that highlights people using or lacking executive functions like planning, forethought, and so on are free and effective ways to help coordinate and integrate your teen's brain.

Faith 101

What would your teenager say in response to the question, "Do you think God wants you to have an exciting life?" How would you answer that question?

In John 10:10, Jesus clearly indicates that the life he died to give us is more than simply plodding along. Various translations indicate that Christ offers us life "to the full," life "abundantly" (ESV), a "rich and satisfying life" (NLT), or "more and better life than they ever dreamed of" (Message). We love how the late Dr. Dallas Willard rendered this verse: "life to the limit."[9]

Unfortunately, many teens see the Christian life as anything but a wild adventure of faith. Many adults suffer from this same misconception. We're certainly not insinuating that everything in life will be fun, but life in Christ isn't routine. We were made for *real life*.

Centuries ago, Iraneus proclaimed, "The glory of God is a man fully alive."[10] Does this describe your life? Can your teen see this is true? Do you need to stop plodding and "let yourselves be pulled into a way of life shaped by God's life, a life energetic and blazing with holiness" (1 Pet. 1:16 Message)?

In a fascinating way, the entire journey of faith begins with a hyperrational decision. When Jesus first called his disciples, they *immediately* left their fishing nets (see Matt. 4:20; Mark 1:18). Certainly, the disciples emphasized the positive possibilities and downplayed the negatives, but they did it because they had faith in the right thing, or rather person: Jesus himself.

The biggest problem with your teen's hyperrational thinking is not that it's there, but rather that he or she often places faith in the wrong things: the approval of people, momentary pleasure, the lust of the flesh, and the pride of life (see 1 John 2:16). What if teens actually believed that the ultimate reward was life to the limit, the life Jesus offers? Perhaps they would weigh what is true, good, worthwhile, and pure more heavily if they perceived us living a life energetic and blazing with holiness.

Try It Today: Take a Risk with Your Teen

When was the last time you did something exhilarating with your teen? When did you last have a breathless-with-fun moment together? Too often on the path of parenting we forget to stop and—in neurological terms—experience the dopamine surge.

During a blood moon, I woke our then thirteen-year-old daughter up at midnight to view the phenomenon. I invited her onto the roof with me, and as she took my hand to climb onto the Spanish tile, she hesitated.

"Isn't it dangerous?" she asked.

"Yes, but I can help you."

Neither of us will forget taking that risk together.

Seize any opportunity with your teenager. Ride the roller coaster. Go parasailing. Ask what your teen is interested in doing and do it. Take a risk and build your relationship.

6

But Nothing Happened

"Mom, there's a police officer at the door."

Words no mother wants to hear.

My (Jerusha's) mom spent the next hour with Officer Grayson and my younger brother, piecing together a story that included an empty house on the property next door, two middle school boys who were convinced that a drug cartel was using the abandoned dwelling and they'd be heroes if they discovered the hidden loot, a collection of broken windows, and other assorted damage. A story no mother wants to hear.

Teenagers notoriously make impulsive and foolish choices. In the wake of their adolescent's risk-taking, parents inevitably want to know *why* their kid would make such a rash judgment, *why* their teenager didn't think things through, and *what in the world* they can do to prevent this from happening again. Are risky behavior, impulsivity, and poor self-control just part and parcel of the teenage experience?

In short, yes.

Drat!

Does that mean there's nothing we can do? Absolutely not!

Understanding what's happening in your son's or daughter's brain can equip you to navigate the unpredictable, impetuous landscape of adolescence and help your teen do so as well. And here's even better news: this involves more than simply surviving; you and your teen can *thrive* as you explore why risk appeals to teens and how to channel that energy in healthy ways.

Bio 101

As we've seen in the past two chapters, the drive to explore novel experiences and hyperrational thinking dramatically influence adolescent decision-making. We observed that lower baseline levels of dopamine and capacity for higher release incite teenage sensation seeking. Overvaluing reward and underestimating risk (hyperrational thinking) complicates matters further. The combination of an under-construction command center (prefrontal cortex) and highly charged emotional center (limbic system) in your teen's brain can lead to behaviors ranging from mildly distressing to outright perilous.

Because brain systems prune, myelinate, and integrate at different rates, developmental time lags occur. This is particularly true of brain structures that excite teenage emotions and urges and those that enable adolescents to keep their impulses in check. Dr. Laurence Steinberg describes this brilliantly: teenage brains are like cars with supersensitive gas pedals and poor brakes.[1] They're magnificent at acceleration and seriously challenged in inhibition. Since we know that the brain's "braking system" (the prefrontal cortex) continues to mature into the early twenties and adolescence begins around eleven or twelve, parents and their teens often endure more than a decade of potential poor-brakes problems. It will help you to expect that teens will make some poor choices and be ready to help them through it.

Expectation impacts parenting in profound ways. Perhaps you've worked hard to train your son or daughter to think about the potential consequences of a decision. It's natural for you to hope that he or she would act consistently with the knowledge you've imparted. If this is where your assumptions stop, however, you'll likely experience disappointment throughout the teen years. You *must* factor in the reality that your adolescent's judgment, planning, impulse control, and discernment are under construction; they are works still in progress. If you've invested the time during childhood to lay a foundation of wisdom, you *will* reap the benefits . . . eventually. Don't be discouraged if you and your teen hit some speed bumps along the way; it doesn't mean everything you've done has been for naught.

If you feel like you failed during your son's or daughter's early days, remember the good news of neuroplasticity: your teen's brain is remarkably pliable during adolescence. Don't lose heart; instead, seize the opportunity to make changes while the brain is malleable! Helping your teen lay a foundation of wisdom and good judgment will require a different approach than it would have in childhood, but God will guide those who ask for his help (see James 1:5–6).

It will also help you tremendously to expect that determining when to do or *not do* something will be difficult for your adolescent. This simple (though far from easy) paradigm shift in your thinking will enable you to approach your teen's impulsivity with greater patience and wisdom. Self-control is a challenge for all of us, and you can best help impetuous teens not by becoming frustrated with their lack of forethought but rather by demonstrating self-regulation in your own life, reinforcing good choices, and showing empathy when your teen blows it.

Remember, the teen brain is highly sensitive to reward (indeed, far more sensitive to reward than to punishment), so find your adolescent's "currency" (what gets him or her really excited) and offer it as an incentive. Address poor choices and disobedience with firm and loving discipline, but don't stop with "giving a consequence."[2] Reinforce appropriate behavior. In addition, repeat "what happens when" stories to your teen, filling his or her mind with the possible outcomes of particular decisions. We don't recommend you do this as a scare technique but rather because the neural equipment to do this for themselves is undergoing serious remodeling.

The teen brain responds well to the repetition of real-life stories, in part because *prospective memory*, an important executive-level function of the prefrontal cortex, does not mature until the end of adolescence. Prospective memory enables a person to determine in advance to perform a task at a future time—for instance, not throwing a rock through the window of an abandoned house since that didn't go over so well last time.

Research consistently shows that a teen's prospective memory develops slowly and unevenly during adolescence. It often appears to be suffering (or even nonexistent) during the middle and high school years. By sharing stories about risk and consequence, adults can act as surrogate prefrontal cortexes for a teenager whose prospective memory is under construction. Don't fall into the trap of assuming "It'll go in one ear and out the other" or "They're going to do what they want anyway." You have a responsibility and an opportunity now that you know the teen brain struggles with an overactive accelerator, a less-than-perfect braking system, and a developing prospective memory. Commit to showing empathy for your teen's predicament, rehearsing truth to him or her, and setting limits when he or she won't. You can bemoan the biological realities, or you can act based on the knowledge you're gaining. Because your prefrontal cortex has been remodeled, we're trusting you can make the wise decision.

Psych 101

The next time your teen acts recklessly, wait before asking "Why?" Reality is, your adolescent may be as perplexed by his or her own behavior as you are. Responding to impulses from an under-construction brain often places your teen in pedal-to-the-metal, brakes-offline situations. If your adolescent knew the answer to "Why?," it would be easier for both of you. Most of the time, however, there's more at play than can be addressed with a simple response to "Why?"

We encourage you to ask open-ended, heart-revealing questions instead. Try one or more of the following:

- What were you hoping to gain by doing . . . ?
- What did you think would happen if you . . . or after you . . . ?
- What has happened since you did or said . . . that you didn't foresee or wouldn't want to repeat?
- What was your plan if . . . happened?

If your son or daughter answers "I don't know" to these questions, don't throw in the towel. Take a deep breath and remember what's happening inside his or her marvelous but currently muddled mind. Offer empathy with statements like, "I can see how you might have thought or hoped that X would happen." Provide an example to fill their prospective memory: "If you find yourself in a situation like this in the future, you could consider . . ."

Doing this in as calm a manner as possible is essential. Remember, your teen's emotional center (limbic system) is highly aroused; your reactivity will only supercharge it! Remaining composed is incredibly difficult when faced with risky behavior. You have the neural wiring to exert emotional self-control, however. Use it.

Emotionally manipulating adolescents into feeling bad about what they've done produces little. As neuroscientist Dr. Deborah Yurgelun-Todd observed, "Good judgment is learned, but you can't learn it if you don't have the necessary hardware."[3] Shaming teens or becoming angry with them in the wake of poor choices is about as effective as making a first-grader feel bad for not being able to multiply fractions. We need to focus our energies in the right place: helping teens strengthen the "hardware" necessary for wise decision-making.

Here are some specific ways to do that:

- **Talk about time.** Adolescents, especially younger adolescents, struggle with the concept of time. When asked about "the future," the typical middle schooler thinks about 3:00 p.m., when school gets out. You can imagine how this might lead to shortsighted decisions! Because time is such an abstract concept and abstract reasoning comes online throughout adolescence, it's often challenging for teens to imagine how their decisions might impact "the future." Even older adolescents, including college undergraduates, need help sorting out how choices may open or close doors of opportunity and how risk-taking today can impact not only tomorrow but years beyond too. Short, frequent conversations with your teen about this will be helpful.

- **Discuss risky adolescent "games" with your teen.** Researchers have tied video streaming websites, computer games, and social contagion (the "copycat phenomenon") to a rise in dangerous "play" among adolescents.[4] We don't include this information to frighten you. Indeed, we think it's a problem that, more often than not, media hype surrounding teenage behavior creates panic rather than fostering understanding and facilitating solutions. That said, as a parent you should be aware of the suggestions for "fun" to which your adolescent is exposed. Educate yourself about these and ask teens if they've heard of the activities, what they think about them, and what they plan to do if friends want to, for instance, car surf, "vodka eyeball," or play the choking game.

- **Focus on self-control, not scare techniques.** As we've emphasized, modifying a teen's circumstances is a better choice than trying to simply "educate" him or her out of risky behaviors, especially if you're prone to panicking and trying to "freak your teen out" of doing wrong. Humans first learn self-control by being controlled; this is an important facet of childhood learning. Your teen, however, is leaving childhood and must begin to regulate him- or herself. This is part of God's design for maturity. It's essential that you not leave teens unsupervised for long periods of time; it's also crucial that you resist micromanaging what they do with their "space." Teens respond best to aiming for something rather than simply inhibiting a behavior through threats or fear. Focus your conversation and activities on the positive outcomes of impulse control (e.g., greater financial stability, relational peace, more opportunities now and in the future) to motivate wise choices.

- **Dig deeper.** Parents often deal with risk-taking and reckless-ness on a surface level, addressing the behavior and applying a consequence. We encourage you, through observation and open-ended questions, to practice discernment and dig deeper. While getting below the surface will not be necessary every time, significant heart issues are behind some impulsive decisions. Risky sexual experimentation, for instance, may point back to a deep loneliness or sense of rejection.

As an example of how to dig deeper, let's consider the adolescent phenomenon of "partying." Parents sometimes dismiss this behavior with a "teens will be teens" mentality. Some believe it's not that dangerous for teens to drink, as long as they don't drive. Others go so far as to purchase alcohol for their teen's group of friends and provide a supposed safe place for experimentation. It's essential that parents be aware of the risks of their own attitudes and choices in instances like this. Here's an example of how digging deeper may influence a parent's and a teen's mind.

- Surface behavior: teens take risks and experiment with alcohol.
- Surface parent reaction: lectures, grounding, preventing teen from going to parties and being with friends who drink, etc.
- Deeper truth #1: *Partying is about more than alcohol.* With even limited exposure to pop culture, you'll find that teens view parties as integral to adolescent life. Most media-portrayed par-ties include alcohol and/or drugs, and—regardless of whether condemning or condoning underage drinking—they also imply that alcohol creates shared memories and solidifies community. In other words, partying is about a longing for experience, connection, and ritual, not just drunkenness. If we're to under-stand teenagers' partying, we cannot focus only on alcohol or other substance use. Teens recount (and thereby relive) stories

of "partying" as a social narrative that unites their group with a shared history. Digging deeper can help parents see the importance of communal experience and encourage us to facilitate opportunities for teenagers to "party" without alcohol.

• Deeper truth #2: *Partying with alcohol and other substances is particularly dangerous for teens.* Despite what some adolescents and their parents believe, drinking (and recreational drug use, including smoking marijuana) during the teen years is *not* a harmless rite of passage. On the contrary, the highly charged reward system and under-construction executive functions of the teen brain leave it incredibly susceptible to the dangers of substance use. Alcohol and other drugs flood the brain's reward system with high levels of dopamine. Remember, the brain's reward system "keeps score" with dopamine, reinforcing behaviors that lead to pleasure. Drugs and alcohol throw off the score-keeping, big-time. The teenage brain, revved up and rearing for reward, is highly vulnerable to chemical influence and quickly becomes accustomed to drug-elevated levels of dopamine.[5] Sadly, the "highs" experienced with substance use become a standard unattainable through the normal joys of daily life. Researchers have also discovered that young people who drink five or more alcoholic beverages a couple times a week (think parties on Friday and Saturday) lose a significant amount of myelin, the "white" brain matter associated with neural integration as well as attention, decision-making, judgment, self-control, and memory. Tragically, these impairments persist into adulthood.[6]

As you can see, digging deeper into the "party" mindset is important because it can help parents determine how to maximize the desire for communal celebration and shared memory while operating on accurate information about how substances impact the adolescent mind. Experimentation shouldn't be dismissed or ignored. The consequences are too far-reaching. More information is available in Appendix A, "The Truth about Substance Use." Regardless of whether you believe your teen abuses substances, please don't skip this important section.

Faith 101

Happily, research indicates that teenagers' risk-taking behavior can yield positive results, benefits that can balance the potential perils. One huge plus is that teens, who lack adult-brain wiring (i.e., inhibition) and generally act more impulsively, discover natural limits in the world around them. Think of it this way: when children learn to walk, they take quite a few tumbles. Scrapes and bruises abound. As much as we'd all like to protect our children from this (or, in teenage terms, the consequences of risky behaviors), they *learn from experience.*

The Bible teaches that "in all things God works for the good of those who love him, who have been called according to his purpose" (Rom. 8:28). In other words, we can trust God to use our children's boundary-testing and independence-establishing risks, even their mistakes, for his good purposes. Please don't misunderstand us; we're not urging you to step back and allow your kid to go off the deep end and make life-altering mistakes so that God can show up and patch everything back together.

We are called to counsel and guide, spurring our teens on in love and good deeds, instructing them in the ways of the Spirit, and intervening in dangerous situations. This is part of our God-ordained responsibility. Another part is stepping back so that our adolescents can learn, even from failures. No good parents want their teen to fail; indeed, we do pretty much everything to prevent it. We also know, however, that in our own lives, failures teach powerful lessons. Taking risks sometimes leads to failure, but failure is never the end of the story with God. On the contrary, in God's hands, risk-taking and the potential mistakes that come with it are opportunities.

When it comes to risk-taking, we encourage you to focus on *discipling* your teen even more than *disciplining*. Discipling your teen means buying up every opportunity that comes with risk-taking behavior, using it to point out God at work. Just as Jesus did with his disicples, tell stories that direct your teen's attention to God. With parables that wove deep truth and daily life lessons together, Jesus was a master subversive teacher. Such "spiritual storytelling" is effective with teens, who are drawn by narrative and no longer interested in "this is just how it is," concrete reasoning.

While seeking to disciple your teen, keep in mind that the more you fulfill your own role as a disciple of Christ, the better your teen will see how to grow in relationship with him. Discipling involves, for instance, consistent, focused prayer, just as Jesus modeled with his disciples; the Gospel accounts reveal that Jesus often stole away to pray intently. Does your teen know you pray?

Discipling is about preparing teens for adulthood, when they'll have to learn from their own mistakes by the grace of God. It's far easier to want to discipline our teens out of risk-taking behaviors, but that is a shortsighted goal; discipleship is for life.

Your teen's desire for risk and adventure is a simultaneous invitation for you to trust in God's goodness to work *all* things together for good and also to press into discipling rather than simply disciplining. God wired the brain to go through these astounding changes so that teens can learn, even from mistakes. He also ordained that parents would be required to grow and change in the process. It's marvelous, though yes, it's also sometimes maddening!

Try It Today: Practice Negotiation

Even if you've already established a curfew, discussing it with your teen is a great way to include him or her in the process of forethought, planning, and judgment, skills that aren't hard-wired into the adolescent brain and thus benefit from practice. When we help teens use their prefrontal cortexes in this way, we help them create neurobiological, psychological, *and* spiritual changes. It's an all-around win.

Note: it's important that you actually negotiate, not unilaterally "lay down the law." Ask your teen what seems reasonable. Listen. Ask follow-up questions. Agree on a time frame to think about it, then reconvene to discuss. Remember to adjust as your teen ages and shows greater responsibility.

Apart from helping integrate your teen's executive functioning, there are four specific benefits of negotiating a curfew in light of potential risk-taking behavior:

- Crazy impulses can become scheduling impossibilities when you have to be home by a certain time.
- If peer pressure is a factor, curfew can be an excuse for your teen (e.g., "Thanks for the invite. Midnight spear fishing could be fun, but my parents expect me home by . . ."").
- Because sleep deprivation impacts a teen's impulse control, establishing a curfew promotes at least some regulation of sleep patterns.
- If curfew is broken, you can use the "time and a half" rule to curb inappropriate behavior. With this, your teen "owes" you time (i.e., has to come in early) the next time he or she wants to go out. It can be a great motivating force.[7]

7

What Do You Want Me to Say?

I (Jeramy) sit down at the dinner table after a twelve-hour workday. I'm 100 percent interested in my family and want to know what's going on in their lives. I'm also 100 percent exhausted and don't feel like prying stories out of my teenage daughters. How can they answer everything with three or fewer words?

"What happened at school today?"

"Nothing."

"Did you learn anything new?"

"It was school."

"Can you tell me something about your day?"

"I don't know."

I try a different tactic. "Let's play the high/low game" (where every person in the family shares a highlight and low point in their day).

As if on cue, both of my articulate, intelligent daughters are dumbstruck.

I'm worn down; it all feels like too much work. At the same time, there's an internal battle brewing within me. I used to know pretty much everything that happened in their lives. They used to race to see who could hug me first. My frustration actually stems from a deep disappointment: my girls aren't as open to me anymore.

Jerusha and I know we're not alone in asking, *Why is it so hard to communicate with teens?*

Perhaps you've been asking yourself that for some time. Maybe grunts and one-liners have replaced what used to be an open dialogue. Have car rides with your teen turned into silent tech zones rather than a time to download the day's events?

Perhaps, like me, you feel fortunate when your teen does open up. I still have great talks with my girls. Trouble is, they usually happen when I'm least expecting it and often when I'm least prepared. For instance, right before bed seems like our oldest daughter's favorite time to come out with a statement like, "The popular girls made fun of me at school today." This is the most revealing thing she's said all week, yet my eyes are so heavy I may have to prop them open with toothpicks so that I can be there for her. In my exhaustion, the best combination of words both to make her feel better and to help her develop resilience threatens to evade me. If I had only thought this through—but how could I have known? This is the first I've heard about it!

Again I wonder, *Why is it so hard to communicate with teens?*

Thankfully, understanding the radical changes in our teenagers' brains and emotions can help us rethink how to best connect with the adolescents we love.

Bio 101

By this point in the book, you know that many radical and pervasive changes occur in an adolescent's brain. You know that neural connections are being pruned in a "use it or lose it" manner, and that the integration of brain systems and the process of myelination (the brain's method of "insulating its wiring" for increased efficiency and specialization) lead to significant changes and profound challenges. A teenager's brain also undergoes significant construction in areas that control language.

Indeed, an adolescent's maturing brain leads to advanced language development. Healthy teens assimilate seven to ten new words per day, producing a working vocabulary of over forty thousand words.[1] As abstract reasoning improves during the adolescent years, the language needed to express and comprehend abstract meanings matures along a similar trajectory. Fourteen-year-olds understand more nonliteral word meanings than their ten-year-old peers, and eighteen-year-olds recognize far more. Adolescents also grow in their ability to use sophisticated language skills such as persuasion and negotiation. Their capacity to relate engaging narratives and understand complex instructions increases as well.

Ongoing education exposes adolescents to advanced language. However, without the maturing neural "hardware" for grasping and utilizing abstract concepts—including metaphor, symbolism, irony, and sarcasm—teens wouldn't be able to communicate in terms beyond concrete realities or appreciate humor in the world. These are essential and marvelous gifts from God which propel your teen into adult life. (Honestly, though, sometimes we wish that irony, sarcasm, and the desire to passionately persuade and negotiate didn't fully develop until teenagers were out of the house!)

Roughly fifteen years ago, researchers discovered that "physical changes in the portion of the brain associated with language learning begin in early childhood but decline dramatically after age twelve. . . . In live testing of [adolescent] brain response to a language skills task, researchers saw a shift from activity in the temporal lobe—normally associated with language—to the cognitive center in the frontal lobe as teens matured."[2] Lead researcher Dr. Jay Giedd found that the temporal lobes, sometimes called the "seat of language" do not reach their gray-matter maximum until age sixteen. Only then do they undergo pruning.[3]

In other words, roughly coinciding with puberty, your teen's language capacity changes dramatically. Across adolescence, growth shifts away from temporal lobes, associated with language acquisition and expression, and toward the frontal lobes, responsible for advanced cognitive processing. As parents, we should expect some communication hiccups as the brain undergoes this essential remodeling. Bottom line: because your teen's brain is under construction, communication will sometimes be a challenge.

Whereas your concrete-thinking prepubescent child may have eagerly dialogued with you about every aspect of the day or looked to you for an answer to every problem, you will likely find that teens, who are learning to use new language and reasoning skills, turn inward and want to figure things out on their own.

Intense neural remodeling can leave adolescents feeling confused. Teens have altogether new (and sometimes disconcerting) thoughts and feelings. Early adolescents don't yet have a vocabulary to express these new emotions and the ideas that accompany them. Teenagers may feel they are the only ones who have ever thought or felt a particular way, that something is wrong with them, or that no one would understand even if they tried to articulate the storm and stress inside. As parents, we have a responsibility to model healthy discussion of feelings and thoughts. We also have a charge to patiently, empathetically, and graciously persist even when communication is difficult.

Before looking at specific ways to foster communication with our under-construction teens, we'd like to note two important facets of neural development and language processing.

The first relates to gender differences. Studies suggest that two areas of the brain—the Wernicke's and Broca's areas—both essential for language comprehension and expression, grow faster in adolescent girls than their male counterparts.[4] Males usually "catch up" in early adulthood, but if you are the parent of a teenage boy, take heart and be patient. Your adolescent son's language skills may be on a slower track than those of your teenage daughters or the daughters of your friends.

The second fact involves the intersection of developing language and the virtual ubiquity of digital communication by teens. Research indicates that the rise of texting, social media, and other forms of technological communication may cause teens to pare down their vocabulary from their capacity of over forty thousand words to a paltry eight hundred.[5] Because digital communication on the scale adolescents now use it is so recent by scientific standards, further study is necessary to determine how pervasive this problem is or can become. Parents simply should be aware of this and encourage communication in other forms when teens are at home, around extended family members, or out in public. Perhaps the whole family can agree to turn off their phones or other devices when they visit grandma or during dinner. Initially, this may be difficult—for you and your teen—but it's worth it. What talking actually does for the teenage brain is truly remarkable, and conversation happens far more readily when digital devices are set aside.

Psych 101

Beyond the neurological remodeling occurring in your teen, the psychological, relational, and social changes happening in and around them lead teens to communicate with their parents in different ways.

Desiring to display independence, teens may no longer wish to process everything with their parents. As we noted before, they sometimes lack the words to express their feelings. Have you ever noticed how many different things a teen describes as "boring" or "stupid"? It's *inconceivable!* You may feel like *The Princess Bride*'s exasperated Inigo Montoya, who shakes his head and mutters, "You keep using that word. I do not think it means what you think it means."

Remember too that teens often feel unsafe sharing embarrassing thoughts or problems, let alone mistakes, with parents who they believe won't be able to handle it. How would you respond to a teen who confesses, "I cheated on a test today. I didn't get caught, but I feel really bad about it"? A parent who can calmly say, "I'm glad you told me. That's obviously made you sad, and it makes me sad too. How can I help you make this right?" will likely earn a teenager's trust on a deep level. We appreciate Foster Cline and Jim Fay's counsel in *Parenting Teens with Love and Logic*: "Remain available without prying. . . . The parental attitude must be, 'Tell me your thoughts; I can handle them,' regardless of what those thoughts may be."[6]

It's normal for your teenager to internalize more and verbalize less. It's going to happen and is an important part of your adolescent's development. Give grace to a teen who is trying to figure out what to share, when, and how. Your adolescent is on a steep communication learning curve.

To foster healthy communication with your adolescent, keep these things in mind:

- **Teens respond best to shorter, more frequent interactions.** This is especially true if you need to talk with your adolescent about something important. Don't think in terms of a "once and for all" approach to conversations about potential problems like substance use and sexual experimentation. The same goes for positive topics like faith, trust, and building healthy relationships.

- **Teenage brains learn by example.** If you want your teen to develop healthy communication skills, model them. Speak with the vocabulary you want your adolescent to use. If you don't want your teenager to gossip, you shouldn't either. To equip adolescents for eventual success in adult life, model how to share thoughts respectfully and graciously. If you want your son or daughter to learn nondigital communication skills, don't default to texting. And make sure that your teen sees you engage in and resolve conflict well (more on this in the next chapter).

- **Close your mouth and he may open his.** Parents eager to communicate with their teens often pepper them with questions. Asking good questions can be a great way to open the lines of dialogue. That said, questions can also feel like hostile inquisition to a teenager whose desire for privacy and sense of self are developing. Instead of filling every space with words, try being quiet now and then. A silent car ride home from school may unnerve you, but it also may be just the ticket for getting your teen to start a conversation. This has been personally helpful for me (Jeramy), as I found myself asking our girls the same questions over and over again. I finally let there be silence in the car or at the table, and my daughters eventually started asking questions or sharing their thoughts without prompting. There's no guarantee this will work with your adolescent, but it's a technique well worth trying.

- **Listen more than you talk.** This is closely related to the preceding tip. Deliberately deciding to listen, to stay focused on what your teen is saying without interjecting your own ideas and solutions, is powerful. Nod and express empathy with a "Hmm" or "Oh." Taking what your teen says seriously will deepen your relationship. It also helps develop your adolescent's capacity to think. Try to understand where your teen is coming from, even if his or her opinions differ from your own. Don't automatically shut down a topic that interests your teen just because it doesn't pique your curiosity. Instead of knee-jerk reacting or correcting, listen actively and ask questions that show interest and elicit understanding (e.g., "That must be hard. Can you tell me what that's like for you?" or "That's interesting. Tell me more."). Try to see *how* a particular thought makes sense to your teen rather than simply evaluating *if* it's rational.[7] While this can be extremely difficult, it's by no means impossible. As parents (with more developed frontal lobes), we can control our impulses to speak and exercise judgment as to when and how to respond.

- **Ask, "Would you like to hear what I think?"** If the answer is "Yes" or "Okay," be concise and consistent. If it's "No," back off for a while. When you do offer counsel, advise without demands or declarations. Obviously we're not talking about avoiding intervention with regard to life-threatening issues; we simply mean that in everyday communication—say, when your teen wants to vent about problems with a teacher, a friend, or a sibling—you can *choose* to wait, listen, ask follow-up questions, and *then* extend the offer of help. Parents of teens often find that the less they give unsolicited counsel, the more their teen asks for advice. You have a better chance of making an impact if you begin by letting your adolescent know he or she has been heard.

• **Use "I," not "you" statements.** Teens are master defenders. If you come at them with a "You always this . . ." "You never that . . ." or "You're so rude/foolish/wrong" list, most adolescents will reject your thoughts out of hand. Instead, tell your teen explicitly what you're thinking or feeling, as well as what you plan to do. For example, "I am disappointed in your behavior. I'm going to my room to cool off. I'll discuss this with you in an hour." It doesn't work to tell teens what they're going to do: "You get in your room right now and think about what you've done to disrespect me. You won't be going anywhere until you change your attitude." Sorry if this comes as a surprise to you, but you can't "make" your teen do, feel, or think *anything*. Using "I" statements and refraining from "you" statements places the ball squarely in your teen's court. When parents continually tell teens what to do, they cannot learn how to tell themselves what to do.

• **If you need to talk about something serious, find an appropriate place and time.** Context makes a huge difference in certain kinds of communication. Trying to hash out "Why?" and "What's next?" at 12:15 a.m., after a third broken curfew infraction, probably isn't a good idea. Neither is having a talk about sexual purity at Starbucks. Interrupting your adolescent in the middle of something to talk *right here, right now* won't lead to the best communication. Exercise patience and set up a time to talk. This will have the added benefit of giving you a chance to think and pray beforehand. Try not to spring a heavy topic every time you and your teen are alone; he or she may not be eager to hang out with you in the future. Finally, don't get into the bad habit of talking only when you've got a bone to pick. As Dr. Michael Bradley writes, "The very sound of your voice can then become a signal to your kid that another grilling is coming. It's tough enough talking to a teen. You don't need them hearing your first words as an air raid siren."[8]

• **Subversively engage your teen.** This is an especially important communication technique with teens who want to exert independence and autonomy with their choices. You can invite your teen to participate in providing the solution by doing one or more of the following:

◊ **Give your adolescent a choice.** Try a phrase such as, "Would you like to do X or Y?" or "Feel free to do X or Y, but Z is not an option."

◊ **Give factual information about the problem and its impact on others.** Try, "Your dishes in the sink make it difficult for me to get dinner ready" and wait for a response. If none is forthcoming, you can add, "What do you suggest should be done about that?"

◊ **Say it in as few words as possible.** For example, point to laundry on the floor, say, "Laundry in here, please," then point to where dirty clothes belong. Most teens will get the point. If you hear a cruel comment or a foul word come out of your teen's mouth, responding with a short phrase ("Ugly words aren't tolerated here") can communicate more effectively than a long lecture.

◊ **Use writing and humor.** Leave a little note for your teen or draw a funny picture indicating what you'd like done. For example: "Dearest Peyton, I'm perishing in a sea of dirty clothes. You're my one and only hope. Please help me before you come to the table for dinner." Important note: never use demeaning or accusatory sarcasm. Teens will mirror the way you communicate with them. If you use biting humor or cutting remarks, don't be surprised if your teen does so as well.

◊ **Employ the magic words.** It's distressing how few parents use please and thank you with their teens. If you need help, ask for it kindly and express gratitude.

◊ **Humbly ask for clarification.** If you're getting the silent treatment, don't automatically assume your teen is being rebellious. Instead, tell him or her you don't want to misread the situation and respectfully ask your adolescent to verbalize thoughts and feelings. This internal storm may have nothing to do with you! Asking for clarification engages your adolescent's under-construction prefrontal cortex (to talk about it, they have to process what they're feeling). This helps teens begin exercising self-awareness and emotional regulation.

Faith 101

Jesus spoke often and powerfully about the importance of choosing our words wisely. As parents, we should take his statement in Matthew 12:34, "Whatever is in your heart determines what you say" (NLT), very seriously and apply this truth in practical ways.

First, we need to recognize that how we communicate with our adolescent children reflects the state of our own hearts. If you are continually frustrated, angry, sarcastic, biting, or quick-tempered with your teen, it's time for a heart checkup. Ask the Holy Spirit to reveal ways in which your speech reflects your heart. Every single one of us can grow in the way we use words. No one has perfectly "tamed the tongue" (see James 3:2). It's important to look at your own patterns of communication before honing in on your teen's shortcomings (see Matt. 7:3–5).

Second, we must consciously and carefully evaluate how our teenagers' words reveal the state of their spiritual health. This should lead not to condemnation or an exertion of power or control but rather to humble prayer, gentle rebuke, and the offer of continual help. Never forget our call as Christians: be slow to speak and quick to listen (see James 1:19). If you find yourself struggling to live out that verse, use the words of Psalm 141:3 as a prayer: "Set a guard over my mouth, Lord; keep watch over the door of my lips."

Everyone experiences communication ups and downs during the adolescent years. Your teen may speak impulsive, illogical, and incendiary words, but take a deep breath; it's essential to get beneath the surface and separate an emotional outburst from a core belief. Your teen will likely say things that drive you crazy; you'll be tempted to disregard his or her thoughts and opinions. Resist this at all costs. Making fun of, dismissing, or failing to recognize your adolescent's faltering attempts to engage in adult dialogue will shut down communication every time.

Remember, your teen's brain is under construction; the neural centers for language are being remodeled. Understanding this can give you compassion and help you discern the best ways to confront and correct poor behavior.

Undoubtedly, this is challenging. Christian parents are never alone, however; the Holy Spirit continually guides, encourages, and convicts us. Pray, "God, what do *you* want me to say?" and then listen to his counsel and act accordingly. Better communication with your teen will follow!

Try It Today: Don't Let the Door Close

If your teen reveals something to you, keep the conversation open by asking a few days later how things are going, expressing your concern, or reminding him or her that you're praying.

Another great way to keep the door open is to ask your adolescent to teach you something or offer an opinion. This is a huge confidence booster to a young adult, who wants to assert independence and competence. Whether you ask for help with technology or for an opinion on what to do in a particular situation, inviting his or her participation in your life is a fantastic way to help your teen develop communication skills while powerfully demonstrating that you love, value, and respect him or her.

8

Why Are You Freaking Out?

"Oh no," moaned our older daughter, Jocelyn. "Dad, I forgot my clarinet."

Jasmine, our younger daughter, instantly exploded, "Are you kidding me? You *always* do this. Now we're going to be late. I *can't believe* this!"

Allow me to set the stage for you: We left for school early that Friday morning because Jasmine had a makeup flute lesson. It was T-minus fifteen minutes until that began, which meant we had just enough—and no more—time to make it. Add to the mix the fact that Jasmine emerged from the womb anxious about being on time, while Jocelyn takes, shall we say, a more laissez-faire approach to promptness. Now top things off with my condition. It had been one of "those" weeks at work—long days, lots of meetings, and some intense situations; since, as a pastor, I work weekends, Fridays are my day off. Let's just say I wasn't in the mood to referee their spite-fest.

"Don't you even *care*?" Jasmine spat at her sister.

"No," Jocelyn scoffed with a little laugh.

Nothing could have infuriated Jasmine more. I honestly thought she might revert to scratching her sister's face. Instead, she loosed a tidal wave of semi-incomprehensible comments on her sister's choices. Jocelyn turned stone cold. Their emotion—uniquely manifested, but equally intense—far outstripped the relatively minor problem we faced. To me, it was completely ludicrous.

I'm sorry to say that instead of leading my girls out of their conflict that morning, I jumped right into it. I was fed up, and I allowed their fight to trigger an emotional grenade in me.

As a dad, when you start with, "Your behavior disgusts me," it all kind of goes downhill from there. I gave full vent to my emotions, and in the moment I felt entirely justified in doing so. In order to get my point across, I laced my words with force; even if I didn't yell, my disdain came across.

I expected that they would apologize, but (inconceivably!) they just sat there. My anger escalated, and so did theirs. When we finally got to school, the car was thick with unresolved tension.

That morning, I chose to act with emotional intensity rather than emotional intelligence. I don't want to do that, and I don't think you do either. The conflict my girls and I faced that morning was minor as far as parent-teenager fights go, but I hope that in being vulnerable and sharing my reaction to this "daily grind" example, I can encourage you that we're in this together. What I've since learned about my teenagers in researching for this book has equipped me to better address the inevitable battles that arise while living with teens. I want to share that with you, knowing God can use it to help us both.

Bio 101

An incredibly complex collection of brain structures nestled deep in the center of the brain, the *limbic system* plays a role in regulating many functions, including basic human rhythms (appetite, sleep, mood, libido) as well as memory, motivation, and emotion. Yeah, it's pretty significant. Some experts refer to the limbic system as the "emotional brain" or the source of emotional life.

Roughly coinciding with puberty, the limbic system becomes more readily aroused, which helps explain why most teenagers experience and express higher highs and lower lows than they have before. Because their limbic systems undergo the emotional equivalent of a race car starting its engine, teenagers often gravitate to emotionally intense experiences, including conflict. Because the limbic system also factors significantly in the development of the social brain, heightened limbic system arousal contributes to a teenager's greater sensitivity to relationships.

Development in your teenager's limbic system is an essential component in his or her maturation toward adulthood. The amazing design of the limbic system allows the brain to respond to the environment with emotion that compels action. It really takes work on parents' part, however, to understand that the emotions adolescents express and experience are undergoing wide-scale remodeling. Your teenager's ability to handle anger and fear, as well as joy, surprise, and pretty much every other feeling, is under construction. Show grace to your emotional teen.

Like all neural systems, the limbic system works in concert with the entire brain to perform its functions. Indeed, the limbic system and the prefrontal cortex (the brain's CEO) constantly communicate; the prefrontal cortex evaluates emotional input and helps regulate associated impulses and the decisions necessary to act. Since we know that the prefrontal cortex develops slowly over the course of adolescence, we should expect that emotional intensity will often outstrip our adolescent's ability to process and control it.

This does not mean that we excuse poor behavior; on the contrary, we should be students of our adolescents' hearts, evaluating how they deal with emotions and graciously helping them make changes. This requires remarkable discernment. As we better understand what our teens are facing on a neurological level, we can show compassion while helping to shape our teenager's heart. We can help our teens learn emotional restraint by keeping our own cool through engaging our adult prefrontal cortex while theirs is under construction.

As an adult, you have a greater capacity to regulate the some-
times-unreasonable emotional responses you may feel. "Teenagers,"
writes Dr. Jesse Payne, "do not have a developed prefrontal cortex
to supervise the onslaught of emotions and drama. . . . When they
feel strongly about something, they will often make a decision based
on their emotions rather than logic."[1] You can exercise control over
your own emotions (unlike me in the story that opened this chapter)
as well as graciously pointing out what appropriate emotional responses to situations might be. In other words, I could have helped
my adolescent daughters by gently and firmly helping them see
that neither cold disdain nor explosive anger is a healthy reaction
to conflict.

To summarize, let's return to the analogy of your teen's emotional
brain resembling a car starting its engine. This particular neural "car,"
throughout adolescence, will remain sensitive to feelings and urges
(think "gas pedal"). This vehicle will also lack fully wired executive
functioning (think "brakes"). Your teen is driving around with a hot
accelerator and brakes that haven't been fully wired to the rest of the
car. As your teen's brain integrates and myelinates, resulting in faster,
more efficient connections, things get easier for the vast majority of
teens (and their beleaguered parents). In the meantime, a great deal
of patient instruction and grace is required.

Happily, heightened arousal in the limbic system can also produce some fantastic outcomes. Channeled in healthy ways, teenage
energy and exuberance often inspire us. Increased emotional intensity associated with limbic system development can enhance vitality.
Simply "shutting off" your teenager's limbic system isn't the answer.
Instead, we have to take a higher road as parents and model for our
children how to process and express emotions.

Psych 101

As parents, we are called to model emotional health to our children,
guiding and instructing them as they respond to different emotional

situations. The trouble is, many parents don't know how to do this themselves.

Indeed, when intense emotions erupt, many parents revert to juvenile methods of dealing with conflict. I've been guilty of it; you probably have too. Sometimes you may feel justified, like I did, in giving full vent to your emotions. *After all, how will they learn if my tone doesn't communicate how serious this is?* you may reason. Don't be deceived; your unrestrained emotional reaction doesn't teach your teenager anything positive.

In order to model healthy emotional experience and expression, consider the following:

- **If need be, walk away.** Or get a drink of water. Unlike when your child was a toddler, you don't have to rely on immediacy to make your point. Adolescents have the capacity to connect past behavior with present consequences. Indeed, it can be highly effective to say, "Unfortunately, I am angry. I don't want to discuss this until I have calmed down. We'll address this later." Give yourself time to evaluate the situation, pray, and come up with a strategy for approaching your teen when you've had a chance to cool off.

- **Name it to tame it.** In other words, know your own emotion and verbalize it calmly. Instead of, "Your behavior disgusts me," I could have tried, "I'm feeling angry and disappointed. I would like all of us to stop talking for two minutes so we can cool down." For some of you, naming and taming will be harder than it sounds. When an emotional volcano explodes inside you, it's sometimes difficult to tease out the feeling or thought at the conflict's root. Finding respectful words to label your own emotion—and doing this using an "I" rather than a "you" statement—engages your prefrontal cortex, which forces your brain systems to work together. You can help your teen to do this as well. After the heat of the situation has cooled, you can ask a question like, "What one emotion are you feeling most right now?" to start a dialogue.

- **Evaluate outcomes.** That morning, I saw my daughters' skirmish as an inconvenience, a disruption to my peace and schedule. I didn't view it as a chance to help them see the consequences of their emotions. In other words, I missed the chance to lead them, to help them evaluate their hearts. Conflict can be an exceptional opportunity for growth. After you've helped your teen to name his or her emotion, try asking something along these lines: "What did you hope to gain through your _____ (use an emotion word like anger, worry, jealousy, etc.)?" Allow your adolescent to answer. Then ask, "What did you actually get?" If you're thinking, "Wow. This is kind of complicated," you're right. There aren't shortcuts to developing heart awareness. But more than any other emotional goal for your adolescent, you should pursue *emotional intelligence*, "the ability to monitor one's own and other people's emotions, to discriminate between different emotions and label them appropriately, and to use emotional information to guide thinking and behavior."[2]

- **Don't be a diversion.** When you lose emotional control, your adolescent diverts energy to evaluating your behavior rather than his or her own. You don't want this. Instead, keeping your cool forces your teenager's feelings and the heart motives behind them to the surface. In a fascinating series of studies, researchers determined that when adolescents fixate on the emotions of others, their ability to process other information weakens. In other words, your angry expression and tone dulls your teenager's capacity to hear the content of your message. If you want to have an effective conversation with your adolescent, don't allow your emotion to distract him or her from what you're communicating.

- **Let your teen have the last word.** This is particularly challenging for me as a dad, especially when I feel right. But foolish pride means having to get in the last word. Going at your teen with a tit-for-tat, "we'll see who wins" mentality actually ensures a lose-lose situation. Mature pride means modeling patience and humility. When the last words to echo in your teen's brain are his or her own irrational ones, it's easier for you to confront this behavior later. "The last word" is something you can actively choose to surrender. In saying this, we don't encourage you to dismiss vulgar or offensive slams uttered by your teen. Even to these, however, you can calmly respond with a statement like, "I will not insult you in return, nor will I stay here to be insulted. We will discuss this later." A good rule of thumb is that the angrier you feel inside, the calmer and quieter you should endeavor to keep your voice. This effort will help balance the force intense emotions usually infuse into your expression—facial and verbal.

- **Lay down your weapons.** When emotions run high, it's easy to lash out with demeaning, accusatory words. Teens automatically counterattack or shut down. Stop participating in the war (after all, fighting is an act of cooperation in which both parties have to keep going). Instead of launching a grenade like, "You're so irresponsible!" when you find out at 9:00 p.m. your teen hasn't started the five-page paper due tomorrow, try naming your feeling and putting the ball back in your teenager's court: "I feel frustrated with this situation. What do you plan on doing?" You can also neutralize arguing by turning statements into thoughtful questions. Instead of "You never put your laundry in the basket! What do you think this is, a hotel?" you can ask, "Where do I expect you to put the laundry? What do you expect might happen if you continue to leave it on the floor?" Direct questions cause teens to engage their prefrontal cortexes; in other words, to *think* rather than simply respond with emotion. As we discussed earlier, teens often don't know the answer to "Why?," so stretch beyond repeatedly asking this. When in doubt, revert to questions that require thought. The more we can help teens use their prefrontal cortexes to regulate emotions, the better.

- **Focus on what you can control.** Remember, you cannot "make" your teen do, think, or feel anything. You can only control your own thoughts and behavior. Because you know this (even though you may not always feel it), focus on what's within your control by telling your teen what you're going to do and not do. Don't waste your breath, energy, or opportunity by telling adolescents what they will or won't do. You can't enforce it, and you lose the chance to influence when you attempt to clamp down. We like using Jim Fay and Foster Cline's simple statement: "I am not going to argue with you."[3] When *you* stop arguing without trying to make them stop, you model for your teens the truth that self-control is possible. When you desperately try to control the situation, you model that this is a parent-approved method of dealing with conflict. In doing so, both of you lose.

- **Factor in extenuating circumstances.** The teenage brain is highly "state-dependent." What this means is that when teens are well rested, well fed, and dealing with fewer stressors, their integrative functions (i.e., the ability of their "rational brain" to keep their "emotional brain" in check) work more efficiently. Conversely, when adolescents are exhausted, hungry, premenstrual (for girls), or under undue pressure, it will be more difficult for their brain systems to work together. Have mercy on your teen. Take into account what may be going on with your teen under the surface. Studies show that people with overall healthier diets and better patterns of exercise experience less conflict in their lives. Those who sleep soundly have less anxiety and report more satisfaction in their interpersonal relationships. Perhaps these factors are playing into your own emotional reactions.

Faith 101

Conflict with your adolescent may very well be one of the greatest trials of your life. Whether marked by vicious rage, snarky sarcasm, passive-aggression, or icy indifference, the emotions your teen experiences and expresses impact you powerfully. God understands this. In fact, as our heavenly Father, he knows well how a parent feels when a child's emotions overrun reason. For such times as these, the Holy Spirit empowers us to act with love and wisdom.

Galatians 5:22–23 describes the benefits of close connection with the Holy Spirit: "The fruit of the Spirit is love, joy, peace, patience, kindness, goodness, faithfulness, gentleness and self-control" (ESV). The closer you choose to walk with God, the better able you will be to display kindness, gentleness, patience, and self-control during the trial of teenage emotionalism.

As much as we'd like to avoid difficulties, God often uses trials to mature us. Conflict with your teenager is an opportunity for growth—in both of you—if you allow God to use it for redemptive purposes. That's why his Word commands us to "Consider it pure joy, my brothers and sisters, whenever you face trials of many kinds, because you know that the testing of your faith produces perseverance. Let perseverance finish its work so that you may be mature and complete, not lacking anything" (James 1:2–4).

Most of us would like to be mature and complete, not lacking anything, *without* having to go through trials of many kinds. That's not an option. We can only view trials with "pure joy" when we see them as opportunities to become who God designed us to be. We believe that you want your teenager to become everything God created him or her to be; you wouldn't be reading this book if you weren't interested in that. The trial of emotional conflict is one instrument God will use to accomplish his purpose in your adolescent's life. Expect it.

Troubles arise when we see a teen's hot "accelerator" (limbic system) and not-fully-wired "brakes" (prefrontal cortex) as an intrusion on our lives. We often respond poorly to our teens because their emotions disrupt our plans and desires. In other words, we try to secure our own happiness at all costs. Though God longs for us to experience joy in life, happiness isn't our highest goal; holiness is. When we genuinely live out this truth, we can view conflict as an occasion for growth in godliness—our teen's *and* our own.

Try It Today

You've probably heard the phrase, "Pick your battles." We'd like to alter that counsel a bit and encourage you to *sort* your battles. If you classify every issue into two categories, either a battle or not, you miss the chance to teach your teen negotiation.

In her excellent book *Inside the Teenage Brain*, Dr. Sheryl Feinstein urges parents to write down the top ten sources of tension with their teenager. What do you and your adolescent argue about most? Go ahead and start your list right now!

Now look carefully at each of these conflicts and sort them into three groups:

1. We need to establish a firm boundary here.
2. We can negotiate.
3. We can let this go.

If you identify all ten conflicts as #1 issues, you may benefit from having an objective outsider (perhaps a friend, mentor, pastor, or counselor) evaluate your list with you. Not every issue requires a top-down mandate. There should be some room for negotiation in areas that create conflict between you and your teen.

You will better train your adolescent to regulate him- or herself if you practice decision-making, negotiation, and the ability to evaluate the outcomes of choices with them. Indeed, allowing a teen to figure out "on his own" that what he thought he wanted isn't all that it's cracked up to be can be an incredibly effective method of instruction.

Over the next twenty-four hours, do this sorting exercise. Then actively let at least one conflict go (perhaps how your teen wears her hair) and negotiate another. You're helping your teen's brain to integrate, so take a deep breath. You're doing great!

9

Why Are You Looking at Me Like That?

Jennifer stood at the kitchen sink, tackling a mound of dishes. The noise of the garage door opening announced that sixteen-year-old Maddi was home. Drying her hands, Jennifer turned around just as Maddi entered the kitchen. "Hi, honey! How was school?"

Maddi tossed her backpack on the counter and opened the fridge. She stood for a couple moments in silence, staring into the fridge, and then shut the door with a sigh. "Mom," she started, "I have to be at Rachel's house at 6:30 tonight to work on our chem project."

In the split second it took Jen to process this information, recognizing that picking her son up from soccer practice, getting to the cleaners, finishing dinner, and driving Maddi to study group couldn't all happen by 6:30, Maddi exploded.

"Why do you always look at me like that? I can't help it that you *still* haven't let me get my license. I've been sixteen for three weeks and I'm still in *car pool*. This is totally ridiculous. You freak out no matter what I ask for."

Jen's temper flared a bit, but she forced herself to speak evenly. "Honey, I was just trying to figure out how I could make it all happen."

"Fine! I'll just tell Rachel she has to do the project by herself," Maddi retorted.

Tears brimmed hot in Maddi's eyes, and Jen cocked her head to the side, totally baffled by the situation and fighting the rising frustration of being completely misunderstood. For some reason indecipherable to Jen, her expression of confusion spiked her daughter's fury further.

"See! You always look at me like I'm an idiot. Just leave me alone!"

Storming out of the kitchen in tears, Maddi left her mother utterly perplexed and more than a little peeved. What in the world just happened?

Bio 101

Statistics show that communication succeeds or fails based on the combination of several factors. The words we speak are only a percentage—often a small percentage—of effective communication. Indeed, according to some research, only 7 percent of our communication corresponds to content, whereas tone of voice and nonverbal cues make up 38 and 55 percent of communication, respectively.[1] A startling 93 percent of our communication is nonverbal!

Most parents of adolescents can recount a tale (or twelve!) of communication gone wrong. When two imperfect humans are in relationship, plenty of "run-of-the-mill" misunderstandings will crop up. That's par for the course. During the teen years, however, the daily irritation and confusion that can accompany communication seem to take on a particularly intense dynamic. Perhaps the situation in your home doesn't typically dissolve into tearful outrage as it did for Maddi and Jen. Your teenage son may get a glazed, apathetic look and sit in stony silence rather than exploding in anger. A combination of eruption and ennui may plague your household.

Bottom line: communicating with a teenager can be complex and confounding. This isn't just anecdotally true; neurobiological studies clearly demonstrate that misconstruing nonverbal cues is *highly likely* during the adolescent years.

If you've ever heard a teen say, "Why are you looking at me like that?" you may be relieved to know that understanding the physiological dynamics at play can help you endure and respond to the nearly universal communication struggle parents face when raising adolescents. As we've seen throughout this book, during the process of neural pruning, different areas of the brain are under construction, being remodeled for greater efficiency, speed, and strength. When certain segments of an adolescent's brain[2] are being refined, decoding nonverbal cues—particularly facial expressions—becomes significantly more difficult for a teenager.

In groundbreaking research,[3] Dr. Deborah Yurgelun-Todd discovered that adults and teenagers interpret facial expressions in very different ways and with very different degrees of success.

Psychologists group human facial expressions into six basic categories. Of course, many nuanced expressions of emotion exist, but the broad categories of anger, fear, disgust, surprise, happiness, and sadness encompass many variations. Adults almost invariably identify these expressions accurately.

Dr. Yurgelun-Todd's team performed fMRI scans of adult and adolescent volunteers while they viewed images of various facial expressions. Study participants were then asked to identify the emotion associated with each image. When presented with a face registering fear, 100 percent of adults correctly categorized the emotion.

What about the adolescents? Only 50 percent deciphered it accurately. A full half of the adolescent participants misinterpreted this facial expression. Some teens suggested the image represented anger or aggression. Others posited shock or confusion. Some simply couldn't come up with an answer apart from "I don't know."

Dr. Yurgelun-Todd also reported that misperceptions were common regardless of the teen's apparent level of sophistication, which means that even adolescents who display mature communication skills in other arenas may struggle to correctly perceive the emotion behind facial expressions. No wonder misunderstandings abound during the teen years!

Other research provides additional clues as to why parents and teens often experience a gulf in understanding. As they studied how adolescents decode basic facial expressions, Dr. Yolanda van Beek and Dr. Judith Semon Dubas discovered that teens often attribute negative emotion even to neutral facial expressions.[4] Additional findings based on fMRIs also indicate that when shown a neutral face, adolescents respond with the "emotional center" of the brain, the limbic system,[5] whereas adults interpret the same facial expression with the brain's center of judgment and reasoning, the prefrontal cortex.[6]

In other words, when determining the emotion behind a particular expression, most adults make a cognitive decision, drawing on the region of the brain where decision-making and executive function rules. Adolescents, however, express more of a gut reaction, using the area of the brain where emotion reigns supreme to decipher facial expression and the emotion behind it.[7]

These are the biological facts, but what does this mean for us as parents?

Psych 101

The first and most important thing we can recognize is that teenagers *will* misunderstand our facial expressions. It's a when, not if, situation. According to the experts, teenagers struggle to identify the correct emotion behind an expression approximately 50 percent of the time. If our adolescent children mistakenly attribute an emotion to us *half* of the time, perhaps we should consider some different modes of communication.

Here are a few basic encouragements:

- **Rise above.** If your teen mistakes your facial expression, an emotional reaction will likely follow. When your teen "flips out," it's difficult to keep your own temper under control. Explosive anger, hurtful accusations, and tearful or icy withdrawals can cause us to feel angry, disrespected, misunderstood, and offended. As the adult in this relationship, you are called to override your emotions using the reasoning portion of your brain. Rising above does not happen effortlessly or instinctively, however. What happens naturally is reactivity. Just because you feel an emotion doesn't mean you have to express it. When we *work on* and *practice* rising above our own feelings, we demonstrate self-control. We also model healthy living by overriding reactivity with rational thinking.

- **Identify your expression.** Naming your emotion is an essential and helpful mode of teaching. Remember, naming an emotion helps tame it. If your adolescent asks you, "Why are you looking at me like that?" responding with "I'm not!" probably won't be helpful. Instead, verbalize what you are feeling and *be honest*. Despite their struggle to identify facial expressions, many teens have a highly-tuned "you're faking it" meter. It may be counterproductive to plaster a forced smile of your face and ask, "What do you mean, sweetheart?" If you feel confused, say, "I feel confused." If you feel hurt, tell your adolescent. If you're angry, state that calmly. Talk openly with your teen. Some parents think it will create further conflict to acknowledge that they're annoyed, angry, or afraid. On the contrary, when genuine emotion is revealed, you can work to overcome it. Name it to tame it!

Imagine with me that your fourteen-year-old son tells you that the twenty-year-old assistant baseball coach who drove him home from practice was pulled over for going 90 miles per hour on the freeway. Your son thinks it's funny. What expression might jump onto your face? A mix of relief that he's safe and fear at what could have been? In those moments, when emotion is rushing around inside of you, your teen is observing. He may say, "Why are you so mad?" Let's say you respond with, "This isn't anger, son, this is fear." He wants to know, "What are you afraid of? Nothing happened." "I'm afraid," you might reply, "because I can't control what happens when you're in the car with someone else. I'm afraid because I can't always protect you and I don't want to lose you. I'm afraid because you seem to think this is funny and it's pretty serious. And I'm disappointed in your coach for endangering everyone tonight." This may not make complete sense to your teen, but your job right now isn't to convince your adolescent that your emotional response is accurate. Your job is to be honest and defuse the emotionality of the situation as far as is possible.

- **Take ninety seconds.** Social neurobiologists study how brain chemistry impacts relationships. Their research shows that emotions follow a predictable ninety-second arc. This means that any emotion you feel will rise and fall within ninety seconds if proverbial fuel isn't added to the fire. If you know that your feelings aren't under control, remove yourself from the situation. Excuse yourself to get a glass of water, go into the bathroom (even if all you do in there is silently scream), or flat-out say, "Look, I need to take ninety seconds here." Some of you may be thinking, "That may work for others, but I've tried the whole counting to ten thing, and my teen just pushes and pushes." Fair enough. This may happen, and it may happen often. Remember, however: you are the adult. Despite what a teen does, you can communicate, "I am trying to get my emotions under control, so I'm not going to talk again for two minutes." Chances are, the first few times you say something like this to your teen, he or she will be annoyed or angered. Hold your ground. After seeing you take ninety seconds a few times, your teen may start to experience the same calming sensation that comes from waiting for this neurological rise and fall. In a noncombative moment, explain the biology behind your ninety-second discipline. You may be surprised at your adolescent's reaction. Flipping out doesn't feel good. Unbridled anger and bitterness are poisonous emotions that leave us feeling worse than when we started. Your teen may see the benefit in taking time to allow the heat of emotion to pass. Ninety seconds doesn't solve the situation, but it

puts out some of the emotional flames and lays the groundwork
for healthier communication.

• **Understanding is not the same as excusing.** Biology is never
an excuse for bad behavior. Your teen will have a more difficult time with emotional regulation during the adolescent
years. As all adults know, however, just because something is
difficult doesn't mean it's impossible. You can have compassion for the difficulty your teen faces in reading emotions and
facial expressions without excusing wrongdoing. The next time
a conflict surrounding communication arises, consider telling
your teen something like this: "You may not understand what
I'm feeling or thinking right now. I am feeling _____
and thinking _____. I'm explaining this to you so you
can understand me and make a decision as to how you'll react.
You and I can discuss this now, but I will control my temper
and I expect you to do the same. If we can't both do that right
now, let's take a few minutes and come back when we're able
to speak calmly." One word of caution: This is a suggestion,
but it's not a formula. Communication is a very individual
thing. Sadly, many parents of adolescents discount potential
solutions without giving them a go. There's no harm in trying!
If your teen reacts disrespectfully, consequences are necessary.
Just remember that compassion is the catchword for the teen
years. Try to keep in mind just how much is happening in your
teen. A little understanding goes a long way.

Faith 101

In order to write this chapter, we looked at every biblical occurrence
of the word *face*. There were almost four hundred references![8] Many,
of course, correspond to the physical appearance of particular individuals, but the Bible also talks about how the face reveals character.
Even more exciting for us was studying the references to God's face
and the blessing that comes when God turns his face toward us.

In Numbers 6, the Lord instructs Moses, Aaron, and Aaron's sons to bless the Israelites with the words, "The LORD bless you and keep you; the LORD make his face shine on you and be gracious to you; the LORD turn his face toward you and give you peace" (vv. 24–26).

Because of Jesus Christ, God's face is turned toward us in love and blessing, now and forever! His face shines upon us with grace. He turns his face to us and gives us peace. Isn't that wonderful?

We can learn two essential spiritual lessons from the biological facts and relational implications we've looked at in this chapter: we are called to (1) trust in the Father's goodness and (2) pass on the Father's grace and peace to our adolescents.

Parenting a teen is difficult work. God alone enables us to do it well. Every day, we need to put our faith and hope in the goodness of our heavenly Father. If you don't believe that God's face is shining on you with grace, if you don't understand that he loves you and sustains you, that he longs to give you peace, you won't be able to model that for your teen. It's not enough to know in general terms that God loves the world. Trusting in his love, grace, and peace for *you* is your source of help and hope.

When we follow the Father's example and turn our face toward our children in love, we pass on the grace and blessing, peace and security our adolescents need. This doesn't mean you will always smile on your children physically (if you try to do that, you'll be faking it a lot, because sadness, disappointment, and anger are part of the human condition). It *does* mean that you can establish that your default position and the desire of your heart will be to love and bless your teen, to give them grace and peace. When your adolescent knows this is the core of your relationship, conflict won't destroy either of you, and misunderstandings will challenge but not devastate.

Try It Today: Smile

According to scientists, the power of a smile is undeniable. The simple act of smiling leads to more joy, both for you and for others around you. Indeed, when we smile, a positive neural feedback loop is stimulated, reinforcing feelings of joy.[9] Truly, "sometimes your joy is the source of your smile, but sometimes your smile can be the source of your joy."[10]

The amazing health benefits of smiling have been documented as well: smiling reduces stress, lowers blood pressure, increases feelings of well-being, and enhances pleasure by releasing endorphins.[11] Researchers also discovered that when we smile, not only do we appear more likeable and pleasant but others also perceive us as more competent.[12] In other words, the more you smile, the more likely your teen will be to perceive you as an enjoyable *and* effective parent.

Still not convinced? Consider this: British scientists discovered that smiling excited the brain as much as receiving a large cash reward.[13]

Now that you know the benefits of smiling, here's your action point: *choose* to smile more and smile often. Bring life to those around you and enjoy the positive benefits yourself!

10

Aren't You Sorry?

After I (Jeramy) dropped the girls at school with the words, "Your behavior disgusts me" ringing in my ears, I muddled through the morning, frustrated and resentful. This was my day off, and their selfishness and bickering had ruined it. Later on, Jerusha and I were slated to outline two chapters for this book. Wouldn't you know it? The chapters were about conflict and forgiveness. That day, God simultaneously displayed his sense of humor and his powerful, gracious conviction.

I knew I needed to apologize to the girls. Regardless of their behavior, I had expressed myself with cynicism and bitterness. I failed to use my adult brain. I didn't exhibit self-control, kindness, patience, and love.

At the same time, I didn't want to absolve the girls of their part in the conflict. I still felt that my frustration was warranted (even if my means of communicating it wasn't). I still wanted to be right. That morning—as backward as it now appears in writing—I actually felt an obligation to blow up in order to get my point across and emphasize their wrong. In short, my pride threatened to block the path toward healing.

As I considered my options, it struck me again how much it costs to truly apologize. I had to admit my own wrong, trust God to work in the girls' lives, and believe that asking for their forgiveness wouldn't undermine my ability to lead them in addressing their own heart issues. Extending a genuine apology requires humility, and surrendering my pride seemed especially pricey.

What costs even more, however, is choosing to hang on to resentment, clinging to the illusion that I can control my adolescents' behavior, and relinquishing the opportunity to influence their lives by modeling humility, authenticity, and empathy. Insisting that my daughters apologize to one another and to me without admitting my own wrongdoing in the situation would result in hypocrisy, and teenagers are particularly adept at recognizing hypocrisy (in everyone else!).

It would cost me far more *not* to apologize, so I did. I spoke to each of the girls individually and asked for their forgiveness. Both of them assumed when I walked into their rooms that I wanted them to apologize to me. It caught them off guard that I started by confessing my own inappropriate expressions of anger. The walls came down, and we were able to talk about what had happened.

Do I wish I had used my adult brain to control my emotions in the first place? Absolutely! Do I believe I would have better influenced them had I kept my cool rather than blowing up and apologizing later? Definitely! And yet, in spite of this, I believe what happened was used for the good of our family. The power of repentance, humility, and forgiveness can transform your family too.

Bio 101

A little over two decades ago, scientists discovered that "certain neurons fire when an animal performs an action, such as a mouth or limb movement, and also when the animal passively observes an identical or similar action performed by another individual."[1] A short time later, these specialized brain cells were deemed "mirror neurons," and studies to determine the presence of a neural "mirror network" began.

While science is far from understanding these fascinating mirror neurons, research indicates that such specialized cells may help humans learn by observation, imitate, and/or recall behaviors (mirror neurons are suspected to play a role in the hippocampus, a portion of the brain which sorts and solidifies memory).[2] Studies also suggest that mirror neurons may help humans interpret the actions of others and show one another empathy.[3]

According to Dr. Caroline Leaf, "We are entangled in each other's lives, and this is reflected in the structure of the brain. We have 'mirror neurons' that fire up as we watch someone else laugh or cry or drink a cup of coffee. . . . Through these neurons we literally fire up activity in the brain without actually using our five senses." In other words, it appears that mirror neurons allow us to experience what someone else does or feels. This ability, to "identify with, and vicariously understand, the internal experiences of another person, making communication more genuine and valuable," is called empathy. Dr. Leaf continues, "When we empathize, many different regions of the brain collaborate in addition to the tiny, miraculous mirror neurons. We have been hard-wired to experience powerful compassion for others."[4]

These mirror neurons also appear to operate when exposed to negative stimulation. For example, if I (Jerusha) struggle with doubts about being an effective mother, my anxiety and fear infect the world around me. My daughters making a comment like, "You never buy any good food," could trigger a storm of negative, "I'm not good enough" neural firing in me. My hungry adolescent expressed her disappointment with disrespectful annoyance, but instead of focusing on her need (hunger) and her heart issue (unkind accusation), my own flood of emotions can be sponged up by my teenager.

We don't consciously determine when mirror neurons fire. Their activation is hardwired by God into our brains. It appears that the neural mirror network can automatically produce imitation, of both positive and negative emotion and behavior. Your teen's brain is constantly observing, evaluating, and reproducing your own behavior. Talk about evidence that parents need to model appropriate behavior!

Scientific research also indicates that for humans to understand the *reasons* behind an action, portions of the frontal cortex—which scientists currently believe do not contain mirror neurons—must fire along with the neural mirror network, helping identify the action and encode it into memory for future repetition.[5] Here's the reason that discovery is significant for teenagers and their parents: if the area of the brain that enables adolescents to rationally determine the motives behind an action is under construction, but mirror neurons in other regions are sponging up the feelings and actions of other people, lots of misunderstandings may arise.

When you experience conflict with your adolescent, assume that mirror neurons are firing. You can help wire into your teenager's brain how to respond to tension wisely. If you swell with anger and react with frustration (which may, in part, be your own mirror network activating in response to your teen's emotion and actions), you'll likely find those negative emotions reflected in your adolescent. If you hold on to bitterness, withdraw, or stonewall your teen after a fight, what do you suppose his or her mirror neurons might do?

Consider also: Could mirror neurons play a role in apologizing? Perhaps the reason admitting your own wrong breaks down the walls around your teen's heart is because your humility is mirrored in his or her brain (even if they don't plan on it or want it to be). While science hasn't definitively proven the implications of mirror neurons, we witness the power of observational learning every day as parents. Knowing that biological underpinnings likely exist helps us recognize the importance of our own choices, especially in the wake of conflict. We desire to set an example of humility and repentance and hope that you'll choose the same.

Psych 101

Taking this high road can be difficult. Keep in mind, however, that you are equipped with an adult brain that can better process what you and your teen did, as well as *why* both of you acted that way.

Your teen's brain is under construction and not as well integrated as your own; his or her ability to empathize and comprehend the dynamics of a situation is more limited. Have compassion and help your adolescent to mature by modeling.

When you determine you should apologize, you can take specific steps to do it well. Though apologizing may feel weak to you, genuine humility demonstrates great strength and courage to your teen. An apology communicates that you respect your teen as a person. Telling your teen that you've thought things over and want to apologize also models self-reflection. To offer a strong, loving apology:

- **Make sure your heart is in the right place.** A heartfelt, authentic apology transforms relationships. An apology offered to make the other person feel bad or so you can point out what the other person did wrong will not help matters and may, in fact, worsen them.

- **Express regret.** This involves acknowledging you hurt the other person. Phrases such as "I'm sorry I treated you that way" can be effective.

- **Acknowledge fault.** An honest apology is self-disclosing. It takes responsibility. Use words like, "I was wrong. It was my fault."

- **Don't try to "make him understand."** A quote widely attributed to Benjamin Franklin sums up the importance of not contaminating your apology with demands for retribution: "Never ruin an apology with an excuse." If your teen quickly apologizes in return, great. If he or she doesn't, give the lesson time to sink in.

- **Find out what you can do to make things right.** This shows you will do what it takes to mend any breach in the relationship.

- **Express the desire to change and take action to do so.** Repentance is not merely saying you are sorry but rather "doing a 180," completely turning from a previous course of action.

This is an essential step because it solidifies a commitment to ongoing growth.[6]

In his many years working with teens and families, Dr. Michael Bradley consistently found that adolescents respect the same things in adults: honesty (especially with regard to mistakes), restraint in the face of their own stormy emotions, courageous self-disclosure (i.e., sharing with your teen how your own mistakes have impacted your life), and setting aside the need to "be right." Teens respect adults who act like real grown-ups.[7]

Bradley also discovered that teens widely *disrespect* the same parental behaviors. At the top of the list: hypocrisy, selfishness, arrogance, cold indifference, sharp-tongued sarcasm, and a controlling, "I told you so" approach to parenting. When you resort to small-minded retaliation, spewing hurtful words in response to his, or when you go stone cold because she's done it *again*, you shrink in your teen's esteem.

If you hypocritically demand that your adolescent apologize, yet never offer an apology of your own, your teen learns the wrong lesson. Adolescents need—and want—parents who "walk their talk," especially when things don't go well. Don't pretend to be something you're not; where needed, commit to change and let your teens watch you grow. Placing your need to be in control and your "right" to be respected above your teen's need to see what true humility looks like will poison your parenting. Your adolescent is watching (mirror neurons are firing!). Show them what it really means to take responsibility for actions and change course.

Faith 101

Many of us have heard or read scriptural encouragement regarding anger and patience. One well-known verse from the book of Proverbs instructs, "A gentle answer turns away wrath, but a harsh word stirs up anger" (15:1). Keeping in mind the potential roles of mirror neurons, this verse shows God's truth written into our very bodies. What we do, and how we do it, is reflected in others.

When we calmly respond to highly charged emotions, we defuse the situation and encourage adolescents to use their developing executive functions. When we apologize, we model how to acknowledge wrongdoing and change course. On the other hand, when we allow our emotions full vent, we kindle more emotional fire. Parents don't carry sole responsibility for maintaining peace at home, but they are called by God to help teens regulate their emotions. Setting an example of self-reflection and courageous admission of responsibility honors God and helps your teen.

If you want to use conflict as an opportunity for growth, consider what happens when your own mirror neurons are on fire. What happens when your teen wounds you and resentment creeps in? Think back to the things teens said destroy their respect for parents: hypocrisy, selfishness, and angry retaliation. In contrast, teens consistently reported that empathy and forgiveness built respect.

Forgiveness sets *you* free from continuing to carry the hurt another person caused you. Your teenager will wrong you and may do so frequently. At times, especially when they offer a heartfelt and humble apology (the kind you are trying to model), forgiveness may flow readily from your heart. On other occasions, when your teen's heart seems hard and ugly, forgiveness may feel far more difficult.

Regardless of whether your teen acknowledges his or her wrongdoing, God urges you—indeed, *commands* you—to forgive. Colossians 3:13 plainly directs, "Make allowance for each other's faults, and forgive anyone who offends you. Remember, the Lord forgave you, so you must forgive others" (NLT). You *must* forgive. Why? Because you have been forgiven of so much.

You do not stand above your teen. You too are in need of forgiveness. Indeed, during the adolescent years, you may find yourself reacting in ways you never imagined you would. Anger, guilt-tripping, accusations, manipulation, and shame may explode from within you. The teen years can expose our own heart issues, problems we'd rather not face. This may make parents feel even less connected to their adolescents, who they see as the source of this new and painful awareness.

God, however, intends this for good; the revelations you experience while parenting your teen can transform you. Don't allow his work to be derailed by fixating strictly on what your teen does or doesn't do. It's all too easy for parents to dismiss their own issues. You may feel angry, defensive, and resentful if your teen points out inconsistencies in your own life. Instead, go to God. Receiving forgiveness from him enables you to extend it to others. As you change, God can use you to change your teen.

On the other hand, lack of forgiveness—along with the bitterness and resentment that come in its wake—corrodes your heart and soul. It separates you from God and from others (see Matt. 6:15). But that's not all; the physical consequences of unforgiveness are medically documented and profound.[8] Withholding forgiveness—especially over a long period—leads to serious physiological and psychological health concerns, including elevated heart rate and blood pressure, increased risk of heart attack, higher chance of problematic cholesterol, greater risk of blood clots, cancer, anxiety, depression, poor self-image, anger, and a litany of other chronic issues.[9] Reading a list like that, it's hard to imagine *choosing* to hang on to the offenses of others, yet that's what many people resolutely do.

Your teen knows whether you are a bitter person or not. He or she sees the way you react to people who hurt you. Your adolescent is observing and learning by evaluating you. Don't proclaim the importance of forgiveness in your faith and then display the exact opposite in your relationships. That hypocrisy will spell internal agony for you and toxic disconnect for your teen.

Practicing, extending, and modeling forgiveness for your teen is not only important for him or her; it also continually sets you free. Perhaps you are holding on to the hurts someone else inflicted on you. Maybe your current or ex-spouse, a family member, a friend, or a co-worker wounded you terribly. Choosing to forgive will not only breathe life and hope into your own heart; it will also change your teen. If you need help with forgiveness, check out this endnote, which lists some helpful resources.[10]

Try It Today

Not surprisingly, teens report that conflict between parents (whether parents are married or divorced) creates major stress in their lives. Your teen needs to see you practice empathy, humility, patience, and forgiveness in your marriage, with your ex, or—if your child's other parent is not around—with those closest to you. Over the next twenty-four hours, consider any ways you've mistreated your spouse or your teen's other parent. If you haven't done so already, apologize and seek forgiveness.

For those of you who are married, keep in mind that marriages often suffer during the teenage years, when tensions can erode loving care for one another. Don't allow this to happen. Repentance, humility, and forgiveness are the antidotes. Spouses of teens too often lose connection with one another as a result of busyness during the adolescent years. They may talk about a lot of things—ranging from daily details to big concerns—without genuinely communicating. Show your teen that your marriage matters by taking the time to connect with your spouse. The health of your marriage must remain a priority. Even in the midst of adolescent crisis, you teach your teen a lot when you maintain a loving relationship with your spouse.

To those of you who bravely single parent, we admire your commitment to your children. Your role is filled with challenges. How you communicate with your ex-spouse and whether you have forgiven him or her impact your teen significantly. If you've not yet begun the journey to forgive, now is the time. Remember, forgiveness sets *you* free from the toxins of resentment and bitterness. Allow God to deal with your ex-spouse; you can be free. You have a unique opportunity to demonstrate for your teen the true power of grace.

Your teen will flourish surrounded by love. Determine today to move beyond conflict with grace, practicing the art of apology, extending and receiving forgiveness.

11

What's Wrong with My Friends?

I (Jeramy) peered across the desk at Mr. and Mrs. Greenfield, both visibly weighed down by concern for their seventeen-year-old son.

"He was doing okay until he started hanging out with *those kids*."

Mr. Greenfield spoke with a harsh and accusing tone; his features contorted with anger. Silent tears rolled down Mrs. Greenfield's face, staining her cheeks with mascara and exhausted grief. The Greenfields had discovered yesterday that their son had been caught smoking pot at the high school football game Friday night. Blake had been suspended for five days, and the Greenfields were beside themselves.

"Jeramy, he met those kids at youth group!" Mr. Greenfield sputtered. I genuinely couldn't tell if he was blaming me or pleading for my help; probably his words included a little of both.

Several days later, I met with Jeannette and Bill, mom and dad to Ashley, a precocious fourteen-year-old who "just didn't fit in" with other kids her age. Ashley was lonely, and Jeannette and Bill were worried.

"I don't know how to help her," Bill confessed.

"There's so much drama with other girls, and they can be really unkind. I know Ashley's a little different, but there's got to be somewhere she fits . . ." Jeannette's voice trailed off sadly.

As a pastor, I've had countless meetings like these. The dynamics of adolescent friendship—with its roller-coaster highs and lows—consumed a good deal of my youth ministry counseling appointments. Parents felt confused, frustrated, and afraid.

Every so often I'd have an uplifting talk with a parent whose teenager had connected with a strong peer group and flourished as relationships deepened. And every week, I watched students scan the youth group crowd, asking with their eyes, "Do I belong here?"

As parents, we simply cannot underestimate the feelings of isolation, rejection, and insecurity that many teens feel. We also cannot ignore the powerful *positive* influence healthy peer relationships can have on our teens.

We understand firsthand—remember, our girls are adolescents—the concerns you may feel regarding friendship, peer pressure, and teen drama. It's exhausting! The chaos and fickleness of teenage girls, the foolishness and immaturity of adolescent boys, the pecking order established on abilities and appearance: it not only makes us alternately angry or sad for our teenagers, it can also touch on memories and insecurities from our own past.

Helping your teen navigate friendships will require you to be clued in but not controlling, patient rather than panicked, and prayerful instead of pushy. Persevering pays off, however. Let's arm ourselves with information and encouragement for the journey.

Bio 101

During adolescence, the neural structures that together comprise the "social brain" undergo significant alteration. When we use the term *social brain*, we refer to the complex neurological architecture that enables humans to relate to one another, to understand the feelings and intentions of others. The neocortex, an important component in the social brain, plays a major role in relationships by helping direct areas of higher social cognition (e.g., empathy, language, regulation of action and emotion, introspection). Since this area is particularly large and well developed in humans, it's evident that we've been hardwired for a life of relationships, not fierce independence.

During adolescence, teens typically begin pushing away from the safety of the home[1] and toward the world outside, particularly the world of peers. As an adolescent's social brain develops, interest in peers and relationships changes significantly. In healthy teens, a move toward peers results in the establishment of friendships they choose and derive pleasure from (even if accompanied by some pain along the way). For teens who struggle, the neural push toward peer relationships may leave them feeling abandoned, alone, and/or angry. As parents, we should be prepared for these eventualities.

While your teen's social brain is undergoing massive remodeling, you should expect that your son or daughter will want to spend more time with friends. During this time, adolescents usually begin to care more what peers think about them as well. Even though it may be painful, trust us: your teen pushing away from you, wanting to be with friends, and trying to figure out where he or she stands with peers is not a referendum on you. These alterations are normal, part of God's good design to equip teens to eventually navigate complex adult relationships, where interpreting and responding to the feelings and intentions of others is necessary. Instead of fighting against this social development, invest your energies in helping your son or daughter develop relationship skills.

Within the last decade, research on the development of the adolescent brain demonstrated neural underpinnings for teenage social drama. Apparently, a "perfect neurobiological storm" for peer sensitivity brews during adolescence: "Improvements in brain functioning in areas important for figuring out what other people are thinking, heightened arousal of regions that are sensitive to social acceptance and social rejection, and the greater responsiveness to other people's emotional cues, like facial expressions" all contribute to the ups and downs of adolescent friendships.[2] As parents who are aware that all this is happening in our teens' brains, we can exercise patience and speak truth to our teens: this storm and stress is part of growing up, and they will make it through, stronger on the other side.

Neuroscience also indicates that being with friends arouses the highly excitable reward circuits in adolescent brains. When teenagers spend time together, dopamine is released. Just being together triggers powerful and pleasurable neurochemicals; no wonder teens want to be with their peers!

On one hand, this explains why some adolescents engage in reckless behaviors together (their brains, as a group, are primed for the release of pleasurable neurochemicals). On the other hand, there's a powerful positive aspect to this neural reality: if teens are spending time in healthy ways with friends and getting pleasure from it, they may be less likely to look for a dopamine rush elsewhere (money, food, sex, or substances like drugs and alcohol).

If you want to maximize the positive and minimize the negative prospects of social development, you'll need to help your teen. You cannot control his or her peer relationships. You can have influence on them, however, by engaging your teen's developing brain. The neural circuits that control good judgment and wise decision-making may not be fully connected in teens' brains, but we can encourage them to tap into their under-construction prefrontal cortex by asking good questions, making connections between certain relationship choices and consequences, and providing opportunities to be with friends in healthy ways.

Psych 101

With every peer experience, with each adult interaction witnessed, with all the media portrayals of friendship watched, teenagers are forming a vision of what relationships look like. The way you conduct your own friendships impacts your teenager powerfully. If you consistently disparage other people behind their backs, don't be surprised if your teenager's friendships suffer from the consequences of gossip. If you're the first to help a friend in need, your son or daughter will likely value selflessness and kindness.

As your teen goes through the adolescent years, you'd do well to evaluate your own relationships. Continue any ways you demonstrate the traits of a good friend; be honest about and make changes in the areas you fail. Ask your spouse or a trusted mentor, pastor, or friend to help you identify ways you could grow. Again, your example isn't the whole story here; indeed, adolescents whose parents have stellar relationships can still make incredibly foolish decisions in friendship. It's essential, however, that you look within as intently as you look at your son's or daughter's relationships.

In order to help your adolescent capitalize on the amazing benefits of healthy friendships while avoiding the pitfalls of destructive ones, keep the following in mind:

- **Acknowledge your teen's good choices.** Parents spend a great deal of time evaluating teenage behavior. Unfortunately, we often focus on negative dynamics. When it comes to friendship, teens need to hear the right and good things they do. When you observe your teen displaying strong character in her relationships, go beyond the general, "You're a good friend." Instead, point out specifics: "I was so proud of how you encouraged Rachel when she didn't make the cheer team." You can also highlight ways your teen's friends show good character: "It was cool that Ben came over to help you study; it's great to have a friend who's there for you when you need it!" Never underestimate the power of your positive attention. Your teen's friendships will grow as he or she figures out what character traits and actions make a good friend. You can help in this process.

- **Cultivate or cut off—help make that call.** Especially with younger adolescents, you can encourage or discourage certain relationships by inviting certain friends and not others to your home. Don't misunderstand this and try to control every dynamic in your teenager's social life. This is not our intention. You can help your teenager cultivate or cut off certain friendships, but you cannot make them be friends with someone or force them to stay away from someone. If you're concerned about a particular friend, ask your teen to help you understand why he or she enjoys being with that person. Find out what makes your teen "tick" in relationship with others and help him or her cultivate healthy relationships whenever possible.

- **Encourage life beyond "likes."** Online networking captivates teenagers, whose social brains teem with growth and change. Sadly, many teens judge their social standing based on how many "likes" their status update, post, or picture collects. If no one comments, teens may feel that no one cares or that what they said was stupid, useless, and so on. It's incredibly dangerous for adolescents to accept this notion as truth. Many adults struggle with this as well. Consistently affirm that your teen's value does not rest on whether people click a digital link to "like" (or "unlike") something or someone. Be honest with your teen if you've ever felt this way. Sharing your own thoughts and feelings about digital communication normalizes your teens' experience and helps them to develop life beyond "likes."

- **Promote face-to-face friend time.** If digital means are your teenager's primary mode of communication, he or she is neglecting a huge amount of essential brain real estate, namely the development of social skills like interpreting and using facial expressions, tone of voice, gestures, friendly touch, timing, and emotion in communication. A good rule of thumb to use with your teens is "People before devices."[3] Consider letting teens know in advance that you expect them to set aside the phone when someone comes over. Texting, posting, and so on can wait while attention is given to the living person in front of them. This may be difficult for your teen at first, but if you establish it beforehand and stick with your convictions, it will become the norm.

• **Don't make value judgments.** Teenagers often say that parents who reject their friends reject them too. While those of us with adult brains know this isn't always true, it *feels* very true to adolescents. You don't know your son's or daughter's friends well enough to say whether they are "good" or "bad" kids (these are never helpful categories anyway), so you sound ignorant and judgmental when you criticize people in these ways. If you feel the need to express concern about a friend, make it about specific behavior and ask your son or daughter to think about those particular circumstances. For instance, instead of saying, "Julia's a gossip and I don't want you around her," it's far better to say, "I'm concerned about having Julia over again, because last time she was here I heard the two of you gossiping a lot. What do you think?" Rather than lashing out at "those idiots who drink," you can choose a comment like, "I hope your friend _____ isn't drinking any more. I hate to think of someone with his whole life ahead of him making the same mistake again." Mr. Greenfield, the father from our opening story, used the term "those kids" as a pejorative to identify other teens whom he believed dragged his son down. This attitude and language alienates teens and limits your ability to influence. Your adolescent's developing brain can start making connections between examples and general trends. Nudge them gently and graciously in this direction, avoiding harsh words or accusations.

• **Limit unsupervised group time.** Just because it's natural to push away from parents and want to spend more time with friends does not mean that parents should leave teenagers alone for long periods of time. Remember, teens benefit from having "surrogate prefrontal cortexes" around, adults who—with adult brains—can help prevent foolish decisions from being made. Think of your presence (even in the other room) like a leaven that keeps the adolescent "dough" from rising too much, too fast. Supervision doesn't mean that you need to be with your teen every moment. You can monitor younger adolescents by, for instance, being at the mall while your daughter shops with friends (even if you're not in the same store) or driving teens and their friends to a sporting event or movie and sitting in another section. For older adolescents, you can extend the amount of solo time according to the degree of responsibility your teen shows. Even really "good kids" can make bad choices when a group of under-construction brains decide to do something foolish. Supervision won't prevent this every time, but it can stop a lot of runaway adolescent brains.

- **Check the clock.** When considering parental supervision, don't limit your investment to weekends. Numerous studies have demonstrated that adolescent experimentation with sex, alcohol, drugs, and criminal activity usually begins between the hours of 3:00 and 5:00 p.m. on weekdays.[4] In other words, the way your teen spends time after school is incredibly important. Sports, lessons, a job, or other after-school activities can help mitigate the potential dangers of this time frame. If your teen must be alone after school because of family work schedules, consider asking a trusted neighbor or friend to check on your teen at a random time. Not knowing when a friend of Mom or Dad may drop by provides some accountability.

- **Address your teen's hurts.** Few adolescents escape the teenage years without experiencing painful rejection. At any age, being rejected wounds our hearts and minds. Scientists have also discovered that the brain mediates social rejection in the same manner as physical pain. In fact, you can actually treat the symptoms of heartache with acetaminophen (the active ingredient in Tylenol)! When your teen is rejected, his or her brain feels the impact like a bodily injury. Don't dismiss the stress of teenage relationships. You don't have to understand things perfectly to show empathy. Even a simple, "I'm so sorry that you're hurting" can make your teen feel supported and consoled.

Faith 101

At this point in the chapter, you may be wondering why we haven't addressed peer pressure. Well, now is the time.

Parents almost universally express anxiety about peer pressure. Like Mr. and Mrs. Greenfield, many parents assume that peer pressure can "make" a good kid do terrible things. Some moms and dads distrust peer relationships altogether, afraid that the "wrong" influence is too great a potential danger.

The apostle Paul addresses peer pressure in his letters to the ancient church at Corinth. In 1 Corinthians 15:33, Paul quotes the Greek poet Menander, who asserted, "Bad company corrupts good character." Paul used this phrase to express the danger of developing friendships with those who live without eternity in mind.

The amount of time teens spend with people whose lives revolve around the material world (money, success, even academics or sports) will impact them. Your adolescent's friendships *matter*. Remember, the neural pathways used most often become the strongest. The more your teen exercises the brain pathways for faith and truth, the stronger they will become. If you want your teenager to develop friendships that "spur one another on toward love and good deeds" (Heb. 10:24), your teen needs to be in close proximity with adolescents who believe the truth and live it out.

Before you start devising strategies to rid your teen's life of "bad company," however, remember that God also calls us to be salt and light in a dark and decaying world, holding firmly to truth and shining brightly in the lives of those who don't yet know Christ (see Matt. 5:13–16; Phil. 2:15–16). You cannot abdicate this responsibility and try to manipulate circumstances so that your teenager will only ever be around other Christians. Not only will your adolescent never learn how to share the good news of Jesus, he or she will also fail to develop the conviction necessary to resist temptation in the adult world.

How do parents approach the difficult balancing act of allowing teenagers to be Christ's light and encouraging them to stay away from bad company? Applying the principles in the Psych 101 section can certainly help. Another important thing—and truly this is the most important of all—that parents can do is help teenagers acknowledge that what's inside them is *always* a bigger problem than what's outside them.

The trouble with the way peer pressure is perceived by parents and portrayed in the media is that it does not tell the truth about the human heart. People don't suddenly make foolish decisions because someone "dared" them or "pressured" them. People—adults and teens alike—make poor choices because they value something more than godliness and goodness. Peer influence simply reveals what's already misaligned in the heart.

Teenagers don't take a drink "because of peer pressure" as much as they determine acceptance and approval are more important in that moment than godliness and obedience. Teens don't bully a weaker or less attractive kid because "all their friends were doing it" as much as they decide that the feeling of superiority, pride, and power over someone else is better than the feeling that comes from doing right.

Your teen's heart is at the very center of every peer interaction, and what's in your teenager's heart determines whether he or she will live with conviction or cowardice. If you only address peer pressure as an "outside force," you're missing the mark. Peer pressure is best tackled by waging the real war: the war for goodness and truth fought on the turf of your teenager's soul.

Adolescents behave based on what is in their hearts, not simply what's happening around them, so have heart-based conversations. Verbally affirm that you believe teens can make good choices and stick with convictions no matter what kind of pressure they face. This gives teens confidence. Remind them that you are on their team and they can talk with you when they're having problems. As teens begin to recognize the way being with friends can bring out either the best or worst in them, they become better able to make wise decisions, even when pressure comes. Help your teen fight the real battle, not against "peer pressure" but against the crookedness of heart upon which peer influence feeds.

Try It Today: Love Your Teen's Friends

In his excellent book *Have a New Teenager by Friday*, Dr. Kevin Leman describes his home as "a place where anybody can come and get some love, attention, and a listening ear."[5] Would your teen identify your home in this way? Do your own kids like to be at home? Do other kids feel welcome and affirmed when they come over? Do you care about the other teenagers with whom your teen spends time? We cannot simply be concerned about our own teenagers. We must also cultivate Christ's love for their friends.

Make a list of your teen's closest friends. Ask God to give you love for each one. Pray for every friend your teenager invites over or spends time with. In time, you'll notice your love for them and their comfort around you increasing. Start today!

12

It's Not Like We're Getting Married

Over the course of my adolescent years, nothing perplexed me (Jerusha) or my parents more than dating. Guy-girl interactions had changed radically in the twenty-some years since my parents dated, and trying to figure things out as I muddled along was far from an effective strategy.

During my junior high days, if you liked a boy and he liked you back, you "went around." Technically, you went nowhere; that was just the nomenclature. By eighth grade, I had "gone around" with two guys, one of whom nearly had a panic attack at my thirteenth birthday party when he couldn't find a plug for the blow-dryer he brought to style his hair after swimming. True story.

I never thought of the relationships I had in junior high as "dating." They were mostly conducted on the phone in agonizingly stilted conversations and at school lunches, where I did my best to avoid revealing that I had absolutely no idea how to relate to a boy. Things didn't get any less confusing in high school.

After graduating from college, I read a ton of books on relationships and grieved the mistakes I'd made. I wanted to do things right and decided not to date for six months. Two weeks before my "relationship fast" was scheduled to end, Jeramy asked me out. I told him we'd have to wait two weeks; I'm so glad he stuck around! Our dating relationship was healthy, fun, and—since both of us were committed to our faith—it was also God-honoring.

That's certainly not the norm today. The modern relationship scene is dismal. For many, dating has become synonymous with a hook up and break up mentality. The concept of courtship attracted some Christians who wanted to avoid heartbreak and "guarantee" healthy marriage, but significant problems arose with both of these approaches.

As frightening as guy-girl relationships can be for teens and their parents, we have to wade into the complexity. In order to have healthy relationships later in life, our adolescent children need to learn to interact with the opposite sex. You and your family will need to settle on the details of an approach (we don't advocate one way but rather the application of sound, biblical principles), but this chapter will equip you to help your teenager to choose wisely, respect others, and learn how to relate to the other half of the world.

Bio 101

Do you remember when getting cooties didn't scare you anymore, and in fact, the idea kind of intrigued you? Most likely that occurred during your adolescence, and it wasn't the result of a conscious choice but rather of subtle changes over time.

Our bodies and brains have been wired for attraction, and when chemical signals that stimulate this begin to course through our bodies, we feel pulled toward people we may have previously avoided at all costs. This happens naturally in adolescence, when increasing levels of hormones spark sexual development and a desire for bonding. Neurochemicals in the developing "social brain," which we previously observed propel teenagers to move away from family and into the world of peer relationships, also contribute to a growing desire to know and interact with the opposite sex.

These drives are natural, by design, and healthy. Challenges surface as teens attempt to integrate biological impulses with under-construction relationship skills. A less-than-fully-connected prefrontal cortex leaves a teenager's decision-making, planning, and good judgment regarding relationships lacking. Parents can and should coach their adolescents in building healthy relationships, even if what we'd rather do is lock our children away, ostensibly to prevent them from doing something foolish.

If your goal is simply to keep your adolescent from making relationship mistakes, you're setting your sights too low. Of course we don't want our teenagers to get hurt or to hurt others. Still, clamping down and trying to control our teens' responses to the opposite sex isn't the answer. Keep in mind that regardless of your personal stance on dating, you won't be able to prevent your teenager's neurochemicals from doing what they are designed to do: move your teen toward adulthood. Instead, you can help your teen learn to navigate these changes wisely.

When humans—including adolescents—think about romance or experience it with another person or vicariously through watching or reading about relationships, the brain releases phenylethylamine (PEA for short), a neuromodulator that shares stimulant and psychoactive effects with its chemical cousins, amphetamines. As with other amphetamines, surging PEA gives people a "kick," a great—though not lasting—sense of well-being.

Large quantities of PEA amplify physical and emotional energy and cause the brain to release dopamine. PEA flows through our bodies with romantic thoughts or experiences and can make us "unrealistically optimistic" about relationships, according to Drs. Beverly and Thomas Alan Rodgers.[1] This "high" can occur whether or not we're in a relationship with the object of interest.

Apply these facts to the lives of teenagers: regardless of whether they're allowed to date or ever do so, adolescents will experience significant chemical changes, kindling the fire of romantic interest. This means that no parent—even those who forbid dating—gets off the hook; we all have a responsibility to teach our teenagers how to navigate romantic feelings and relationships well. Simply telling your teen he or she can't date until a certain age isn't enough, nor is having a "once and for all" talk about the subject. Instead, knowing that what's going on in your teen's brain is complex, completely new to younger adolescents, and every bit as perplexing to older ones should secure your compassionate parental help.

Psych 101

As has become our custom in this book, we want to start by encouraging you to evaluate your own approach to relationships. What you believe about romance, love, and marriage impacts your teen far more than you may like to believe. Adolescents listen intently to how parents speak about these issues (even if they pretend they couldn't care less). Moreover, your teen observes how you live, the kind of movies and TV shows you watch, and the magazines and books you read. Each influences your teen's perception of opposite-sex relationships. If what you say you believe is inconsistent with the way you live, your teen—hypersensitive to hypocrisy—will spot it. Because of this:

- **Point out cultural messages.** Remember, shorter and more frequent conversations are effective with teens. Make a comment here or a statement there about how dating, relationships, romance, and marriage are portrayed in the media. You don't have to turn your teen into a relationships expert in one talk; you can't do that anyhow! Just keep the conversation going. Almost every movie—even "innocent" animated ones—includes messages about romance. Teach your teenager to recognize cultural ideals and determine whether they're consistent with a biblical worldview. If they're not, help your adolescent see how and why.
- **Don't follow your heart,** and teach your teen not to follow his or hers. One of the most destructive messages of our day can be found in virtually every medium: print, screen, and music.

Adults know that following your feelings can lead you astray, but the idea that your heart always tells you the truth and will guide you to what's best and right for you is so pervasive that even the smallest of media consumers—toddlers—can parrot "follow your heart" stories and songs. If you've never noticed this theme or have never brought it up with your teen, it's not too late. The world will provide you with plenty of opportunities to point this out! Watch a movie together and you'll have fodder for at least one conversation.

- **Ask and listen.** Regardless of his or her age, your teen already has some opinions about dating, romance, and relationships in general. Most of us assume we know what adolescents think without ever actually discussing it with them. Why not ask for your son's or daughter's opinion on dating? You may be surprised by some of his or her thoughts. If you choose to have this conversation, note that this is *not* the time to convince him or her of your superior wisdom. This is strictly an exploratory, fact-finding mission, so listen attentively. Ask follow-up questions as long as your teen remains open. Since you don't have an agenda in this other than to listen and learn what's in your teen's heart, if he or she shuts things down, that's okay. Anything you have heard and learned can inform your approach for future conversations, as well as your prayers.

- **Offer advice rather than issuing mandates.** Trying to "reason" a teen out of chemical attraction is fruitless and frustrating. Fortunately, neurochemicals like PEA—the amphetamine-related neuromodulator—naturally wax and wane, so the object of your teen's affections won't remain as perfect in his or her eyes after some time. Trying to force your teen not to think about or have feelings for someone can actually stoke the neurochemical fire within. We must exercise patience and gently offer counsel. The quickest way to alienate your son or daughter is to criticize someone he or she thinks is "the one." Instead, ask teens questions that cause them to think. We can also teach our teens the essential lesson that we don't have to act on every feeling of attraction we have. Indeed, we should be honest with our teenagers: getting married doesn't mean you're never chemically attracted to someone again, so learning to evaluate and control physical responses is incredibly important.

- **Recognize the influence of your past.** Studies reveal that parents, particularly mothers, who made relationship mistakes in the past tend to be stricter as their teens mature. In fact, moms who were promiscuous in their own adolescence consistently showed greater mistrust of their teenage children, even if their teens' behavior warranted no distrust.[2] If you feel overly anxious about your teen entering the years when relationships and romance become important, ask yourself why. Learning from your own past is not the same as assuming that your adolescent will make identical errors. Seek advice from a trusted mentor, pastor, or counselor if issues from your past return during these years.

- **Be appropriately vulnerable.** Teens respond incredibly well to honest, courageous, and humble parental sharing. Of course, there are appropriate and detrimental ways to do this, so talk through your decision with a spouse or close friend before speaking with your teen. I (Jerusha) have talked to our girls from the time they were young about how I thought getting a guy to like me would make me feel better about myself. My flirtatious ways led to a lot of pain for me and for those around me. Sharing with our daughters—at the right time and in the right context—the mistakes we made and the consequences that followed is a priority for Jeramy and me. In this way, God redeems our past, allowing what was ugly to become a source of strength and protection for our teens. The same can be true for your family.

- **Provide opportunities for your teen to interact with the opposite sex.** Your adolescent cannot develop healthy relationship skills without practicing them. It's important for your teen to spend time with members of the opposite sex in healthy contexts.

Group settings can be great for this, as can after-school activities and youth group events. Don't be afraid to have teens
of the opposite gender in your home. Indeed, if you want to
influence your teen's choices, you need to know the people he
or she hangs out with. There's great freedom in normalizing
friendships between young men and women. Ironically, it's when
Christians prohibit the development of relationships between
the genders that adolescents and young adults find themselves
woefully unprepared to interact with the opposite sex.

- **Discourage exclusive relationships.** Adolescents who pair off
  often fail to explore same-gender friendships, extracurricular
  activities, hobbies, occupations, and service. Statistics also show
  a connection between exclusive dating in early adolescence and
  sexual experimentation. Parenting expert Dr. Jim Burns notes,
  "Exclusive dating at younger ages . . . sometimes revs up the
  engines too soon and leads the way toward early sexualization.
  Kids make sexual decisions based on emotional involvement that
  exceeds their maturity levels. I have observed many really good
  kids at too early of an age get way over their heads and hearts
  in exclusive relationships."[3] Letting your son or daughter hang
  out with the opposite sex doesn't mean that you must condone
  exclusive relationships.

- **Don't try to bake cookies at 500 degrees.**[4] No matter how fantastic your recipe is, you're almost guaranteed to burn cookies
  if you try to bake them at such an extreme temperature. In a
  similar manner, placing undue pressure on guy-girl relationships leaves people burned. In an effort to avoid mistakes in
  dating, some parents try to control relationships with strictly
  enforced rules. In this highly intense environment—somewhat
  akin to a 500-degree oven—developing healthy relationship
  skills can be challenging. In some ways, it forces people to
  decide before even having coffee together whether or not
  someone is a potential mate. Broken courtships are often as
  painful as severed engagements for this reason. Be aware of

the potential problems that any relationship model might introduce. Don't choose a method simply out of fear or a desire
to control things. Your adolescent's relationship future is far
too important for that.

- **If your teen is hurting, don't minimize the pain.** Some parents
  dismiss their adolescent's feelings as "puppy love" or "teen
  drama." It's essential that we recognize the wounds our teens
  feel in relationships are *very real*. In fact, a great deal of anxiety,
  depression, substance abuse, and even suicide can be connected
  to unrequited affection. Explain to your teen that it's normal
  to hurt when you feel rejected. You may have less energy, be
  less motivated, and want to either pig out or stop eating altogether. Assure your teen that these feelings pass with time,
  while affirming that you hurt because they are hurting. Parents
  who tell their teens to "get over it," or worse, mock their teen
  during this time actually make things worse.

Faith 101

To love and be loved is one of the most universal human longings. In
the name of love wild, wonderful, and wicked things have been done
by men and women of every race, status, and era. If we reflect on our
own past honestly, each of us can see ways in which the yearning to
be loved has motivated us—both positively and negatively.

As Christians, we believe that God created us—literally wired
our bodies and brains—in his image (see Gen. 1:27). Because God
is love (see 1 John 4:8), our nature reflects this beautiful facet of his
character. We love others and long to receive love because the Author
and Perfecter of love made us. We experience incredible glory in this!
We also know terrible pain when love is withheld or the brokenness
of this sin-stained world infects our relationships. Many people look
to another human to meet their need for love and affirmation, but
the love for which they pine—unconditional, unselfish, and unending
love—cannot be found in relationship with another person.

At this point, your teen probably cannot understand, let alone articulate, this universal ache to be loved, pull to look for fulfillment in people who cannot provide it, and longing to give love to someone else. These feelings are present, however. They're mixed up with the awakening of sexual hormones and neural development, societal messages and social interactions, but the deepest cries of the human heart are within every teenager looking for a relationship. The affirmation we feel when someone likes us, chooses us, or wants to be with us is powerful and compelling. If you never went out as a young person, you may have questioned whether you were worthy of being loved or would ever find romance. If going out all the time was your method of validation, you may have grounded your identity on being admired or sought after. You may have wanted to "conquer" as many relationships as possible to show that you were desirable and attractive. You might have ached for love because you never got it at home. Imagine that your teen may feel some of these things and have compassion on your under-construction adolescent.

Some of you have never settled into the reality of your complete belovedness. Perhaps you wonder if God could really love you after what you've done. Maybe you're operating with a hole in your heart from abandonment during childhood, a broken marriage, or rejection on some deep level. Please know that adolescents sense this, even if they have no idea what it is or why it impacts them.

The best and most important thing you can do for your teenager when it comes to relationships is to model that your identity is grounded in Christ's undying love for you. The Word of God declares that you are loved with an "everlasting love" (Jer. 31:3), a love that endures and never depends on your accomplishments or worthiness. "'Though the mountains be shaken and the hills be removed, yet my unfailing love for you will not be shaken nor my covenant of peace be removed,' says the LORD, who has compassion on you" (Isa. 54:10). If you truly believe this and allow it to define everything you do, your teen will be so far ahead of the game.

As we live out the truth, we can help teens recognize that the gospel—the truly *Good News*—is that they don't have to look to anyone else for affirmation or validation. Pastor Timothy Keller writes, "The gospel is this: We are more sinful and flawed in ourselves than we ever dared believe, yet at the very same time we are more loved and accepted in Jesus Christ than we ever dared hope."[5] Live this, teach teens this, and it will change the way they approach relationships. You can help teens see that human relationships are a beautiful part of life, but they cannot define us; God's neverending, never giving up, unbreaking, always and forever love for us does.[6]

Try It Today

At some point over the next twenty-four hours, spend time discussing with your spouse or a close friend any fears you have about your child developing relationships with the opposite sex. Bringing any concerns you have into the open is an important step forward. Pray about each specifically.

13

This Is Sooooo Awkward

"Stop the tape and talk about erection."

What? No! This can't be happening!

The interior of our blue station wagon suddenly felt fifty degrees hotter. An uncomfortable cough escaped from my dad's pursed lips, while my mom's neatly painted fingernail moved toward the stop button. I (Jeramy) seriously considered rolling down the window and flinging myself onto the highway.

At some point, Mom must have told my brother and me that we were going to listen to tapes "about growing up" by her Christian parenting hero, but I don't recall any details of that interaction. It wasn't until the recorded voice commanded us to chat—with our *parents*—about "your changing body" that the internal screaming began. *Nooooo!*

Fast-forward about twenty-five years. Jerusha and I received a package from her publisher. Enclosed was the full "help your kids learn about sex" book collection. That night, I read through the first of four books (the one identified as "just right" for their ages). As Jerusha remembers it, I lay the book on my chest, closed my eyes and groaned, "Oh no . . ."

Here I was, youth ministry veteran, dating and relationships author, the guy you might have thought would be confident about talking to his kids about sex. I'd given maybe a hundred purity talks in my time. I'd spoken to teens and their parents around the country. But now it was "go time" in my own family. I understood the deer-caught-in-the-headlights look I'd seen on the faces of so many parents. Perhaps that very look is on your face right now.

Statistics say 95 percent of us had some form of sex education in school. Most of us endured it in either junior high health class, high school biology, or those awkward, "The boys are going to go with Mr. So-and-so and the girls will stay here" special assemblies.

If the various seminars and conferences around the nation I've conducted are an accurate indication, most of us also had little if any dialogue with our parents about sex. The vast majority of people I encounter had significantly more peer than parent sex education. Youth ministry expert Dr. Jim Burns recently observed, "Studies show that almost 50 percent of parents have a conversation about sex *after* their kids have already had intercourse."[1] Don't let that be your story.

Instead of reviewing schoolyard misperceptions and stilted "sex ed" classes, I'd like to focus on neurochemical information you may never have received. During adolescence, I certainly didn't learn about the role oxytocin plays in sexual awakening, curiosity, and exploration.[2]

And though I completely understand the challenge of "You've got to be kidding me" and "This is sooooo awkward" teenage responses to your "Let's talk" efforts, we cannot let one another off the hook. Of course resistance and snarky comments can be exhausting and embarrassing, but we are the parents, and our teens desperately need us to be informed and able to discuss the physical, emotional, and spiritual dimensions of sexuality.

Bio 101

According to neurobiologists, "Oxytocin is important for social memory and attachment, sexual and maternal behavior, and aggression.

Recent work implicates oxytocin in human bonding and trust as well."[3] In layman's terms, oxytocin—the "cuddle hormone"—can make you want to snuggle, remember how good snuggling feels, and do whatever you can to experience that again. It can also (positively) stop you from doing things that would prevent future snuggling, such as tame aggression, or (negatively) incite jealousy. Since oxytocin can also intensify our feelings, when this hormone is present, it can enhance a sense of bonding with whomever one is with, regardless of how genuine and lasting the emotional connection may be.[4]

The release of oxytocin increases dramatically during the adolescent years. Most research indicates that oxytocin affects females more intensely than males, which may explain, at least in part, the greater emphasis adolescent girls place on bonding in relationships.[5]

Now that you know this, what can you do?

- **Channel oxytocin's positive power.** Clinicians counsel parents to provide adolescents (particularly girls) with nurturing opportunities that stimulate the healthy release of oxytocin. Something as simple as petting an animal or caring for small children can release oxytocin and satisfy the desire for connection and bonding.

- **Don't withhold affection, even from your surly teen.** It becomes awkward for some parents, especially dads, to show affection to their children during the adolescent years. If this describes you, we'll be blunt: get over it. Appropriate physical affection in the home meets powerful physiological needs while teaching healthy boundaries. Some of you suspect teens would rather die than hug their parents, but finding ways to be affectionate is essential.

- **Ride it out.** Studies using fMRI scanning show that when pictures of a preferred member of the opposite sex are viewed, regions of the brain linked with well-being and pleasure light up. Dopamine surges, creating a natural high, and oxytocin release follows, stirring up greater desire and affection. Parents, remember this biochemical reality. Your adolescent *will* be vulnerable to powerful feelings, some of which will baffle you. Others may infuriate you, but don't overplay things. Research shows that left on its own, the teen brain stays in this heightened physiological state for a much shorter period than the adult brain. Only after this initial rush are teens able to engage their under-construction frontal lobes to logically reflect on the relationship, weighing risks and benefits.[6] If a parent rushes in during the emotional surge, ranting and raving, it can further stimulate response from the emotional center of the brain, thus short-circuiting a teen's ability to reason and judge. Most of us would prefer, for instance, that our teenage daughter *not* date the bouncer from Hell's Ink tattoo parlor, but trying to reason with her when biochemicals are running rampant can be counterproductive. It requires tremendous discernment and patience to time conversations wisely.

• **Keep in mind that sexual curiosity doesn't equal sexual activity.** As the level of sex hormones in your teen's body rises, interest and curiosity will increase as well. Don't assume, however, that expressing interest or curiosity means your adolescent is sexually active. This is where open communication becomes significant. Ask questions, listen, and observe attentively.

• **Finally, don't buy into cultural lies.** During adolescence, as the brain prunes neurons and reinforces the neural pathways used most often, what your teenager sees and does matters, bigtime. What your son or daughter is exposed to sexually (in the media and in relationships) impacts the rest of their lives. Society would like us to believe that media doesn't affect us and "teens are going to do what they want, so we better just mitigate the consequences." Don't accept these lies. The age at and way in which adolescents begins to explore sexuality does impact their future. The shows and movies they watch, as well as the websites they visit (and we're not strictly talking pornographic ones here), reinforce certain brain pathways. Throughout the day, teens assimilate a great deal of information about sexuality: conversations with peers, media exposure, physical desires, and *your input*. Don't let your input be an empty set. You can play a role in the development of your adolescent's sexual brain. I know it can be uncomfortable. Ask the questions anyway (e.g., "Do any of your friends sext each other?"). Your teen may feel like I did all those years ago, ready to throw open the car door and perish on the highway, but he or she will also know that you care and are aware.

What Statistics Teach Us about Teens and Sex

Sexual content in film, television, and music continues to increase. In television programming aimed at teens, more than 90 percent of episodes have at least one sexual reference, with an average of 7.9 references per hour.[7] Note: these aren't "adult" shows, but programs aimed at teens.

- According to one study, young adolescents exposed to sexual media content, including that on the internet, were 2.2 times more likely to have had sexual intercourse when reinterviewed two years later than were peers who took in a less-sexualized media diet.[8]

- Nine in ten teens agree that most young people have sex before they're really ready, and nearly two-thirds say once you've had sex with a partner, it's hard to say no in the future.[9]

- Recent studies indicate that the risk for depression is "clearly elevated" for sexually active teens of either gender.[10] Twenty-five percent of adolescent girls who had sex became clinically depressed within three months of the experience.[11]

- Clinicians report that the roots of sexual issues facing adults often date back to painful teenage experiences.[12] Research revealed a correlation between abstinence in the teen years and better mental health at age twenty-nine and at age forty.[13]

Psych 101

We don't include statistics to startle or scare you. Instead, our aim is to connect your parenting with the physiological and psychological reality of your adolescent's life. Your teen hears time and again that the pleasures he or she can get from sexual expression are what really matters. "You shouldn't feel bad about wanting to feel good," some would have your son or daughter believe. The problem is, at least psychologically speaking, feeling good for a few moments can lead to feeling bad, sometimes for a very long time.

Most adolescents don't understand that sex is more than just a physical act. Watching juvenile, narcissistic sexual antics on-screen; listening to the highly sexualized chatter of pop stars or musicians; glancing at the no-boundaries, no-rules, "we'll teach you how to get the best orgasm of your life" magazines, all the while desperate to be liked and feel good—this is what your adolescent faces, each and every day. As Dr. Michael Bradley wisely wrote, "Teenage sex represents a terrible confluence of volatile developmental and emotional issues simply waiting for a match to ignite them. These 'vapors' include new and powerful hormonal rushes, peer acceptance needs, rebelliousness, curiosity, nurturing, intimacy, desires to please [and] desires to dominate."[14]

Your adolescent's emotional drive for love and acceptance is inextricably tied with his or her blooming sexuality. Don't forget that—ever. It's easy to come down on a teen discovered with porn or freak out after walking in on a make-out session. Your emotions are not ill-placed, but the timing and the way you express your feelings will make a huge difference. You can get to a heart level and find out what's compelling your teen, or you can miss the opportunity altogether. The choice is yours.

Reviewing his multiyear, participant-observer study of adolescents, Dr. Chap Clark wrote,

> My conclusion after reflecting on the data from this study is that
> adolescent sexuality, and perhaps all human sexuality, has more to

do with a desire for relational connection and a safe place than with
a physical, albeit sometimes pleasurable, activity of the body. Many
midadolescents are almost desperate in their loneliness, with few opportunities to share or even deal with the effects. Sexual activity and
desire are obviously related to the natural drives and hormonal changes
of this phase of life, but buried underneath any hormonal drive there
is an even deeper, more profound need that uses sexuality and sensual-
ity to heal. Today's midadolescents . . . are crying out for attention
and affection. Expressions of popular culture occasionally concede
that this may be true for girls but rarely if ever cast boys in this light.
I consistently observed, however, that midadolescents boys are just
as vulnerable and desperate as girls but may not be as aware of their
need for care and affection. Sexual behavior and sexual fantasy are
immensely powerful in that for a very brief time they can ease the pain
of disconnection and loneliness as they mimic authentic love. This is
why unbounded, indiscriminate sexual activity for adolescents is even
more dangerous and potent than most adults recognize. Adults limit
the power of "sexual urges" to changing hormones, but in reality far
deeper forces are at work.[15]

Because of this, we need to equip our kids with more than a "just
say no" approach to sexuality. As Dr. Andrea Solarz puts it, "For most
teens, telling them to 'just say no' does not help them to deal with
sexually stressful interpersonal situations in which they are anxious
to be liked. Instead . . . help the adolescent identify and practice
strategies in advance for dealing with or avoiding these situations."[16]
You may think your teen is smart enough to see an "I've never loved
anyone like you, and there's only one way to show you" come-on for
what it is, but don't assume that an adolescent's developing prefrontal
cortex can sort through the emotions and neurochemicals surging at
that highly charged moment. Discuss with your teen what he or she
might do and say in various circumstances.

In addition, help your son or daughter identify hypocritical messages the media promotes with regard to gender, sexuality, and physical affection. Talk about the double standards faced by young men
and women. Develop strategies with your teen, who will most likely

be invited to view porn at some point during the adolescent years (more on this in chapter 23). In taking steps like these, we can wage war for our teens' emotional and sexual health.

Finally, keep in mind that for some adolescents, very little sexual mystery still exists. The barrage of sexual images, metaphors, and allusions; the readily available sexual stimulation from music, film, and television; and the general, overtly sexualized environment, let alone the sheer glut of free pornography only a click away, have served to desensitize a lot of adolescents to the beauty God created in sex. Unfortunately, for some teens, sex has become so commonplace and mundane through overexposure that its value has declined as its ubiquity has increased. Parents can equip teens with a grander view of sexuality—God's view.

Faith 101

God created sex and has a lot to say about it. The Bible is full of references to human sexuality, ranging from the proscriptive to the poetic. Taken as a whole, God's Word with regard to sexuality is positive and powerful. Nipped and tucked and served up in youth groups in tiny morsels, however, Christian ideas about sexuality can confuse even the most committed young believers.

For the purpose of this book, we challenge parents: avoid reinforcing common myths about sex and using Christian scare tactics to keep your kids "safe." Don't try to convince your teen that:

- **You'll automatically feel guilty if you have sex.** If you encourage your teen to use the presence or absence of spiritual guilt as the measure of whether something is right or wrong, you're on a very slippery slope. Teach your teen that his or her feelings about sex don't change the truth that sex was created exclusively for the passionate and committed love relationship called marriage.
- **Sex is a bigger deal for guys than girls.** In our adolescent years, boys and girls were split up so that girls could talk about modesty and boys could talk about "it." Sadly, many churches still

operate on the idea that lust is a "guy" problem. Lust isn't a male problem; it's a human problem.

- **The Bible's message is simply "don't 'do it' before marriage."** This particular myth has two implications:
  ◊ One, it leads many Christians to believe that all God cares about is their virginity. Even in the church, "technical virginity" has become an acceptable goal. How tragic! God cares about your son's or daughter's entire sexual being: body, mind, and spirit. In some ways, a teen's most important sexual organ is the brain, for with it he or she will make every sexual decision, pursue or reject sexual expression, and carry the consequences throughout life.
  ◊ Two, your adolescent has been robbed if this is the sum total of what he or she learns about God's view of sex. Take the time to understand and communicate God's truth to your teen: God designed sex for joy, for comfort, for nurture, and for procreation. It can be a blazing and beautiful fire. Fire in a fireplace is amazing. Fire raging over acres of forest is terrifying. God intended sex for the fireplace of marriage. Help your son or daughter see the benefits of keeping it there.

- **There's nothing I can do about it.** As a parent, you are *not* helpless. Sexual temptation is particularly powerful for many young people, so parents need to help teens be strategic. Don't let your teen be deluded into thinking you're "out of it" when it comes to sexuality. In 2 Timothy 2:22, the apostle Paul urges his young protégé to "flee the evil desires of youth." We can and should encourage our children to do the same. The battle is, after all, for more than their bodies. This battle is for their hearts and souls as well.

Try It Today: Keep It on the Table

Bottom line, a one-size-fits-all, mechanics and spiritual messages rolled into one talk about sex doesn't work. If you're going to connect with your adolescent and be part of his or her healthy sexual development, you've got to establish an ongoing dialogue.

Take a moment to ponder the important questions pastor Paul David Tripp asks in his book *Age of Opportunity*:

> Do your teenagers feel comfortable raising this topic with you? Have you given them a mixed message, on the one hand saying that sex is a wonderful gift from God, and on the other hand communicating fear, reticence, and avoidance? . . . Do you know what your kids know and what their source of information is? Do you know where your teenager struggles with sexual temptation and how [they're] doing with that struggle? . . . [Are they] able to critique the distortions of the surrounding culture? Does your teen have a heart for sexual purity or is s/he pushing the limits of biblical modesty and propriety? If you do not have ready answers for these questions, you have not kept the topic on the table as it needs to be.[17]

Sometime over the next twenty-four hours, use what's right in front of you to bring the subject up. Make a brief comment about a TV show or billboard. Ask a simple question. It doesn't have to be a "big talk." Knowing that you're not afraid to discuss sex gives subconscious security to your teenager, so keep the conversation going.

14

But It's Mine

One Saturday, Joshua Becker dragged the contents of his garage—dusty and bedraggled—into the driveway. Around lunch, a neighbor, who had spent the entire morning wrestling her own yard into submission, noticed Becker's consternation: the pile of thises and thats his family had accumulated over the years had already taken four hours to sort, hose off, and place back in a more orderly fashion.

"Ah, the joys of home ownership," the neighbor commented sarcastically.

Becker responded with, "Well, you know what they say, 'The more stuff you own, the more stuff owns you.'"

"That's why my daughter is a minimalist," the neighbor replied. "She keeps telling me I don't need all this stuff." Though Becker had never heard the term *minimalist* before, the idea of getting off the consumer treadmill struck a chord in him. He went inside to share the brief interchange with his wife, and her response mirrored his own: "I think that's what I want."

Years later, after writing a popular blog and several books about the joys found in escaping the grip of material possessions,[1] Becker still considers that Saturday morning a turning point. We interviewed

Joshua Becker a short time ago, and he graciously shared some thoughts on raising adolescents in a consumer-driven, material-obsessed world. Becker encourages parents to teach teens that living well doesn't mean pursuing the ever-shifting targets of *more* and *better*.[2]

Becker told us that until he started physically removing "stuff" from his life, he couldn't see the burden his possessions had become. He observed, "After taking the third vanload of stuff to Goodwill, I had to ask myself, 'What caused me to buy *vanloads* of things that I didn't truly need?'" Once the physical clutter of his life decreased, Becker began to see the emotional and spiritual clutter around his heart: jealousy, greed, resentment, and selfishness had motivated him to strive for *more* and *better*.

Believing that young people are drawn to the idea that abundant life doesn't consist of abundant possessions, Becker wrote a book for teens called *Living with Less: An Unexpected Key to Happiness*. He invites adolescents to consider that living for what's *more important* rather than simply for *more* brings greater joy and long-term satisfaction. This reflects his faith in Jesus, who invites all of us to live this way by choice rather than mandate (see Mark 10:17–27).

Some parents scoff at the idea that teenagers could willingly choose to reject the materialistic, consumerist mentality of the world, but Becker speaks to standing-room-only crowds of adolescents. Even at their age, many teens sense that having doesn't lead to happiness.

The trouble is, adolescents are also bombarded—virtually every waking moment—with cultural messages that success and satisfaction can be quantifiably measured. Add the neurobiological reality that purchasing and consuming arouse the brain's reward circuit, as well as the truth that envy and greed are rooted deep in the human spirit, and parents can easily see the predicament teenagers face. Is there a way to help teens navigate a me-centered, it's-mine world? By the grace of God, yes. It starts with understanding how materialism rewires the brain.

Bio 101

In fascinating research using fMRI scans to observe the neural responses of participants during a simulated shopping task, a team of
neuroscientists studied the way purchasing, and even anticipating
purchasing, material goods impacts human brains. The results have
powerful implications for the parents of teenagers.

When adolescents viewed images of particularly desirable products
(e.g., electronic devices or tasty foods), activity in the nucleus accumbens (NAc) increased significantly. You may recall from an earlier
chapter that the NAc plays an important role in the brain's reward
system, mediating dopamine release and the cognitive processing of
pleasure, as well as motivation and reinforcement learning. With the
mere thought of getting something enjoyable or enticing, the human
brain lights up, and dopamine floods neural circuits.[3]

A related study, however, demonstrated that these "positive emotions associated with acquisition are *short-lived*. Although materialists still experience positive emotions after making a purchase,
these emotions are less intense than before they actually acquire a
product."[4] Additional research projects have confirmed that desire
produces powerful neurochemical responses in us, but these effects
diminish not only with time but also with actually possessing a product. Looks like the quip, "You always want what you can't have, and
when you get it, you don't want it anymore," actually has neurosci-
entific backing.

Partnering with popular author Martin Lindstrom, neuroimaging
expert Dr. Gemma Calvert provided further, fascinating information
about the impact of consumerism on the brain in *Buyology: Truth
and Lies about Why We Buy*. Dr. Calvert studied the neural activity
of subjects exposed to images not just of desirable products but of
specifically recognizable brands (Apple, Ferrari, Coca-Cola, etc.).
Considering what you just read, it probably won't surprise you to
learn that the brain's reward system became aroused when viewing these images. In Dr. Calvert's experiment, fMRI scans showed
increased activity in the caudate nucleus, an area of the brain highly

innervated by dopamine neurons and closely connected to the VTA, another important structure in the brain's reward system.

Here's what may surprise you: when neuroscientists asked people who consider themselves "devoutly religious" to describe their relationship with God and then exposed them to religious images while performing fMRI scans, the *exact same* area of the brain—the caudate nucleus—lit up. Dr. Calvert's team reported, "Bottom line, there was no discernible difference between the way the subjects' brains reacted to powerful brands and the way they reacted to religious icons and figures. . . . Clearly, our emotional engagement with powerful brands . . . shares strong parallels with our feelings about religion."[5]

From a neurological standpoint, this helps explain the quasi-religious fervor people attach to power brands (e.g., Apple, Hello Kitty, and Harley-Davidson). Indeed, in his book *Brand Sense*, Lindstrom applies the research he conducted alongside Dr. Calvert, recommending to marketers that "a brand should attempt to create a following akin to the obsessive adoration a sports fan feels or, even, in some respects, the faith of a religious congregation." Lindstrom asserts further, "Evoking something resembling religious zeal . . . is one objective of the next generation of products and advertising."[6]

The Japanese cartoon character Hello Kitty, which has raked in billions of dollars for the Sanrio Corporation, successfully embodies this. The power of the Hello Kitty brand extends beyond backpacks, electronics cases, plush dolls, clothing, and household items. Hello Kitty also has a help line, prayer sites, and private Hello Kitty counseling sessions![7]

If this sounds crazy to you—and it certainly did to us when we first encountered it—consider some of the benefits a religious faith gives people and compare those to what strong brands provide. Religions and brands both offer people a sense of belonging (a binding sense of community), a charismatic leader or figurehead (think Steve Jobs or Walt Disney), opponents (note the ongoing battle between Mac and PC users), evangelism (sharing a passion with others to inspire belief in them), symbols, and sensory appeal. Some of you have begun to internally argue with us: religious fervor and true relationship with God are different; a brand cannot offer what intimacy with Jesus can. You're absolutely right, and that's the point.

The release of pleasure-inducing chemicals and the neural firing of reward-focused brain structures can momentarily trick our brains into believing that a product or brand can satisfy us. Even thinking about getting something we like, whether a Godiva chocolate or the latest generation Apple device, stimulates activity in our brains. But we must remember, and we must teach our teenagers: this *does not last*. In fact, we must reinforce what research proves—possessing often *diminishes* the pleasure. Fleeting gratification from the material world disappoints us eventually. In order to keep experiencing the dopaminergic rush, we have to chase after the next thing.

During the adolescent years, many teenagers own less than they do during any other stage of life. Teens don't have near the amount of physical "toys" as children, and they haven't accumulated the mountains of stuff most adults labor to organize, arrange, care for, and maintain. As a result, we believe this season in your teen's life presents a unique and fantastic opportunity to look at what lies behind the "it's mine" mentality. If you can choose to confront materialism during your child's adolescent years, your teen will be better prepared to face the adult world.

We've seen the specific neurological reasons why things and brands entice us; let's turn now to what happens in the mind, heart, and soul when people choose materialism or contentment.

Psych 101

Materialism involves the *focus* of our attention, desires, and energies. It's an insatiable desire to get and a preoccupation with possessing what we believe will make us happy. Materialism also implies the *choice* to view physical things and consolations as more important than other values. Even if one doesn't make this decision consciously, it's made nonetheless. Ultimately, the measure for success becomes equated with how many objects, comforts, and considerations one can amass. In bumper-sticker lingo, it's a "whoever dies with the most toys wins" philosophy.

Sociologists have studied human desire for many years. Their central questions: Why do we *want*, and why does our *wanting* never lead to what we think it will provide—lasting satisfaction? In his book *The High Price of Materialism*, Dr. Tim Kasser reveals,

> Existing scientific research on the value of materialism yields clear and consistent findings. People who are highly focused on materialistic values have lower personal well-being and psychological health than those who believe that materialistic pursuits are relatively unimportant. These relationships have been documented in samples of people ranging from wealthy to poor, from teenagers to the elderly. . . . The studies document that strong materialist values are associated with pervasive undermining of people's well-being, from low life satisfaction and happiness, to depression and anxiety, to physical problems such as headaches, and to personality disorders, narcissistic, and antisocial behaviors.[8]

Let's break this down and evaluate the scientifically observable pros and cons of materialism. Cons: lower levels of happiness, pervasive undermining of well-being, depression, anxiety, physical complaints, and social problems. Pros: a temporary burst of chemical pleasure that fades quickly. Considering this, it's hard to imagine anyone choosing a materialistic mindset. And yet, as a popular blogger asserted bluntly, "It sounds horrible, but we all do it to some extent, even if we don't go overboard."[9]

In one sociological experiment, people were repeatedly exposed to consumer messages, words associated with material goods and acquisitions (e.g., *buy*, *status*, *asset*, and *expensive*), as well as images of luxury goods (things considered "out of reach" for the average person). Study participants not only became more anxious and depressed but also exhibited increased selfish and competitive behavior, a lower sense of community responsibility, and "disinclination to trust other people."[10] Researchers concluded that since the average person views roughly 250 cultural advertisements a day (everything from billboards while driving to pop-ups while web surfing), we can safely assume that the temporary effects evidenced in this controlled study are triggered in all of us, every day.

Imagine how all this affects your teenager, an adolescent whose brain is under construction and who doesn't yet have the neural connectivity to evaluate and reject cultural messages designed to promote insatiable desire, selfishness, social competition, and distrust of others.

If you want to escape cultural manipulation yourself and help your teenager live with greater personal satisfaction, less anxiety and depression, and a more pervasive sense of well-being and social connectivity, here are some practical steps you can take:

- **Shop less.** A national survey reported that the typical woman makes 301 trips to a store annually, spending an average of 399 hours and 46 minutes shopping for everything from peanut butter to purses. Factored over sixty-three years, the average woman will have shopped for eight and a half years before hitting retirement age. Yikes! When we shop, we're exposed to far more consumer messages, our brains are continuously primed for spending, *and* our teenagers see us coming home with enticing bags and boxes. It's all very titillating. We can consciously choose to break this cycle, however. Of course we need to shop for food and clothing, but do we need to spend an average of 100 hours and 48 minutes looking for clothes and 49 hours window-shopping *every year*? If you want your teen to put less emphasis on things and live for more than the latest technology release or fashion trend, shop less.[11]
- **Practice gratitude.** Research shows that people focused on material goods and comforts have social, personal, and physical problems. Grateful people, on the other hand, complain of fewer psychosomatic problems (i.e., anxiety, depression, headaches, stomachaches), have more satisfying relationships, and

accomplish more in school and other goal-oriented pursuits.[12] They also show greater empathy and express less aggression.[13] We don't think it's a stretch to say that all of us want our kids to be healthier, happier, and better able to relate to others. If gratitude is a key to that, why not start today? What if at every meal that you ate together (not just at Thanksgiving), your family members articulated something they were grateful for that day? Gratitude isn't just an expression; it's a *practice*. It's something that has to be intentionally implemented into your lifestyle because it won't happen naturally. The natural bent of our hearts is toward desire, selfishness, and discontent. Even if for a while your teen says the same thing over and over, they will hear you expressing gratitude, and a genuinely grateful heart is infectious.

- **Give the gift of experience.** Instead of adding more "stuff" to your life, gifts of experience strengthen relationships and remind us that true life is experienced *together*, not through things. Take your teen to a concert or to get a pedicure. If you're able to save for it, consider a getaway for big occasions (a sixteenth, eighteenth, or twenty-first birthday, for example). Since spending time with family members is more important than another "thing," you can encourage others to give the gift of experience as well. Be creative and enjoy the memory making!

- **Slow down.** It takes time to live in contentment. A busy, hectic life is conducive to seeking fulfillment in temporal pleasures. The more stressed you are, the more stressed your teen is, and the more entertainment, material possessions, and comforts will appeal. As Dr. Richard Swenson observes, "We can learn to voluntarily take segments of our lives off-line, to voluntarily step off the default cultural treadmill from time to time to regain our equilibrium. It is not mandatory to participate in everything progress throws our way."[14]

- **Live generously.** Like gratitude, generosity is a practice that fights the pull of consumerism and materialism. It sounds ironic and it certainly flies in the face of the messages with which we are constantly bombarded, but the more people give—of not only money but also time and energy—the more satisfaction they report with life. There's a reason the phrase, "It is more blessed to give than to receive" became popular apart from its biblical origins; it's a truth we can *feel* down to the very cellular level. Generous people express deeper peace, a stronger sense of well-being, and fewer physical complaints. Model this for your teenager, help him or her to practice generosity, and talk about the benefits you can see as a result. Here's one practical way to do this: after your teen receives birthday or Christmas gifts, encourage him or her to choose a few things to give away. This keeps gratitude for what has been given and generosity to others closely connected in teenage minds.

Faith 101

"Beware, and be on your guard against every form of greed; for not even when one has an abundance does his life consist of his possessions" (Luke 12:15 NASB).

Jesus spoke these striking words after a man tried to involve him in a family inheritance dispute. Uttering the ancient equivalent of "Show me the money!" this man wanted Jesus to settle his financial problems and give him security. People have longed for the same from the genesis of humanity, and the endless striving for comfort and confidence has led many down the path of envy and greed. We need to be on our guard, and we need to teach our teens the same wariness and wisdom.

Envy and greed often sneak up on us. Most Christians wouldn't identify themselves as materialists. After all, people of faith know better, don't they? Unfortunately, many Christians live as "practical atheists" when it comes to their personal finances, and they model a fixation on what can be accumulated and accomplished for the teenagers who live with them.

When we make decisions about money, business, success, entertainment, or really anything else without considering God's truth, we operate as practical atheists. Alternatively, we can communicate to our ever-watchful, ever-judging teens that we are committed to looking at stuff and success differently.

G. K. Chesterton famously wrote, "There are two ways to get enough. One is to continue to accumulate more and more. The other is to desire less."[15] When we choose to desire less, we escape entrapment. We aren't *owned* by stuff.

Sadly, most Americans don't choose to live this way. Despite what our dollar bills claim, adolescents see adults live with an "in things we trust" rather than "in God we trust" mindset.

Augustine taught that God desires to give good things to us, but our hands are usually so full of material things that we cannot receive his gifts of grace.[16] When we throw off everything that hinders, however, as Hebrews 12:1 commands, we are able to receive what God longs to give us: not "one more thing," but the *one thing* that truly satisfies and can never be taken from us (see Luke 10:38–42).

We must *practice* letting go. We must *decide* to stop grasping, clinging, and clenching, and to tell our teens the truth about what constant striving does to us. We can also talk about the cost of getting what we want. In the colloquial, you might say, "If the grass is greener on the other side of the fence, you can bet the water bill is higher."

When stories come up in the news or situations present themselves (which happens almost every time we're at the mall!), point out to your teen what envy and greed do to people. Both reduce us. They wrap us up in tiny, self-centered packages of what we desire and what we perceive as our needs. Bring to their attention how most of the things people wanted *so badly* last Christmas eventually end up at the dump or Goodwill.

Things don't last forever; science verified this hundreds of years ago in the second law of thermodynamics. According to this principle of entropy, given enough time, the universe and everything in it will dissolve into complete chaos. Once again, however, science simply affirmed truths God proclaimed ages before: "The world offers only a craving for physical pleasure, a craving for everything we see, and pride in our achievements and possessions. These are not from the Father, but are from this world. And this world is fading away, along with everything that people crave. But anyone who does what pleases God will live forever" (1 John 2:16–17 NLT).

Let's help our teens truly *live*. Teach them to get enough by desiring less.

Try It Today: Talk to Your Kids about Debt

Many—perhaps even most—Americans live shackled to debt. Whether you condone or condemn debt in principle, no one claims that living with massive amounts of debt is healthy, makes you happier, and lowers your stress. On the contrary, studies show again and again that the more debt people incur, the less they enjoy life. Adolescents should learn this before they begin handling their own money.

Credit companies have spent years developing, marketing, and now distributing cards to teenagers. Their strategy: create child consumers who grow up to be adult debtors. Don't allow this to happen to your teenager.

If you've struggled with debt and can speak to your teenager from firsthand experience, seize this opportunity to let God use something negative for good. Sharing your mistakes can be life-changing and perhaps life-saving for your teenager. Regardless of whether you've endured financial struggle or enjoyed financial success, speaking honestly with your teen about the weight of debt is essential.

15

Hold On, I Just Have to Send This

Fourteen-year-old Jason clearly did not want to be sitting in my office that afternoon. I (Jeramy) had received a call from his distraught mom a couple days before.

"Jeramy, I don't know what to do. We fight about *everything*. Can you please talk to him?"

As a youth pastor, I got calls like this frequently. I never knew if setting up a meeting would lead to a transformative talk with a teen or a frustrating exercise in trying to engage the equivalent of a human wall.

My time with Jason fell into the latter category. Not only did he seem angry that his mom had dragged me into "their stuff," he also spent more time looking under the table at his phone—which was lighting up like a pinball machine—than at either me or his mother. After about ten minutes of trying to battle for Jason's attention, I politely asked if he would please put his phone away.

Apparently it took an extraordinary amount of energy for Jason not to roll his eyes; his face contorted with the effort. With a resigned sigh, he stuffed the phone into his jeans. *Bing-bing-bing*. Jason's cell continued to send Morse-code-like signals from the depths of his pocket, alerting him of incoming texts.

What happened next I could neither have predicted nor believed possible. With his hand resting on top of his pocket, Jason started texting through his jeans. He was so keenly aware of every button on his phone that he felt confident sending messages without looking at the screen. To this day, I'm not sure if Jason thought I wouldn't notice or if he just didn't care. I simply asked that he completely turn off his phone until our time was over.

Since I met with Jason, technology has skyrocketed from being a problem to being *the* problem for many families. Even with limits and filters, guidelines and agreements, technology remains a major source of contention. Understanding what's happening in our teenagers' brains won't entirely eradicate the tension of navigating technology well, but it *will* give you greater peace, wisdom, and a strategy to move forward.

Bio 101

According to recent studies, average teens are exposed to between seven and eight and a half hours of electronic media per day.[1] Much of this is spent in digital multitasking (e.g., texting while watching videos online or social networking while doing homework on the computer). Not surprisingly, the near-constant digital input our teenagers receive impacts their brains in striking ways.

As you now know, how teens choose to spend their time shapes their brains. When adolescents focus their attention in particular ways, energy and information flow through neural pathways and into their entire body through the nervous system. With every incoming digital signal, your teen's brain fires, activating specific circuits. The more particular pathways are activated, the more they're strengthened ("hardwired"). Thus your teen's brain is radically changed by spending hours using technology or being exposed to it.

Digital media stimulates the brain's reward system, and because the teenage brain is particularly sensitive to pleasurable titillation, all it takes is the latest digital message, app, or game to send it into delighted distraction. If the reward center of the brain is overused, however, the experience of gratification decreases. Neurologically speaking, striving for too much pleasure diminishes your ability to enjoy it. Instead of recognizing this, most under-construction teens seek increasingly greater stimulation, trying to recapture what eludes them, hungry for another "like," a new social media friend, or the chance to defeat the next level.

The current generation of adolescents, ages twelve to twenty-five, are both incredibly tech savvy and incredibly tech sensitive. In some ways they're victorious over technology, and in others they're dangerously vulnerable to it. Adolescents are susceptible to all of technology's influences: the good, the bad, and the ugly. One of the ugliest realities is that the insatiable need for stimulation accompanied by diminished satisfaction is the basis of addiction.

An activity can become addictive if it (1) provides pleasure and gives relief from unpleasant emotions, (2) requires increasing activity to satisfy, (3) makes a person feel uncomfortable or distressed when access is denied, (4) creates conflict with people or life responsibilities, (5) becomes difficult to set aside, despite attempts to do so, and (6) ultimately dominates someone's life, both in what they do and what they think about. Do any of these descriptions apply to your teenager's tech usage?

Dr. Susan Moeller discovered that most students, when asked to abstain from media for twenty-four hours, reported disturbing feelings about their tech-free day. Across twelve countries, one thousand students expressed similar sentiments: "I was edgy and irritated . . . and insecure." "I began going crazy." "I felt paralyzed." "Emptiness overwhelm[ed] me." "My phone has my whole life in it. If I ever lost it, I think I would die."[2]

Clearly, technology has a major hold on today's teens.

We know of very few people who would argue that unlimited tech use is healthy for teenagers. But how much is too much? At what point does the brain's reward system become flooded and less able to enjoy other pleasures, including conversation, without animation and alerts? When do the demands of the digital world exceed the brain's capacity?

We spent some time discussing these issues with Dr. Jay Giedd, father of four adolescents and the neuroscientist whose pioneering research on the brain forever changed the way the world understands teenagers.

"Is technology good or bad for teens?" we asked Dr. Giedd. His answer:

> Both. The adolescent brain is wired to change and to tackle problems. Our digital world is challenging people to adapt at unprecedented rates. With heightened neuroplasticity, teens are uniquely positioned to do this. Technology allows adolescents instant access to information and enables them to become more globally aware than ever before. These can be incredibly positive things.
>
> That said, teens must be taught how to sift through large amounts of data, identifying what's true and useful, discarding junk and ignoring "noise." This is no small feat. Formerly teens were taught to memorize information; now they need instruction in using instantly-accessible information to solve problems and tackle challenges. We also need to look intently at what's being hard-wired into their brains.[3]

Does the way a teen uses technology benefit his or her life (relationships, character, academics, communal responsibility, etc.)? Most likely the answer is "sometimes, but not always." How can we use technology for all it's worth, optimizing the positive potential and diminishing negative effects?

Because electronic media is such a huge topic, we've divided the issues into two chapters. The structure for these chapters will differ slightly. Instead of a "Psych 101" section, we'll tackle specific technology concerns individually. This chapter will deal with cell phones, social media, and internet browsing. We'll tackle TV, film, music, and video gaming in the next.

Your Teen's 24-7 Companion

The cell phone wields tremendous power in teenage life. Statistics show that 77 percent of adolescents own a phone and approximately 40 percent have a smartphone.[4] Teenage girls typically spend more time on their phones—both talking and texting. But factoring in data for both genders, the number of texts sent and received averages out to 3,853 per month; that's well in excess of 100 texts every day.[5]

Studies have shown that almost half of adolescents experience feelings of anxiety and insecurity when their text messages go unanswered, and 73 percent feel "panicked" if they misplace their phone.[6] How can parents help teens manage this virtually omnipresent technology?

The first and perhaps best way is to have them deliberately turn off the device at prearranged times. Choosing to turn off the phone demonstrates that life can be lived without it. Making dinnertime a no-cell time frame and setting a "bedtime" for your teen's phone are good places to start. Of course, the practice will work best if you set aside your device at the same time.

Turning off the phone before bed results in significant benefits, while not doing so leads to detrimental effects. Using a cell phone to text, talk, or surf the web at night has been linked to poor sleep habits (more on this in chapter 20) as well as depressive symptoms. Since approximately 80 percent of smartphone users and 53 percent of conventional cell phone users leave their device on twenty-four hours a day, millions of teens are suffering from fatigue and mood disruption as a result of never disconnecting from their phones.[7]

Studies also show that adolescents who are heavy cell phone users have shorter attention spans, make more errors in memory-based tasks, learn slower, and retain less than their peers.[8] Excessive cell phone activity can also be dangerous. Increasing incidents of traumatic brain injuries can be linked to texting while walking, and digital use while driving has surpassed drunk driving as the leading cause of teenage accidents and fatalities. Some research indicates that driving while texting is *six times more dangerous* than driving drunk.[9] Finally, while we will discuss the impact of pornography specifically in chapter 23, it's essential to mention the peril of instant access on cell phones. Many teens first view porn on a mobile device, and since they stimulate the brain so violently, these salacious images can be burned into an adolescent's memory. Reduced use equals reduced potential for negative influence or harm.

How you use your cell phone also influences how your teen uses his or hers. If you're habitually telling your teen to wait while you finish your message, post, or level, don't be surprised if you often get a "Hold on, I just have to . . . " response. Many of the physiological and psychological effects we've outlined thus far—fear of being disconnected, anxiety when someone doesn't respond to a message, and a sense of emptiness when no technology is available—apply equally to adults as they do to teenagers. Please show your teen that technology doesn't rule you.

Another excellent way to help your teen use his or her cell phone well is to practice the "People first, devices second" rule. People are infinitely more important than apps and alerts. Most adolescents won't be able to see this instantly, so anticipate a learning curve. It's okay for teens to struggle. Help them succeed by suggesting an activity or topic of conversation that interests them and encourage their efforts.

Networked

Parental approaches to social networking differ widely. Some prohibit it altogether, others monitor it heavily, and some believe it's "no big deal."

Many of our daughters' peers had social network accounts prior to age thirteen. We drew a line by showing our girls the user agreements, clearly indicating thirteen was the minimum age to establish an account. We told them we wouldn't lie so they could be "connected." Judging by our daughters' reactions, it was as if we'd decided to become Amish.

To us, things seemed very straightforward: it would involve lying to allow our girls on any of the typical social networks at that time, so there was nothing to "choose"; it simply wasn't an option.

On her thirteenth birthday, however, our oldest daughter wanted to open an account on the photo sharing site her friends used. We'd researched this and talked to others, and we decided to sign up for our own account so that we could monitor her posts. We talked to her about online etiquette, privacy, and ethics, and we limited her access.

After a couple of years, we can report on the positive and negative aspects of allowing her to be networked. From online artists, she's learned some fantastic techniques. The cool facts she's gleaned and gorgeous images she's come across have given us fodder for great conversations. We've laughed a lot, and shared humor is a huge blessing for our family.

We've also seen firsthand how easily trashy comments or pictures can slip onto the feed, as well as how "likes" and comments (or lack thereof) impact teens. People "like," repost, or comment on something online for a variety of reasons, but it always goes back to their personal preferences: Was that interesting, shocking, funny, or important *to me*? As Dr. Gary Chapman and Arlene Pellicane note in their book *Growing Up Social*, "It's hard enough for adults to deal with disparaging comments online or a lack of comments, which communicate, 'No one is interested in me.' Imagine how hard it is for children who don't yet possess the emotional maturity to cope with the digital world."[10] Online "likes" are conditional, but teenagers need more *unconditional love* in their lives, not more appearance- and performance-based admiration, which easily leads to insecurity, anxiety, and resentment toward others who are "liked" more.

Studies demonstrate that heavy usage of social networking sites leads to envy, triggering both physiological and psychological symptoms of depression in adolescents. This was particularly true for those who "strongly agreed" with the following:

- "It is so frustrating to see some people always having a good time."
- "Many of my friends have a better life than me."
- "Many of my friends are happier than me."[11]

When adolescents perceive life is better for "everyone else," dissatisfaction with their own situation increases.

Research also indicates social networking trains teenagers to become undisciplined adults. Scientists have linked social networking to lack of self-control, since it "interferes with clear thinking and decision-making, which lowers self-control and leads to rash, impulsive buying and poor eating decisions. Greater social media use is associated with a higher body mass index, increased binge eating, a lower credit score, and higher levels of credit card debt for consumers with many close friends in their social network."[12] Obviously, those are not the character traits we want our teenagers to develop! Our teens—whose ability to evaluate cause and effect is under construction—need help recognizing that constant exposure to advertising triggers the desire to eat or shop excessively.

Adolescents also need help navigating the additional pressures ever-widening social circles can create. According to one study, the more "friends" a person has online, the quicker social media becomes a source of stress.[13] As more and more "friends" or "contacts" are added, teenagers begin to treat those with whom they are "connected" as commodities. If they don't like what someone says, they hide or "unfriend" them. There's no need to work through relationship difficulties when you're on to the next click. Increasingly, teenagers avoid the natural challenges of friendship by hiding behind technology. Teens who train their brains to use electronic, "srry 4 htng on u" messages shortchange their ability to interact with people face-to-face, now and in the future.[14]

We recommend the ABCs of handling social media well: awareness, boundaries, and communication.

Be *aware* of your teen's social media habits. Even if you don't allow your teen to be on the most widely used networks, he or she is likely watching videos online, reading posts and emails, or being exposed to social networking with their friends. Because of this, all parents—both those with strict limits and those with looser ones—need to be aware of how social media plays a role in their teen's life.

Establish *boundaries*. It's best to do this before your teen starts using social networking, but boundaries can be set up at any point. Though daunting, it's a battle worth fighting. For younger adolescents, identify specific times when they can and cannot be online. Since older adolescents need to learn self-regulation, gradually releasing control over your teens' choices is essential. If you've helped them develop self-restraint along the way, you can trust that their decisions will be good much of the time and that when they fail (which they will!), they can learn from it.

Finally, *communication* with your teen about social networking is nonnegotiable. Ask them to show you the funniest thing they've seen recently or whether they've learned anything new online. Eventually these conversations about social media will enable you to ask about negative things they've seen or experienced online. Talk about your own social networking, sharing your thoughts and emotions. This normalizes conversation about online activities, making it more likely that your teen will talk with you in the future.

Surf's Up . . . *Always*

Internet surfing is more than a pastime for teenagers; for many, it's their primary source of knowledge and entertainment. The massive amount of wonderful information available to adolescents and the sheer volume of possible distractions (many of them brain-numbingly silly) is overwhelming.

As noted previously, every digital click and alert signals the brain to respond. For teens, with highly charged reward systems, every computerized "surprise" (e.g., new video or website) primes the neural pump for pleasure. But when there's so much available, teens end up drinking from a proverbial fire hydrant. The human brain—adolescent or adult—simply cannot process continuous stimuli and information.

According to Nicholas Carr, author of *The Shallows: What the Internet Is Doing to Our Brains*, deep thinking becomes increasingly impossible as the online world overwhelms neural circuits with fleeting

Did You Know?

The most popular video streaming website in the world recently published statistics about its virtual omnipresence. Boasting more than 1 billion users who generate billions of views *every day*, this website uploads 300 hours of video *every minute*.[15] According to a *Variety* magazine survey, its "stars" (popular video creators) are more influential amongst teenagers than mainstream celebrities.[16]

More than 1.3 million applications are currently available in the iOS App Store, serving 155 countries around the world. More than 300 million users visit the App Store each week. In October 2014, a new record of 7.8 million *daily* downloads was set.[17]

Google now processes an average of 40,000 search queries every second, which translates to over 3.5 billion searches per day and 1.2 trillion searches per year worldwide.[18] Teenagers can surf approximately 920 million active websites at any moment of any day, in any location that has an internet connection.[19]

and temporary information. "Our ability to learn suffers, and our understanding remains shallow. . . . When we go online, we enter an environment that promotes cursory reading, hurried and distracted thinking, and superficial learning," which is "the type of thinking technology encourages and rewards."[20]

The online world also reinforces what Dr. Kathy Koch calls the "I Am the Center of My Own Universe" myth, a falsehood teenagers already tend to believe.[21] Because the online world is structured around each person's "preferences," it's easy for teens to find the virtual world of perpetual entertainment and personal relevance exciting and enjoyable. In the real world, limits to individual autonomy and responsibility encroach on the "what I want, when I want it," "only if it makes me happy" mentality.

Teenagers must learn they're *not* the center of the universe. They should also spend more time in the real world than in the digital one, which means limiting web surfing. I know it's not easy, but that's no excuse. It takes discipline to teach your teenager to limit him- or herself, but thankfully God gives us the wisdom and courage we need as parents to set these boundaries and stand behind them.

Faith 101

The Bible consistently enjoins God's people to "pay attention" to wisdom. The book of Proverbs admonishes us to "pay attention and gain understanding" (4:1), while the book of Exodus reminds us to "pay no attention to lies" (5:9) and the book of Jeremiah reveals what happened when God's people "did not listen or pay attention"—they went their own way and suffered greatly (17:23, 27).

The powerful digital world has made it more difficult than ever to pay attention. According to Joseph McCormack, author of *Brief: Making a Bigger Impact by Saying Less*, the average person's attention span has decreased by 40 percent since the year 2000. Typically, people now pay attention for approximately eight seconds before becoming distracted, tuning out, or choosing to refocus on the original source.[22]

Eight seconds. Wow.

In Search of Balance author Dr. Richard Swenson adds, "We have no longitudinal attention span today. Instead, we have 'continuous partial attention.' Technology has enhanced our productivity and simultaneously destroyed our depth."[23]

The endless stream of information to which we're exposed on smartphones, tablets, computers, and other digital devices tells us what to pay attention to and what to think about. Entire days can easily go by without a teenager *choosing* what to think about or *choosing* to pay attention to what really matters. Neural circuits contributing to faith, hope, and love need stimulation and attention so they can grow healthy and strong.

Research shows that not only has attention span decreased, but people rarely pay attention to one thing at a time. Among teenagers, electronic multitasking has increased by 120 percent in the last ten years.[24] Adolescents often pride themselves on being able to do "lots of things at once," but studies show that effective multitasking is a myth. Paying careful attention to multiple things at once is impossible; multitasking inherently "decreases our attention, making us increasingly less able to focus. . . . This opens us up to shallow and weak judgments and decisions, and it results in passive mindlessness."[25] Surely it is our responsibility as Christian parents to help our adolescents learn to pay attention to what matters. Model paying attention to one thing at a time, especially to life's most important dimension: a relationship with God.

Your teenager's prefrontal cortex is under major construction during the adolescent years. And guess what helps activate it? *Deep thinking.* Focused attention also improves connections within and between nerve networks, particularly in the frontal and middle regions of the brain, including the emotional limbic system. Neural integration in these areas helps teenagers tremendously.[26] It also increases concentration, decreases switching between tasks pointlessly, makes necessary transitions between tasks more effective, decreases emotional volatility, and results in increased completion of projects.[27] What teen wouldn't benefit from this?

God wrote his truth in us on a cellular level. We perform better, feel better, and live better when we pay attention, as he commands us to do.

Help your teen pay attention to the right things by ensuring an appropriate environment and providing opportunities. When attending to one task (i.e., homework) is important, disallow electronic multitasking, unless it's listening to calming instrumental music, which studies show actually aids in concentration. Consider reading a passage of Scripture at the dinner table or before bed. Buy your teenager a devotional to read on his or her own.

Rewarding teens for memorizing Scripture gives them an attractive reason to pay attention to the truth. There are few ways you could better spend your money, as the investment is eternal and kingdom-building. And because God's Word *always* accomplishes its purpose, *never* coming back void (see Isa. 55:11), you can trust that eventually your teen will discover the reward of knowing God's Word for its own sake.

Try It Today: Start Writing a Tech Agreement

If you're like most parents, supervising tech usage is difficult. One way to help teenagers take responsibility for monitoring themselves (an important task in adolescence) is to collaborate with them in writing and agree to a tech use "contract." This also increases adolescent buy-in. Negotiating a tech agreement will require you to compromise in some ways, so before you broach this subject with your teen, remember to "sort" your battles (review the steps on page 97).

Here are some important areas to address in a tech agreement:

- **Privacy.** Research shows that 59 percent of teens "interact with strangers online and overshare information, even though they realize that these activities can put them at risk. . . . This could be because 33 percent of them [teens and tweens] say they feel more accepted online than in real life."[28] Discuss this with your teen and then remind them (often) that giving out or posting phone numbers, email or home addresses, and other personal information, like whereabouts or employment locations, is never acceptable.

- **Propriety.** Identify inappropriate web content, including cyber-bullying, pornography, and online gambling. It's also important to emphasize that you expect your teens not to text or post anything they wouldn't say to someone face-to-face. Finally, reinforce with adolescents that if they encounter disturbing images or text online, they can talk to you about it.

- **Payment.** Let your teen know that if excessive tech use results in fees, he or she will be responsible for them. This helps to avoid most "You never told me . . ." arguments.

- **Parental privileges.** Calls or texts from parents take priority and should be answered within a reasonable time. Request that driving adolescents pull the car over to respond. Your teen should also give you access to his or her screen history, text messages, and passwords. This makes some teenagers uncomfortable, and parents often feel bad about insisting on this rule, but studies reveal that 45 percent of teens would change their online behavior if parents were monitoring it. Your adult brain is a parental privilege—use it and let your teen know that you're watching because you care about them!

For more information about helping your teen make wise digital choices, we highly recommend *Growing Up Social* by Dr. Gary Chapman and Arlene Pellicane and *Screens and Teens* by Dr. Kathy Koch.

16

It's Not That Bad

If pressed to defend their entertainment choices, adolescents usually offer one of two defenses: "It doesn't affect me" or "It's not *that* bad."

Neither science nor common sense supports this. Media affects *every single one of us*: what passes before our eyes and through our ears becomes imprinted on our brains.

I (Jerusha) grew up in a media-saturated home. My dad writes music for film and television, as well as chorus and orchestra. My mom loves nothing more than a novel in her hand or a good audiobook. My brothers, sister, and I all played instruments, sang constantly, read voraciously, watched TV and movies, and played video games. Music of all genres, cinematic and literary references, even Nintendo theme songs wove my childhood together.

Media is not the enemy, nor is abstinence from it an answer for the very real and present dangers modern pop culture presents. Instead, we invite you to learn and practice discernment with regard to media and entertainment. As you discern wisely, your teens will learn likewise.

Bio 101

Our brilliantly and complexly designed brains separate, judge, order, and distinguish relentlessly, allowing us to make sense of the world. This process of observation, perception, and determination can be summed up in the term *discernment*. Every day, your brain provides sensory feedback and helps you decide what to do, when to do it, and how it should be done. You and I are perpetual discerners.

In today's media frenzy, people rarely apply the neural skill of discernment. Instead, they flip through channels, browse stations, skim magazines, or pick up a game controller without giving much thought to their decisions. Many of us operate on autopilot when it comes to media choices.

If our brains were static and inflexible, we wouldn't need to pay attention to the media we consume. It wouldn't affect us; it wouldn't matter. But this is not our neural story. On the contrary, our brains are incredibly malleable, and never more so than during adolescence.

As we noted previously, adolescence is a period of heightened neuroplasticity, the brain's remarkable ability to adapt based on exposure. During the first season of neuroplasticity—from birth to three years old—we make very few choices for ourselves. Caretakers shape our environment, exposing us to what they deem important, convenient, or manageable. The story shifts during adolescence, when we become responsible for more of our own decisions and have a greater degree of autonomy regarding what we see, hear, and play.

For this reason, the heightened neuroplasticity of adolescence and a teenager's near-constant exposure to media input require tremendous discernment. As Dr. Daniel Siegel so brilliantly summarizes, "What we focus our attention on and what we spend time doing directly stimulate the growth of those parts of the brain that carry out those functions."[1] Our teenagers *literally* grow and shape their brains as they watch TV and movies, play video games, read, and listen to music. In the words of Dr. Laurence Steinberg, who has spent decades researching adolescents, "Adolescence is probably the last real opportunity we have to put individuals on a healthy pathway and to expect our interventions to have substantial and enduring effects."[2]

Every scientific experiment with teenagers confirms the incredible sensitivity—body, mind, and spirit—of this time period, so we cannot settle for an "it's not *that* bad" approach. We must devote careful thought to and concentrate strategic action on helping teenagers optimize media decisions. The experiences of adolescence matter . . . a lot. Don't simply allow teens to be molded by what they are exposed to; teach them to direct the molding.

In a sense, each of us can be a neuroplastician, sculpting our own brains as we decide what to attend to and absorb. As teens mature, their brains move from being highly plastic to being less pliable and more difficult to transform. Don't allow this highly significant time period to fly by in a flurry of mindless media choices. Neuroplasticity is an amazing gift, but it also carries tremendous weight: *we can shape our own brains!* The positive and negative implications are enormous.

Thankfully, our brains have been equipped with both astounding malleability *and* the power to discern. Your teen has been designed to distinguish between what is good, bad, better, and best. This is the gift of discernment, and teenagers can learn to apply it to media choices.

As in the last chapter, the structure of the following pages will differ from the typical "Psych 101" format. We've placed TV and movies in one section. We'll discuss music, print media, and video games individually.

What's On?

People no longer have to arrange their schedules around favorite shows or movies. Instead, they exercise the power of personal choice through instant streaming apps, on-demand programming, and überconvenient home recording options. We've been given the "right" to decide when, where, and for how long we watch. It's all quite intoxicating.

We chose that word, *intoxicating*, with specific purpose. Exercising the perceived powers of control and choice spikes the pleasure potential and primes the pump that pushes us to pursue it again and again and again. Perusing a media menu, even if it hasn't changed that much since last time, gives us a sense of discovery; it's a virtual treasure hunt that promises to take us away from our stresses, at least for the length of a program or film. Super-sensitive-to-rewarding-stimulation teens are exceptionally susceptible to this draw.

In order to help your teen discern well with regard to film and television, you've got to have more in your arsenal than simply "don't watch movies or programs rated _____." Instead, establish an ongoing dialogue around the following questions:[3]

1. **Does this promote truth or lies?** Every show or film presents a worldview. Most modern media weaves together some truth and some falsehoods about life, relationships, and so on. The trick is to evaluate the worldview and determine if truth ultimately triumphs. For instance, watching an R-rated film like *Schindler's List* is not the same as watching a program that titillates with violence or, worse, glorifies it. Look for films and television that tell the truth about good and evil, consequences and opportunities, friendships and family. Even if they don't fit 100 percent with your worldview, films or programs can speak truths into your teen's life.

2. **Do I want to be like these characters?** Watching hours of programming or films that present antiheroes, currently a very popular choice for protagonists, impacts your teen. Choose programs and films that have characters your teen can clearly emulate or reject. Confusing characters (i.e., they're bad, but only because of their tortured past) are more difficult for some adolescents to understand. Teach your teen to watch the way the characters speak to and about people, how they treat others, and whether character traits that will eventually make your adolescent a responsible, contributing member of society are encouraged.

3. **What does this say about family?** Films and television often degrade marriages or family members. Fathers may be portrayed as lazy, fat, clueless buffoons and moms as harried and out of touch. "Look at sitcoms," Jim Fay and Foster Cline write. "Almost all of the humor is based on watching frustrated authority figures try to control situations they can't."[4] The family is the basic building block of society; watching programs and movies that tear at the fabric of the family doesn't edify anyone.

4. **What does this say about faith?** Let's imagine your teen watches an average of ten hours of media a week. That would be, say, a bit on school nights plus a movie or several programs each weekend (in case you're wondering, this is far less than the national average). Even in this amount, your teen would be watching close to four thousand hours of television and film over the course of his or her adolescence. During that time, your teen may rarely (or never) hear God, the Bible, or faith mentioned in positive, affirming ways. How important does faith seem after these *thousands* of hours? As Paul David Tripp wisely notes, "During those hours of cultural bombardment, [your teen] is usually relaxed and not thinking critically. . . . It would be the height of naiveté to think he will remain uninfluenced."[5]

Just as you wouldn't allow your teenager to eat only Pop-Tarts and Mountain Dew, you cannot allow your teen to consume *only* a diet of mindless media. Help your teen discern well.

The Soundtrack to Your Teen's Life

God designed music as one of life's greatest pleasures and most powerful forms of expression. Strains of melody and harmony wash over our neural cells, impacting the very wiring of our brains. Indeed, when we asked pioneering adolescent neuroscientist Dr. Jay Giedd what promotes myelination—the "insulating" of brain pathways to make them more efficient and integrated—his answer was immediate: music!

According to youth expert Dr. Jim Burns, music and the artists who create it meets three basic needs for teenagers: companionship, acceptance, and identification. Since many teens spend a great deal of time listening to music or reading about their favorite bands, they become virtual companions for adolescents. Because neither music nor musicians reject your teen, the sense of being accepted when listening to music of their choice is a powerful force for teenagers. Finally, in music and with musicians, teens find an outlet for their emotions, as well as an articulation of ideas and feelings they may not have been able to express otherwise.[6]

As a parent, it's important that you identify the influential musical "voices" in your teenager's life. Listen to the songs your teen chooses and read the lyrics. Do this so that when you have the chance, casual, and crucial conversations with your teenager about music, you'll know what you're talking about. You'll be immediately dismissed if you base your comments on rumors and stereotypes, or if you pigeonhole the music or musicians ("All her songs are about . . ." or "They *always* or *only* . . .").

Remember your goal: to encourage teens to evaluate *on their own* what they hear and how it impacts them. Your adolescent must do this in his or her adult life, and learning it during these highly neuroplastic teenage years is critical.

You can use the lyrics or tunes to stimulate developing discernment. If you're concerned about particular songs, initiate a casual (rather than confrontational) conversation about the selfishness, violence, or sexuality communicated by the band or lyrics. Keep in mind that censoring your teen's music, thereby creating musical martyrs, will be less effective than using what your teen chooses to expose the truths and lies about life presented by cultural voices.

As always, it's important for you to evaluate your own music choices before judging your teen's. Share with your adolescent what you discover. Vulnerability, courage, and honesty are highly prized virtues among adolescents. Use that to your adult advantage.

The Pen Is Mightier Than You Think

Many parents falsely believe "my teen doesn't read that much." Because the written word surrounds us, even if your teen isn't reading books for pleasure, he or she is exposed to far more of the written word than you may think. Our teens are continually bombarded with cultural messages in what they read: you're only really alive when you're in love with someone; if you follow your heart, it will show you the way; and a tragic love story is the most exalted of all.

Think of some of the most popular young adult fiction of the past decade: books featuring mythical, star-crossed adolescent lovers; teenagers with terminal illnesses who find love "before it's too late"; adolescents who overcome tremendous odds (societal, political, or familial abuse and neglect) in order to unite, survive, and—at least in the final book—overcome. The ideas and emotions teens are exposed to and experience while reading not only shape their minds in the present but also weave together the neural and moral fabrics from which their future choices arise.

Even cursory reading can produce powerful effects in a revved-up teenage brain. One sociological study revealed that adolescent girls felt guilty, depressed, and anxious after looking at a fashion magazine for *only three minutes.*[7] Surveys indicate 83 percent of adolescent girls read fashion magazines (online or in print) on average 4.3 hours per week. *Seventeen* alone boasts a readership of 11 million. The influence of adolescent-targeted print media should not be underestimated.[8]

If you haven't read the cover of one of these magazines in a while, you may be shocked by what you'll encounter. Glaring and explicit sexual references are just one issue. According to a former editor, the *acknowledged purpose* of these magazines is "to convince women that something is wrong with them (e.g., hair, body, sex life, etc.) so that they can sell their product (i.e., the content of the magazine) to fix it."[9]

Lest you parents of teenage boys think your son is immune, be aware that increasingly common media presentations of "super-guys"—stronger, fitter, and more competent than your average Joe— are taking their toll on adolescent boys. Recent studies on teenage males show rising levels of personal stress resulting from comparisons with media stars in print and on film.[10] Considering what's available for them to read (or watch or play), it's no wonder our teenagers are confused. They didn't write the books, the screenplays, or the advertisements; adults are responsible.

You can't constantly stimulate an under-construction teenage brain and then act surprised when a teen feels angry, sexually charged, suspicious of authority, or longing for the kind of love he or she reads about. We recommend you review and apply the same questions used to evaluate film and television to the books or magazines that you and your teen want to read.

Game On!

Video games are neither inherently good nor inherently evil; as a result, we cannot issue either a blanket recommendation or repudia-tion of them. Instead, as with all other forms of media, we urge you to exercise discernment.

In the past, playing video games was perceived as an isolating activity that promoted a sedentary, selfish lifestyle. These stereo-types no longer apply to many digital games. Indeed, with the rise of MMORPGs (Massively Multiplayer Online Role-Playing Games), social gaming has eclipsed lone participation, and full-body involve-ment is often required to advance in the complex worlds designed by brilliant technicians. Healthy levels of video gaming can develop quick thinking and spatial skills, as well as hand-eye coordination and sensory integration.

That said, computerized games tend to emphasize rapid responses in the brain instead of encouraging thoughtful decisions. As Dr. Sheryl Feinstein affirms, "teens who engage in excessive violent video play have underactive frontal lobes during and long after the game has been unplugged. This means logical, reasonable thinking is muffled and fast; reactive thinking is stimulated."[11] In other words, during *and long after* playing certain video games, the prefrontal cortex—the brain's CEO and the very last area of your teen's brain to mature— functions even less effectively.

Designed for perpetual multisensory stimulation, video games flood the brain's reward centers with the pleasure-inducing neuro-chemical dopamine. Though it frustrates some gamers to acknowledge, this is similar to the way drugs or alcohol produce an appealing "high." More and more gaming is necessary to produce the same "rush" of dopamine release. Some people think only certain games do that, but this biological reality does not apply only to first-person shooter games; MMORPGs also have this effect on the brain.

First-person shooter games, however, additionally and actively stimulate areas of the brain that control aggression and reactivity— particularly the amygdala, which is already "large and in charge" in the typical teenage brain. Young men, especially, have naturally heightened activity in the amygdala during adolescence, so additional stimulation is hardly necessary.

It's essential for parents to separate the activity (gaming itself) from potentially destructive motives (why your teen games) and con-sequences (if gaming is out of control and leading to other concerning behaviors). Dr. Douglas Gentile, pioneering researcher on video game impact and addiction, offers wise words to parents: "It's not that the games are bad. . . . It's that some kids use them in a way that is out of balance and harms various other areas of their lives."[12]

According to one study, as many as 40 percent of online video game players admitted to playing as a way to escape from the real world.[13] Using escape as a coping mechanism is a key component of addiction, whether someone escapes through drugs, gambling, or video games.

Research also consistently shows—and by this we mean *over two thousand scientific studies agree*—that ongoing exposure to violent video gaming increases the risk of aggression and reactivity, decreases empathy and sensitivity, and can ultimately lead to an anxious, suspicious, and harsh view of the world.[14] The National Institutes of Health, the American Medical Association, the American Academy of Pediatrics, the American Psychological Association, and the Surgeon General's office have all issued statements that *content matters*: media violence influences adolescents in powerful ways. Indeed, "video games are especially dangerous because a child is not passively watching a violent act; he is participating in it. . . . Games also create a system of reinforcement. A child is rewarded for destructive behaviors again and again."[15] If your teenager has a steady diet of aggressive, violent media, he or she will be affected. Science, sociology, and anecdotal evidence all prove this.

If you're wondering how much is too much, start by identifying the amount of violent media your teen is exposed to. Don't trust estimates. Spend two to four weeks writing down whenever you notice your adolescent playing a video game, watching a TV show or movie, visiting a webpage, or listening to music that includes violence. Most of us don't estimate very well. We tend to minimize how much time our teens actually spend with technology.

You can then evaluate what your child is like before, during, and after gaming. Do you like the way this game makes your teen feel and/or act? Do you notice any patterns? Observation and honesty are key here. Finally, watch carefully for signs of unhealthy attachment. If a teen breaks family rules, lies or manipulates in order to play more, chooses games over friends and family, becomes enraged when asked to stop, has hand and wrist pain, or has disrupted sleep or poor personal hygiene because of gaming, a problem exists. If you suspect a serious problem, you can find help at www.video-game-addiction.org.

Thankfully, the vast majority of teens won't progress to addiction. Instead, for most, the key is discernment: judging between good, bad, better, and best when it comes to video games, then deciding wisely and committing to uphold those choices, even when being tired, sick, or stressed out might lead you to make an exception.

Faith 101

The Random House dictionary defines pop culture as "activities or commercial products reflecting, suited to, or aimed at the tastes of the general masses of people."[16] TV, film, music, print media, and video games make up a large part of pop culture.

Driven by aggressive marketing and targeting teenagers, who are huge media consumers, pop culture is pervasive, constantly changing, and entertainment focused. Teenagers especially tend to unite around pop culture phenomena.[17] Viewed through a spiritual lens, pop culture is entirely of this world.

Enjoying the amazing, thrilling world God created is good, but it was never meant to be our source of lasting peace and joy. The more teenagers find their place by participating in and identifying with pop culture, the less time and energy they have to invest elsewhere.

According to Proverbs 23:7, "As he thinks within himself, so he is" (NASB). It's both a biological reality and a spiritual truth: how we choose to direct our thoughts shapes the very course of our lives. Dr. Caroline Leaf, after three decades of research on this topic, asserts, "In the busyness of life and the flurry of everyday activity, we expose ourselves to the possibility of developing a chaotic mindset with the net result of neurochemical and electromagnetic chaos in the brain."

Dr. Leaf's prescription: deliberately choose to take "a Sabbath in the brain." This counteracts the neural and emotional overstimulation of pop culture. "It is like a mental rebooting process to reconnect with who we are and with our Savior to bring perspective to the issues of life."[18] Pop culture keeps us constantly spinning, striving, and seeking. Teach your teen to take a break from the chaos.

Also, share with your adolescent the truth that "everything is permissible, but not everything is beneficial" (see 1 Cor. 6:12). We've been given tremendous freedom by the Lord, and regardless of age, stage of life, or socioeconomic level, every person shares this freedom: we can choose how to focus our minds.

The temptation to justify negative choices—"It's not *that* bad," "It doesn't affect me," or "It's just a little thing"—is common to adults and teens alike. Consider, however, the shrewd observations of François Fénelon: "'It is a small matter,' they say. That is true, but it is of amazing consequence to you. It is something you love enough to refuse to give it up to God. It is something you sneer at in words, so that you may have an excuse to keep it: a small matter—but one that you withhold from your Maker, which can prove your ruin."[19]

Let's model for our teens that we refuse to be ruined by small things like TV, movies, or games that continually focus our minds on the here and now. Instead, let's teach our teens to choose what builds up, rather than simply trying to figure out "How bad is too bad?" What you choose and what they choose *matters*.

Try It Today: Plan a Media Sabbath

A few weekends ago, both our girls lost their tech privileges. We ended up playing games, getting outside, and enjoying the time. Even they admitted it was fun! We didn't have to force these activities; they happened naturally because there was space and enough "restlessness" in our adolescent daughters to prompt the question, "Do you guys want to do something together?"

When the option to watch or play something is always present, our teens tend to default to that. Perhaps you and yours do the same.

Plan a family media sabbath. Tell your teens you're doing an experiment to determine, "When technology isn't an option, what will we do?" They may grumble, but who knows what wild things may happen?

17

How Do I Know That's True?

For Christian parents, statistics can tell a grim story. Take these, for example: somewhere between 40 and 50 percent of adolescents actively involved in church youth groups disconnect from God in college. And 80 percent of these teens intended to continue living a life of faith—only 20 percent predetermined to walk away—which means somewhere between intentions and daily decisions, a major breakdown occurs.[1]

Like for many of you, reading those stats ignites a fire of concern in us. How do we help our teens develop a faith that lasts, a faith that survives not only college but also the adult world of temptations, trials, and troubles? Sometimes it feels overwhelming.

As a teenager's ability to think abstractly develops, most likely he or she will begin to explore and evaluate previously held beliefs. Even though they're not the first people to ask existential questions such as "Why do bad things happen to good people?" and "How do I know any of this is true?" teenagers often *feel* that they're the first (if not the only) ones to struggle with such issues. Because these ideas occur to them "all of a sudden," teens often believe their experiences are entirely unique. They also may assume that having questions automatically means everything they've held true is under suspicion until proven to their satisfaction.

Please take a deep breath and know that all of this is normal. In fact, it's essential. Your teen cannot develop an authentic faith without wrestling with the complexities of truth and life, hope and heartache. Looking at stats and walking through these years may spark fear in you, but we encourage you to read this chapter with a settled peace. God chose you to parent your teen, but he is your teenager's Savior. *His* power, mercy, and love will protect your teen. Ultimately, whether adolescents stick with faith or walk away is up to them and God. In order to be part of his work in your teen's life, it's important that you know and can share with your teen the blessings of faith. Amazingly, the benefits start in your brain.

Bio 101

Close to two hundred independent scientific studies indicate that faith makes a noticeable difference in the structure and functioning of the brain. One prominent researcher, Dr. Andrew Newberg, has studied the impact of faith on the brain for over two decades. Focused on the connection between neurology and spirituality, his experiments utilize brain imaging to observe and evaluate both the practice and experience of faith.

After twenty years of empirical study and despite the fact that he professes no personal relationship with God, Dr. Newberg asserts, "Faith in its broadest sense is the *best thing* you can have for the brain."[2] In providing a framework for life and for understanding the world, faith creates what Dr. Newberg calls an "interconnected meshwork" that links brain and spirit with hope and health. Faith literally does a body good.

Both Dr. Newberg and Dr. Daniel Amen, neuroscientist and best-selling author, affirm that the *practices* of faith—prayer, meditation on Scripture, acts of charity and compassion, and so on—change the brain. Indeed, writes Dr. Newberg, as acts of faith "become a part of how your brain functions . . . you can do them more easily and you want to do them more. You become 'wired' for it. Whether meditation, prayer, reading the Bible, discussing the Bible, or Bible studies, they change your brain, making you more receptive."[3] In other words, the more you invest in your faith, the more your brain changes; those brain changes mean an increased desire for the things of God and a greater receptivity to God through his Word, prayer, and engaging with the world.

Nobel laureate Dr. Eric Kandel first discovered that neurons never stop "learning," and the implications for faith are profound. Because human brain cells alter with every stimulus, what we do, what we believe, and how we live out those beliefs on a daily basis transform us on a cellular level. It's amazing to consider that as we engage in spiritual practices, neurons that fire together actually wire together, and we grow closer to God. Conversely, claims Dr. Amen, the more you give in to temptation, the more likely you are to give in to it in the future. Remember, neuroplasticity—the brain's remarkable ability to adapt and alter based on experience—cuts both ways.

Neuroscience shows that practicing faith, not merely assenting to it, makes a profound overall difference in anyone's physiology. Dr. Newberg's team also discovered a benefit that we can apply to teens in particular. When participants in his experiments added a component of meditation to their life (such as focusing on a passage of Scripture), significant changes in brain functioning occurred. "Specifically," noted Dr. Newberg, "we saw increased activity in the frontal lobes."[4]

The frontal lobes! The very area of the adolescent brain that wires together last; the area of the brain involved in executive functions like judgment, forethought, planning, and self-control; the area that integrates with the rest of the brain to balance emotion with wisdom—the frontal lobes are changed by the practice of faith.

At this time in your teen's life—when abstract reasoning develops, questions of *why* reign, and executive functions are periodically on or offline—right now is the time to encourage a personal practice of faith. Teenagers must begin to experience, choose, and know God on their own so that their brain and spirit can fire and wire together. This is the process the apostle Paul describes in Romans 12:2: "Do not conform to the pattern of this world, but be transformed by the renewing of your mind. Then you will be able to test and approve what God's will is—his good, pleasing and perfect will."

Of course, we don't practice faith simply to develop a healthier brain. God "has saved us and called us to a holy life" (2 Tim. 1:9). The word *holy* literally means "whole." God is interested not merely in your teen's belief and right action but in his or her entire life being set apart, healthy and whole for him. As parents, we might be tempted to settle for well-behaved, successful kids who grow up to be responsible and happy adults. The call of God on every teen's life is *far* greater than this, and he has wired each teenage brain for faith, hope, love, and truth. Let's look at some specific ways you can encourage this now.

Psych 101

Our body, mind, and spirit are intricately and inextricably connected. We cannot separate what's happening in our brain from what occurs in our emotions and soul. God created us to be integrated beings. The connections between faith, God-honoring psychology, and biology are astounding!

In an earlier chapter, we discussed the role of mirror neurons, how they interact with the environment around us and influence our mental and emotional states. Here's an example: when you see someone smile, that expression is reflected physiologically in your brain. In a manner of speaking, part of your brain smiles in response to another person's joy.

According to Dr. Newberg, mirror neurons can play an important role in the communication of faith. If someone speaks about God in loving and confident ways, "those traits are similarly now reflected in the brains of all that are listening."[5] Dr. Newberg also points to hope and enthusiasm as essential components of faith that become mirrored by those around us. *If you want your teenager to be excited about faith, model joy in and eagerness for relationship with God, the practices of faith, and fellowship with other Christians.* If all your teen hears are your complaints about church, believers who have disappointed or betrayed you, or that you're too busy to pray or read the Bible, don't be surprised if he or she mirrors this back to you. The same goes for expressing negative perspectives about God, which Dr. Newberg found activates the emotional amygdala and causes the stress hormone cortisol to be released in the brain and bloodstream. In excessive amounts, cortisol blocks or breaks down neural connections in the brain. What the people around your teen communicate and believe about God plays a role in making or breaking certain neural pathways.

Mirror neurons, of course, cannot tell us the whole story. They may help us understand the importance of modeling, but most of us know parents with committed and joyful lives of faith whose teenagers have gone off the rails. So many factors converge in a teen's life, each strengthening or undermining faith. Parental modeling, strong friendships with other believers, and positive understanding of God are essential components, but each individual—including your teen—must respond to God on his or her own.

Ironically, if we could guarantee that our adolescents would live faithful lives by watching our own righteous living, we'd be in a worse predicament. Why? Because all of us fail in front of our children, multiple times every day. We cannot control our teenagers' faith choices. The only area over which we have control is our own commitment to God.

That's why it's absolutely crucial that parents know what they believe and why they believe it. Your teen's adolescent years provide an amazing opportunity for both of you to grow in faith. If you commit to engaging with the questions and doubts your teen brings up, everyone will benefit. The teenage years can be a win-win faith situation if greeted with a "roll up your sleeves and get into the grit" anticipation rather than "what if" and "if only" anxiety.

As you get ready to dig in, here are some specifics to remember:

- **Break the 88/95 cycle.** According to research conducted with eleven thousand teenagers, only "12 percent of youth have a regular dialogue with their mom on faith or life issues. In other words, just one out of eight kids talks with their mom about faith. It's far lower for dads. One out of twenty kids, or 5 percent, has regular faith or life conversations with their dad." In addition, "approximately 9 percent of teenagers engage in regular reading of the Bible and devotions with their families. So not even one out of ten teenagers looks at Scripture with their parents. When it comes to matters of faith, mum's usually the word at home."[6] You can break this cycle. Determine that you will be part of the percentage of parents who regularly talk with their teenagers about life and faith. In order to do this well . . .

- **Have more frequent, shorter conversations about faith.** Some teenagers may be ready for protracted ponderings on theology, but most are not; their brains simply don't have the wiring for it. Instead, adolescents are brilliantly positioned—neurologically, emotionally, and spiritually—to engage in ongoing dialogue about faith. Regularly asking questions and making comments about God, the Bible, church, fellowship, and prayer normalizes these things for a teenager and keeps them "on the radar." Highly sensitive to what's right in front of them, teenagers benefit from continual reminding (though not nagging) that God makes a difference in daily life. Of course, if you live as if a relationship with God is a Sunday thing and Monday through Saturday all bets are off, your teen will mirror this.

- **Ask thoughtful questions.** *Sticky Faith* authors Dr. Kara Powell and Dr. Chap Clark brilliantly advise, "never explain something to your kid if you can ask a question instead."[7] Jesus himself was a master question asker, consistently drawing others into dialogue, wrestling with issues of life and faith by asking questions. In his power and by his grace, we can do this with our teenagers, but it means we've got to get beyond "What did you learn at church today?" or "How was youth group?" More often than not, you'll get unsatisfying answers to stock questions like these. Instead, share with your teen something you learned at church and ask his or her thoughts on it. Sometimes you'll get an "I don't know" or a disgruntled moan, but other times you'll start a dialogue that neither you nor your teen will forget. In order to have that opportunity, you've got to try and try again.

- **Open the door for questions and doubts.** Your teen has questions and doubts. It's not a matter of *if* as much as *which ones* and *how much they impact his or her daily life*. Adolescent doubts usually focus on God's existence, the purpose of life, why there's so much suffering in the world, and whether they can be forgiven for bad things they've done. Teens also question their personal value, whether they could recognize God's voice if he did speak to them, whether people who seem really good will go to hell, and if certain sins are actually *that* bad.[8] Many adults wrestle with these issues; imagine trying to process them with a brain that's being progressively remodeled. We should have great respect and compassion for our teens! You've had doubts and questions before; try to remember what that was like and be honest with your teen. Talking about your own struggles gives teenagers the freedom to share their questions with you. You don't have to have perfect answers to everything. Indeed, according to Drs. Powell and Clark, "The greatest gift you can give your children is to let them see you struggle and wrestle with how to live a lifetime of trust in God."[9] Show your teens that you choose faith and pursue truth.

- **Help your teenager think biblically.**[10] Be careful that Bible stories and verses memorized don't remain disconnected factoids. Thinking biblically involves a distinct and integrated worldview based on a growing understanding of the whole truth of Scripture. The life of faith concerns more than knowing about God; it must include living wisely in light of God's truth. Your teen can't stay inside God's boundaries if he or she doesn't know what they are. Without a "no matter what" heart commitment to doing God's will, however, knowing commands won't lead to life transformation.

• **Encourage a 1 Timothy 4:7 life.** Researchers discovered long ago that repeated physical activities such as juggling and piano playing rewire the brain. More recent studies confirm that cognitive repetition—specifically memorization and meditation—also stimulate myelination, an essential facet of brain remodeling.[11] Remember, myelin insulates neural wiring so that your teen's brain can work in a more efficient and integrated manner. When the Bible commands us to *train* or *discipline* ourselves for godliness (see 1 Tim. 4:7), it reveals a truth God wrote into our very cells. As we practice spiritual disciplines, our brains are myelinated—better connected and more effective. Amazing, isn't it? Prayer, Bible study, and memorization really do matter. Motivate and reward your teen (remember how reward-sensitive adolescents are!) for practicing the disciplines of faith. Eventually—because, as Isaiah 55 promises, God's Word never comes back void—being close to God will become its own reward.

Faith 101

The vast majority of teenagers don't abandon faith because of Jesus. Most don't walk away because they actively disbelieve in God. Instead, circumstance, convention, and confusion prey on teenagers. We need to clear these away and focus on who God truly is. For many teens, this process uncovers a performance-based, rather than gospel-laced, Christianity.

Because humans want results (and preferably immediate and measurable ones), we often subject our faith to quantifiable standards. The thinking goes, if you read your Bible X number of times per week or pray for X number of minutes per day, you'll get closer to God. The trouble is, teenagers who engage in this kind of faith jump on a treadmill of spiritual performance: if you "slip," better hop on the treadmill and "run it off" with some extra prayer. If you're a "good girl or boy," you have peace and feel worthy. If you're not, well . . .

Our teenagers' faith *will* fail if it is based on a "do good/don't do bad" approach to life. The true gospel is about so much more than making us good little boys and girls. Jesus doesn't simply "fix" our sin problem; he transforms every aspect of our being. Our teenagers must experience this true gospel of redemption and deliverance, developing "wholehearted trust in the God who is entirely trustworthy."[12] As Hebrews 10:23 proclaims, "Let us hold tightly without wavering to the hope we affirm, for God can be trusted to keep his promise" (NLT).

If you're not living this gospel, you can't pass it on to your teenager. If you're on the spiritual treadmill, stale or suffocating Christianity may be plaguing you. If, on the other hand, you live in daily connection with the God of grace, mercy, and compassion, who doesn't just save you *from* sin but also saves you *for* new life, you will model a faith that withstands the tempests of life because it is based on what God does, not your performance.

Try It Today: Avoid the Easy Road

Next time your teenager deals with a difficult issue, resist the urge to apply a biblical Band-Aid. Let's imagine your son or daughter is being bullied at school. You could quote Scripture to your teen, encouraging him or her to turn the other cheek and forgive with a kind of "do the God thing and move on" approach. That's the easy road. The more difficult path is to help your teen trust Jesus in circumstances that hurt and scream for justice.

In his book *Thinking, Fast and Slow*, Nobel laureate Dr. Daniel Kahneman explains that the brain learns most effectively when it experiences challenge. Being too comfortable, Kahneman discovered through extensive research, suppresses analytical functioning in the brain.

Kahneman divides the brain into two systems, which work together to operate at optimum efficiency. System 1 continuously generates "impressions, intuitions, and feelings. If endorsed by System 2, impressions and intuitions turn into beliefs and impulses turn into voluntary actions."[13] System 1 functions even when a person is relaxed (e.g., "zoning out" in front of the TV). System 2, however, must be active for us to learn, because it governs our ability to test assumptions, evaluate ideas, and establish new patterns of thought and action. Kahneman's research shows that the brain shifts into System 2 functioning when stretched beyond its comfort zone.

We cannot take the easy road of spiritual platitudes and weekly rituals because our brains will default to System 1 thinking. When challenged—whether through problems at school or church, a broken relationship, academic struggles, or some other trial—your teen must switch to System 2 brain functioning. His or her assumptions can be scrutinized, beliefs can be solidified, and transformation of the mind is made possible. Don't try to avoid or whisk away the discomfort that comes with living in a broken, sin-stained world. Instead, engage in the struggle. This activates your teen's capacity to learn and grow.

This may be a mental shift for you. When your child was small, you solved most of his or her problems and eased the way. During the adolescent years, however, as teens face challenging situations, they must learn—more and more—to use difficulty and discomfort as the fuel for thoughtful action.

For example, if your son or daughter fails to complete a project and asks you in desperation the night before to "cover for him" or "help her," the best thing may be to state, "It's unfortunate that you waited this long. What do you plan to do about this?" Placing the ball back in your teen's court engages System 2 thinking.

Asking older teens to take responsibility for managing their own schedules is another way to do this. That way if a practice or event is missed, it's not "your fault," but rather an opportunity to have your teen make the necessary explanations or apologies. Uncomfortable? Perhaps. Good for your teen? Definitely!

18

It's Not My Fault

Teenagers are highly self-absorbed and rarely self-aware; it's one of the greatest mysteries surrounding adolescents and arguably the most frustrating aspect of parenting them. Considering the amount of time teens spend thinking about themselves, one might hope they'd develop the capacity to evaluate their behavior and make changes as needed. Yeah, right. As most parents of teenagers will attest, this kind of self-reflection seldom—if ever—occurs to the vast majority of adolescents.

When I (Jerusha) woke up on my sister's high school graduation day, I had one thing in mind: my outfit for the ceremony. I was singing in front of roughly two thousand people and—in my sixteen-year-old brain—looking great was top priority. Wearing one of my "old" dresses wasn't going to cut it, so I went into my sister's room to go through her closet.

Jessica wasn't having it. Whether she was annoyed with me for barging into her room or found it ridiculous that I was more concerned about how I looked than about celebrating her big day, I honestly don't remember. A sarcastic verbal exchange escalated into a shouting match, which ultimately dissolved into—it's humiliating for me to admit this—an all-out cat fight, during which my sharp fingernails left an ugly scratch on Jess's face. On her graduation day. My mom rushed in to mediate, and after ascertaining the basic facts, she expected me to apologize for lacerating my sister's cheek. Of course, that would've been the right thing to do. Instead, I blamed Jessica for inciting me. If she hadn't been so selfish with her clothes, none of this would have happened. *She never thinks about anyone but herself*, went my faulty reasoning. I persisted in this argument, the height of irrationality! I'm utterly chagrined recounting these circumstances.

Like my teenage self, many adolescents will blame anything and everything before acknowledging their own culpability. It's a human weakness that started in the Garden. Blame-shifting and responsibility-shirking have plagued every human heart since, and this problem often comes into sharp focus during the teenage years.

Bio 101

In light of the amazing information we've shared about the teenage brain, some might be tempted to blame biology for the issues adolescents and their parents face. We sincerely hope you won't. As we've reiterated again and again, understanding our bodies doesn't excuse behavior. It can give us perspective, increase our compassion, and guide our approach to parenting, but what's happening in your adolescent's brain doesn't define him or her.

In the not-so-distant past, genetics became a popular scapegoat for a wide variety of behaviors, ailments, and attributes. According to some theorists, genes and their expression determine everything from intelligence to physical health to personality profiles. Gratefully, science has progressed beyond this simplistic approach. After all, if humanity is reduced to a chemical chain, it's impossible not to be anxious about—even obsessed with—which genes are good or bad.

In the words of Dr. Francis Collins, former head of the Human Genome Project and director of the National Institutes of Health,

"Fortunately, ten years of intensive study of the human genome have provided ample evidence that these fears of genetic determinism are unwarranted. It has shown us definitively that we human beings are far more than the sum of our genetic parts. . . . Genes are not all-determining factors in the human experience."[1]

The same is true of the human brain. Despite what some claim, we aren't merely the sum of our neurons. Your adolescent's brain doesn't *force* him or her to do anything. It may make certain things more desirable to your teen or certain patterns of behavior more probable, but your son's or daughter's brain does not generate behavior.

We've highlighted the significance of neuroplasticity in various chapters, and as we discuss personal responsibility, it's essential to emphasize again that teenagers *can* change on all levels: physiological, emotional, and spiritual. The adolescent brain is constantly altering based on environmental stimulus and experience. Because of this remarkable truth, the more adolescents are exposed to self-reflective thinking—first being guided in this process, then required to do the mental work alone—the better able they will be to assume responsibility rather than shifting blame.

Psych 101

Here are a few things to keep in mind if you want to help your teen develop self-awareness and guide them in the process of reflecting on their behavior and acknowledging wrongdoing.

Be aware of popular excuses. Adolescents are master excuse-makers. Teens may claim they "didn't hear you" or "didn't know that's what you really wanted." If you've assigned a chore he or she detests, you may hear later, "There wasn't enough time." Forgetting is a convenient excuse for almost anything, and when it comes to behavior issues, pointing out someone else's failings (often yours!) is a favorite strategy. In order to help your teen get beyond blame-shifting, be on the lookout for popular excuses and direct attention back to the issue at hand: your teen's responsibility.

Don't get distracted. This second point is closely related to the first. Along with being master excuse-makers, adolescents are also prodigious attention-diverters. When a parent points out behavior that's out of bounds, teenagers often respond with defensiveness or hurt feelings. Some teens try to turn the tables on their parents, accusing them of being unfair, never listening, or always jumping to conclusions. Expect these kinds of smoke screens. Spending time justifying your parental response diverts energy and focus from the business at hand: getting to your teen's heart. Oftentimes, you can defuse defensiveness with humility. Speaking directly with teenagers—"I sense a lot of tension here, and that won't help us resolve this issue, which is my primary goal. Could you explain why you are so angry or defensive?"—requires them to evaluate their emotional response.

Engage the mind to transform the heart. Stop telling your teen what he or she did. Ask questions instead. And not just, "What were you thinking?" questions but rather challenging, revealing questions that teenagers wouldn't think, or wouldn't want, to ask themselves. In doing this, your goal is to expose your teen's motives, thoughts, assumptions, and desires. For lasting change, your teen's *heart* must be transformed, not just his or her behavior.

Asking good questions engages the prefrontal cortex and encourages neural connectivity and integration. This, of course, is crucial for under-construction teenagers. God designed our brains to work with our emotions and our will to shape our character. Asking questions helps teenagers participate in this process and ultimately equips them to do it on their own. Parental declarations of what a teen did wrong (and why) lead to adolescent defensiveness or passivity. Engage your teen's mind by inviting him or her to interpret events rather than relying on your constant analysis.

In his powerful book *Age of Opportunity*, Paul David Tripp outlines some excellent heart-searching questions. After establishing the basic facts around a situation, Tripp encourages parents, you can ask teenagers questions like these:

- What were you thinking or feeling at the time?
- Why was that so important to you?
- What was it that you were afraid of in that situation?
- What was it that you were trying to get?
- Why did you become so angry?
- If you could go back and do something differently, what would you change?[2]

Open-ended questions engage teenagers' brains in evaluating their emotional response to the situation (what they thought and felt), any actions they took in response to their feelings (what they did), the motives and desires that prompted these responses (why they did it), and what happened as a result. Parents can follow up with a question like, "What would we expect of you in this situation?"

Initially, most teenagers have a difficult time answering questions like these. It's not natural! It's helpful for parents to anticipate that this process of self-reflection will take time to develop. We don't have to push for immediate results. Instead, be gracious: "I can see why it would be difficult to sort this out. Why don't you think about it and we can chat later?"

Set self-reflection up for success. Punishments handed out unilaterally, without compassion, don't lead to heart change in your teen. A logical consequence, communicated with empathy, "allows our kids to figure out for themselves the cause-and-effect patterns of how their decisions and behaviors lead to certain consequences; it allows them to know that we love, support, and feel empathy for them in their situations but will not bail them out; and it allows responsibility to develop in them as they work through their difficulties and solve their problems for themselves."[3] The most successful times of self-reflection for your teen may come after you compassionately fit consequence and crime together.

Address the pleasure principle. If you ask teenagers what they want out of life, happiness will rank at the top of the list. Teens who "just want to be happy" think this is a reasonable goal. They don't realize that someone's pleasure often leads to someone else's pain. Teens need to be trained to ask themselves, "What will it cost other people for me to be happy in this situation?" You can help by pointing out how this works in daily life. This isn't a time for a "Woe is me! I do so much for you and you don't even realize it!" lament. Rather, this is an opportunity to help engage your teen's mind and heart. Consider asking questions like, "In order for you to go out and have fun with friends, what do you think your _____ (e.g., mom/dad/siblings) would have to give up?" As always, remember this is a process, and don't get frustrated if a grunt and "I dunno" follow your initial attempts. Being patient and persistent leads to an eventual payoff.

Give yourself the extra fifteen minutes. It takes time to engage your teenager's heart. If your schedule is so jam-packed that you don't have time to ask thoughtful questions and wait for your teen's response, something's got to change. Every blame-shifting excuse, as maddening as it may be, is an opportunity for you to draw out your teenager's heart. Whenever your teen wants to shirk personal responsibility, you have a chance to help him or her develop self-awareness. In this process, not only is time crucial; self-control is as well. Your natural reaction to teenage blame-shifting probably isn't patience and humility, but parents are called to exhibit these very traits. Our own bad behavior distracts teens from looking at their hearts. If you do flip your lid, ask for forgiveness. A humble acknowledgment of wrongdoing models the process of self-reflection for your adolescent. Thankfully, you don't have to manufacture patience, gentleness, or self-control. You can't white-knuckle your way through parenting a teen! Ask the Holy Spirit to produce his fruit in you, enabling you to teach your teen how to take responsibility and act accordingly. He promises to do this for those who ask (see John 15:7 and Gal. 5:25).

Faith 101

Teenagers exemplify the truth that self-absorption doesn't lead to self-reflection; instead, it leads to self-consciousness. Self-awareness and the ability to act upon it come ever and only from *God-consciousness*.

Adolescents typically live in extremely present-driven, physically focused, and problem-centric ways. What's right in front of them consumes their energies, and teenage life often gets reduced to what I want in this moment (i.e., "my will be done"). This lack of God-consciousness makes teenagers poor self-reflectors and master blame-shifters. The Bible makes it clear: when the mind is focused only on the here and now or the pleasure one can derive from it, godliness is impossible. "The mind governed by the flesh is hostile to God; it does not submit to God's law, nor can it do so. Those who are in the realm of the flesh cannot please God" (Rom. 8:7–8).

For this reason, we must help teens not only acknowledge their sin but also abhor it. If they can detect sin but still don't detest it, their hearts can be misled. Satan is actively focused on deceiving your teenager. He wants your adolescent son or daughter to think, "_____ really isn't that bad." He diabolically presents what's dangerous, what's destructive, and what ultimately leads to death (in other words, sin) as an attractive and appealing option.

According to the Scriptures, there are only two options when confronted with sin: the first and more common human tendency is to justify the self and quench the conscience. The other is to repent, which means agreeing with God and being realigned with his truth. Your teenager stands at the crossroads of this choice every time he or she does wrong. Make no mistake: the teenage years are a battle. But they are not a battle *with* your adolescent; they are a battle *for* his or her heart.

First Peter 5:8 minces no words: "Be alert and of sober mind. Your enemy the devil prowls around like a roaring lion looking for someone to devour." Jesus told us that the devil comes to steal, kill, and destroy (see John 10:10). He is a liar and the father of lies (see John 8:44), the accuser of God's people (see Rev. 12:10). He doesn't play fair, and your teenager is in his sights.

Instead of fighting with your teenager, fight the real battle, the battle beyond flesh and blood (see Eph. 6:10–18). Helping your adolescent understand that sin always destroys is part of the real war of the teenage years. Self-absorption makes teenagers particularly vulnerable to the "I can handle this" deception. Only God-consciousness, which leads to authentic self-awareness, enables a teen to see that the true problem is not what's outside (i.e., everyone and everything else), but rather what's inside his or her heart.

It's always easier to see the speck in someone else's eye than the log in our own (see Matt. 7:3–5). You may clearly see selfishness, materialism, rage, greed, the lust of the eyes, and the pride of life in teenagers, but they will not see these things clearly. It's absolutely essential that you spend time praying that God would reveal your teen's own heart to him or her. So often we sabotage the Holy Spirit's work in teenagers' hearts by swooping in to declare "what's wrong with" them. It takes tremendous discernment and patience to wait for God to move, to speak and act only in accordance with him, trusting that his plan is far better than any strategy we might conceive. Be a warrior for your teen on your knees.

As you fight this battle for your teenager's heart, expect that your adolescent will struggle. You will too. You are both sinners in a broken world. You are fighting in a great war, and it's tempting to fight everyone *except* the real enemy. Allow your teenager to see that you are engaging in an ongoing battle with sin and the author of sin. Identify with his or her struggle. There's nothing your teenager has done or could do that you're immune to; by the grace of God, you may not have made the same mistakes, but you are fully capable of them. If your teenage son knows that you are fighting *for* him, if your adolescent daughter knows that you are a soldier in the war against sin *just like her*, an unbreakable bond is forged. The gospel comes alive when you start with "I see why that appealed to you," rather than "How could you?" or "Why would you?" and conclude with, "By God's grace, there's a better way" rather than "You'd better . . . or else."

Most adolescents long to be caught up in something bigger than themselves. That's why teens love being with friends, doing outlandish things. That's why some of the most brilliant and successful entrepreneurs started dreaming as teenagers. Some teens literally do change the world with their energy, enthusiasm, and exuberance.

Too many adults settle for much lower goals: getting to the next vacation, the next raise, the next whatever. Comfort, control, and happiness are the aims of their daily lives. Teenagers rush onto the scene with all their sound and fury, and it's easy to see their inability to self-reflect and their constant blame-shifting and responsibility-shirking as a protracted hassle, encroaching on parental well-being and family harmony. We must reject this thinking.

Give teens a bigger picture, a vision of glory greater than theirs. God's purposes for their lives extend far beyond becoming a functioning adult, having a nice Christian family, or enjoying a good career. When your teen blames someone else or gives you a lame excuse, seize the opportunity. Take the extra time. Fight the real battle and reach beyond your personal happiness and ease for the greater good of God's glory. We urge you, as the apostle Peter did, "Let yourselves be pulled into a way of life shaped by God's life, a life energetic and blazing with holiness" (1 Pet. 1:15 Message). A life energetic and blazing with holiness is impossible to resist, even for the most skeptical teenager.

Try It Today: Delay the Next Consequence

When your teenager was much younger, you likely heard the advice that in order to connect consequences with behavior, discipline needs to occur immediately. This is very good counsel for parents of small children, but adolescents are capable of tying past behavior to current consequences. For that reason, discipline doesn't demand immediacy.

In fact, when you're in a pressured, emotionally volatile situation (i.e., dealing with a rule-breaking teen), coming up with an on-the-spot consequence can be less than ideal. It's often effective for parents who want to help their teenagers develop self-awareness to say, "I'm disappointed in this behavior. There will be consequences, but I want to think about what would be best. I would like for you to spend some time thinking about it too. I'll come and find you at

_____ (indicate a time), and we can discuss what you were thinking and feeling and what you plan to do differently next time." Giving a specific hour is helpful, because you can bet the proverbial farm that your teen won't forget; he or she will be thinking about what happened for at least part of that time frame.

Our judicial system wisely works this way. Judges hear the facts surrounding a case at one time and issue a sentence at another. Engaging with your adolescent can be intense and impassioned. When you dole out discipline on the spot, you may get stuck with a poorly chosen consequence or find yourself repealing a decision later. Needless to say, both end badly.

Try delaying the next consequence. It gives everyone a chance to cool down and process. Remember, teenage self-awareness takes time to nurture and practice. Choosing the best time to respond—when the situation has stabilized and there's been an opportunity for reflection—helps everyone. Delayed consequences are often more memorable and instructive than immediate ones, which can get lost in a storm of anger, defensiveness, or apathy (theirs or yours!). Delaying consequences engages your teen's mind to transform his or her heart.

19

I Can't Take This!

During my senior year of high school, Mr. Erskin—one of my absolute favorite teachers—observed, "Jerusha, you don't just burn the candle at both ends. You cut the candle in half and light all four ends on fire." I took this as a compliment, never imagining that a life furiously ablaze might have consequences down the road.

At seventeen, I was taking six honors classes and preparing for a battery of advanced placement tests. If I passed them all, I'd enter college as a sophomore. It seemed reasonable to make sacrifices—like sleep—to get through the homework, exams, and academic hoops.

Of course, life would've been boring if school was *everything*, so I took a position in student government, joined the vocal ensemble and various clubs, performed in two drama productions, danced at a private studio twice a week, pursued my piano certificate of merit, and attended church.

If colleges wanted "well-rounded," I was it. I might have joked, "I eat stress for breakfast," but actually I ate nothing; I was too busy for that nonsense.

My academic and extracurricular load caused me to live beyond my limits—constantly. And though your teenager's life may look nothing like mine did, research shows that in the twenty-some years since I graduated from high school, stress hasn't decreased for teenagers. Indeed, every indication is that adolescent stress continues to increase exponentially.

With homework, sports, rehearsals, lessons, community or church activities, and the ever-present draw of hanging with friends, many teens are beyond harried. Adolescents who don't participate in extracurricular activities face mounting pressures too. Staying digitally available 24-7 takes its toll on everyone. Dysfunctional family dynamics, economic pressures, and the barrage of reports—often sensationalized—about world crises, natural disasters, and terrorism intensify stress for today's adolescents. While many people associate teenagers with laziness and apathy, stress—along with the physical and emotional exhaustion that accompanies it—plagues more teens today. Teenage life in the twenty-first century is complex and confusing.

Complicating matters further is a significant physiological fact: the teenage brain is uniquely vulnerable to stress.[1]

Bio 101

According to neuroscientist Dr. Frances Jensen, "Teens simply don't have the same tolerance for stress that we see in adults."[2] One major reason: THP, the hormone usually released by the body in response to stress, and which modulates anxiety in adults, actually has a *reverse effect in adolescents*. Where adults experience a calming sensation as the body produces and circulates THP, in teenage brains THP is often ineffective in inhibiting anxiety. Neurobiologically speaking, stress breeds more stress in the teenage brain.

As a result, teens are far more likely to suffer from stress-related complaints like headaches and stomachaches. Since the human body's response to stress often includes the suppression of immune system functioning, tapped-out teens get sick more frequently. They're also far more susceptible to stress-related behaviors like nail biting, hair pulling, eating disorders, and cutting. Stress—both the emotional experience of it and the body's inability to process it—plays a major role in teenage illness. Research indicates that between 75 and 90 percent of all medical visits can be traced to the impact of stress on the body.[3]

No one lives with zero stress. Our bodies were designed to deal with moderate amounts of stress frequently and high amounts on occasion. With average amounts of stress, the brain releases adrenaline, enabling our bodies to react with alertness and focus. Moderate amounts of adrenaline can even sharpen your sensory experience and memory. The trouble is, most people live with far greater stress levels than the human body can sustain long term.

If the body is overwhelmed by stress, it responds by releasing large amounts of cortisol, a hormone that lingers in the bloodstream far longer than many other neurochemicals. Excessive cortisol has been connected with increased heart rate and blood pressure, impaired thinking, disrupted memory, and immune system dysfunction. Teenage brains, in particular, struggle to process cortisol; it takes a teenage body longer to bounce back once cortisol has flooded its circuits. This is especially true of adolescent girls, for whom new and higher levels of progesterone negatively impact the body's ability to process cortisol.[4]

One of the pioneers in stress research, Dr. Hans Selye, coined the phrase *adaptive energy* to describe how the body deals with stress. According to Dr. Selye, adaptive energy is the reserve strength the body utilizes to get through stressful periods. Too many teenagers—and adults!—force their bodies to use reserves to get through daily life, when that adaptive energy should be preserved for crisis.

If a teenager lives at an emergency level all the time, physical and emotional consequences are inevitable. Remember, living a 911 life doesn't have to look one particular way. A teen with very little going on in his or her schedule may be maxed out by internal stress that's harder to see. Discernment is crucial.

Put simply, too much stress is detrimental to the body and brain. It also wreaks havoc on the mind and spirit.

Psych 101

Let's consider some ways to help teenagers deal more appropriately with stress.

Go compassion crazy. Most parents underestimate the stress in their teenagers' lives. Before researching for this book, we had no idea how stress specifically impacts teenage brains. Discovering the facts gave us greater compassion for our adolescents, and we pray it does for you too. If we verbally minimize or dismiss our teenagers' stress, it's highly unlikely that they'll come to us when times get tough. Teens are constantly subjected to comparison and competition—at school, on the athletic field, in extracurricular activities or lessons, even within social circles. It's stressful! Our chaotically busy culture also rips at the fabric of families. Busyness steals the time it takes to listen, the energy to care, and the power to love. A grace-filled home acts as an antidote to these toxic forces. Don't dismiss your teen's stress, even if it seems minimal to you; instead, go compassion crazy!

Check your own stress quotient. We interact with a lot of involved, loving parents. We also see *a lot* of stretched-thin, stressed-out, can't-take-it-anymore moms and dads. Despite endless books, blogs, and best intentions to live "more balanced" lives, most adults have runaway schedules. Teenagers suffer from the fallout of our stress. If you're running ragged, you won't be able to help your teenager learn to deal with stress. You simply won't have the time. The eminently wise Dr. Dallas Willard regularly counseled others to *ruthlessly eliminate hurry* from their lives.[5] Busyness makes us less available for the true purposes of parenting: character building and soul nurturing. Living at break-neck speeds destroys communication and connectedness, already in short supply during the teen years. Living frantically costs too much, for everyone, so start ruthlessly eliminating busyness from your life.

Find your why. Today, living a full-throttle life is the norm. Chaos in our schedule creates chaos in our homes, though, so why do we stay on the culturally conditioned treadmill? Just because teenagers have the option to do lots of great things doesn't mean they *should*. Why is your family doing what you do? Have you ever asked that? If you have a ready answer, is your *why* worth whatever it may cost you? It may, in fact, be worth it; we can't evaluate that for you. Instead, we encourage you to calculate your why for every activity and do a second round of ruthless elimination. This second time around may look different.

Aim for 80 percent. In his book *In Search of Balance*, Dr. Richard Swenson describes this brilliantly. "If we are at 80 percent capacity," Swenson writes, "there is some space between our load and our limits. If we are at 100 percent capacity . . . we have no wiggle room, no reserves, no buffer, no leeway. There is no margin left for error."[6] Life is a constant balancing act of limits and loads. When we decide—and it requires a conscious determination—to leave room in our lives, we can deal with the unexpected. Because we aren't maxed out at 80 percent, we have the physical, emotional, and spiritual resources to face daily ups and downs. If we live at 100 percent capacity and something goes wrong, life's dominoes topple and everything goes haywire. If you or your teen are maxed—or worse, overloaded at 120 percent—you have zero, possibly even a negative amount of energy and availability. For much of my life, I (Jerusha) would have considered it an outrageous waste to live at 80 percent. "Doesn't God at least expect us to live at 100 percent? Doesn't he want us to use our gifts and talents to the fullest?" I would have thought. Now I wonder, "What if God wants us, more than anything, to live *available* lives?" If you or your teen are currently at 100 percent capacity, you're not available; instead, you're terribly vulnerable.

Do a performance review. People typically associate performance reviews with being evaluated, but we're encouraging you to review how much stock you put in your teen's performance. To live with healthy amounts of stress, your adolescent needs to know that performance doesn't define his or her worth. Unfortunately, many parents live the lie—often subconsciously—that people who contribute more or achieve at higher levels are more valuable. As we ruthlessly eliminate hurry in our lives, we must also brutally eradicate performance-based thinking. The stress many teens face is directly related to the expectations they sense (often from parents). Unattainable ideals create unbearable physical and emotional dissonance in a teenager's life. Help your son or daughter develop an identity apart from achievement, and stress will decrease.

Faith 101

Humans don't naturally lead balanced lives. We're constantly stretching beyond our limits, testing the boundaries, and experiencing frustration and heartache when confronted with our inherent weaknesses. Most of us don't like being so *human*: finite, vulnerable, and limited.

God, in his infinite wisdom and grace, designed us with the capacity to do wonderful things. He also placed parameters on our lives. We have physical limits: no one has access to more than twenty-four hours in a day; we have varying degrees of health and strength; and despite what our modern culture hopes, we cannot extend our lives beyond what God ordains. That's why Moses prayed, "Teach us to number our days, that we may gain a heart of wisdom" (Ps. 90:12). We especially appreciate the way various translations render this verse: "Teach us to realize the brevity of life" (NLT) and "teach us to consider our mortality, so that we might live wisely" (NET).

For teenagers, who see their "whole life" in front of them, it's difficult to imagine how present choices will determine the course of their lives. But as adults, we know very well that decisions matter. Choosing to gain a heart of wisdom, to number our days, remembering that life on earth won't last forever, is a decision that affects everything else.

At church, waiting in line to pick up kids from all manner of activities, even at the grocery store, parents talk endlessly about the need to slow down. Life is "crazy busy" and we just need "more balance," they lament. It's only when we embrace mortality—not merely that we don't live forever, but also that we have limits—that we live wiser, more balanced lives.

Before we can even begin to pursue balance, however, we must address a deeper heart issue. Teenagers (and most stressed-out adults) don't have as serious a balance problem as they do a *center problem*.[7] One cannot maintain balance without a solid core, a fixed center. Like our solar system, with the sun providing a durable center around which the planets orbit, we must have a fixed point around which the various activities and experiences, joys and stresses of our lives orbit. Most people are out of balance because they either aren't sure what the fixed point in their lives should be (so they try out various relationships, accomplishments, and activities) or they know what their center should be but don't consciously order their lives around it. The latter applies to many Christians, both teenage and adult.

The *only* solid and lasting center for life is the immovable, immortal, and infallible God who created us, loved us even unto death, and promises that his plans for us are good (see Jer. 29:11). If you center life on anything else—to any degree—your orbit will be off and balance will remain elusive. When everything revolves around, connects to, and is evaluated by the standards of the One True Center, whether life speeds up or slows down for a season, the core stands firm and balance is possible. This is what it means to order our days with wisdom.

The Bible describes God as the Author of peace, order, stability, and strength. Discontent, irritability, exhaustion, and burnout are not of God, so if you are experiencing them, you've got a center problem. When we're healthy and connected with the Lord, we recognize this problem and adjust accordingly—we cut back somewhere, look for opportunities to be refreshed by God, and accept that in our weakness, God's strength is perfected (see 2 Cor. 12:9–10). When we're on overload, we can't even see that our center is off; instead, we try to better arrange the orbiting forces, which is about as effective as arranging deck chairs on the *Titanic* would have been.

In our own lives, and with our teenagers, we need to evaluate the solidity of our center. Teenagers, who lack the prefrontal cortex capacities for long-term planning and analysis, need the help of adults, who can use their adult brains, to ruthlessly eliminate hurry, rightly order schedules, and accept limits. Teens will not do this on their own. You can act as a surrogate prefrontal cortex when it comes to stress and making decisions—some of which may be unpopular with your adolescent—to live wisely, with less stress.

The *Message* translation of Matthew 11:28–32 reads,

> Are you tired? Worn out? . . . Come to me. Get away with me and you'll recover your life. I'll show you how to take a real rest. Walk with me and work with me—watch how I do it. Learn the unforced rhythms of grace. I won't lay anything heavy or ill-fitting on you. Keep company with me and you'll learn to live freely and lightly.

Learning the unforced rhythms of grace, living freely and lightly . . . now doesn't that sound good?

Try It Today: "Time-In"

Like us, you may have used time-outs to discipline little ones. Removing children from a situation and requiring that they sit quietly often worked well to break a pattern of behavior. Typically, teens don't get time-outs. They also don't get much "time-in."[8]

A positive spin on the time-out concept, a "time-in" is set aside for rest and recharging, completely unstructured and unhurried. Think of it as a mini sabbath.

God ordained that his people take an entire day every week to rest from their work. Some biblical scholars believe the implication was that God's people should also rest from *thinking about* work on the Sabbath. We think that's brilliant!

Scientific research demonstrates that when people are spontaneous and have fun, their brains grow and strengthen neural connections.[9] Intentionally setting aside time when nothing needs to be accomplished, when unwinding is the only goal, is not only good advice; it's also a pathway to better health and neural integration (both of which are hindered by stress and desperately important for teens!).

It's essential for your teenager to have downtime, every day. Of course, not all downtime activities are created equal; if you're playing a game or watching something that's adrenaline pumping, it may not recharge the body's batteries. Encourage your teen to do something that relaxes the mind—listening to music, drawing, taking a walk or bike ride, jumping on the trampoline—for no reason other than to give the brain a break.

In order for you to teach your teen the value of this, you need to believe in it yourself. Deliberately *schedule* your own time-in over the next twenty-four hours. Even ten minutes can make a massive difference!

20

I'm So Tired

Few things annoy me (Jeramy) quite as much as a tech alert going off right as I'm about to fall asleep. To this frustrating noise I awakened last night from a half-slumberous state.

"Was that tea caffeinated?"

It was our teenage daughter. Her bedroom was less than twenty yards from ours, but—of course—she chose to ask me via text message whether the iced tea we had at dinner was keeping her awake.

Before I could even respond, two other texts buzzed through, both composed of only one character, repeated in quick succession: "???????????"

Between Jerusha and I, we received twelve such texts over the next thirty minutes. Even after we assured her the tea was herbal and couldn't be the culprit in disturbing her sleep (and mine), our persistent adolescent continued to harangue us with details about her sleeplessness: "Don't want to keep you up . . . Guess I'll just be really tired tomorrow."

Final text: a frowny face emoticon.

Yeah, that's how I felt too.

There are times 10:45 p.m. rolls around on a weeknight and she isn't tired—*at all.* "I just *can't* sleep," she bemoans. Inevitably, I mentally fast-forward to the next morning, when I know it will be torture to get her up for school. I try not to let her sleep habits rankle me, but she often keeps Jerusha up, and let's just say, when Mama don't sleep, ain't no one in the house happy.

The erratic, odd, or downright poor sleep habits of adolescents are a frequent cause of distress for parents. Whether the concern is that teens work into the waning hours, buried under an avalanche of homework; that they stay up until 3:00 a.m. playing video games or watching movies every weekend, then want to sleep past noon; that they seem to initiate serious discussions only after 10:00 p.m.; or that they are virtually unable to wake up on time for school in anything resembling a good mood, issues with sleep are common and significant.

What is it with teens and their crazy sleep cycles? According to the *Washington Post*, "It may be tempting to blame this behavior on computers, cellphones and coffee. And, in some cases, those are the prime reasons for nocturnal teen behavior. But . . . researchers over the past decade have learned that a teen's body is different than those of younger and older people" and that as a result, adolescents' natural sleep rhythms differ profoundly.[1] Understanding how the body, mind, and spirit of an adolescent influence and are influenced by sleep benefits everyone, particularly those interested in a good night's rest. Let's start by looking at the biology of sleep.

Bio 101

Most of us know from personal experience that losing sleep makes us feel terrible and a good night's rest can boost not only our physical strength and readiness to face the day but also our emotional stability. Sleep, or lack thereof, even impacts our life of faith. While the benefits of sleep are readily evident, scientists continue to discover more about the significance of sleep. Studies clearly reveal that sleep plays a vital role in metabolic and immune functioning, memory consolidation, and learning.

Indeed, the quantity and quality of sleep profoundly impact learning and memory. Both are compromised by sleep deprivation but can be enhanced by healthy sleep habits. Harvard scientists report, "Sleep helps learning and memory in two distinct ways. First, a sleep-deprived person cannot focus attention optimally and therefore cannot learn efficiently. Second, sleep itself has a role in the consolidation of memory, which is essential for learning new information."[2]

Though the exact mechanisms aren't perfectly understood, it appears that during sleep our brains sort and stabilize information acquired or recalled throughout waking hours, strengthening neural connections that form our memories and enabling us to build upon them through continued learning.

Researchers at Harvard Medical School also indicate, "One of the most recent and compelling explanations for why we sleep is based on findings that sleep is correlated to changes in the structure and organization of the brain. This phenomenon, known as brain plasticity, is not entirely understood, but its connection to sleep has several critical implications."[3] Because adolescence is a period of heightened neuroplasticity, this connection between sleep and neuroplasticity is particularly important for teens.

Safe to say, sleep is incredibly important.

Statistics, however, reveal that the vast majority of people don't make sleep a priority. In the United States, staying up all night to study, work, or party not only is acceptable but may even—depending on the situation—be encouraged. Going without sufficient sleep carries serious consequences, however.

In the short term, a lack of adequate sleep can affect judgment, mood, ability to learn and retain information, and may increase the risk of serious accidents and injury. In the long term, chronic sleep deprivation may lead to a host of health problems including obesity, diabetes, cardiovascular disease, and even early mortality."[4]

Dr. Jesse Payne articulates well the significance of adequate sleep for adolescents. He writes, "For young people, sleep is especially important. During sleep, our body releases growth hormones and also works to repair any damage that may have been done to it during the day. Also, during sleep our brain grows and develops critically important brain synapses (connections) between nerve cells, which help our brain run more efficiently and productively."[5]

Physicians and sleep researchers almost universally agree that adolescents need a lot of rest: between 8.5 and 9.25 hours of sleep per night. Dr. Daniel Siegel explains,

> When I [use] the word *need*, what I mean is that for optimal brain growth, for optimal memory consolidation of the day's learning, for optimal insulin function and food metabolism to keep fit, for optimal immune function to fight off disease, for optimal response to stress to deal with life's hassles, and for optimal mental functioning with effective abilities for focusing attention, thinking, remembering, problem solving, handling your emotions, and connecting with others in relationships, you need at least the lesser amount of your range of sleep.[6]

I don't know about you, but I certainly want my adolescent children to have the physical and emotional reserves that Siegel describes. Most teens do not.

The US Centers for Disease Control reports that approximately 69 percent of high school students get fewer than eight hours of sleep on school nights, and roughly 40 percent get six hours or less. Studies from the National Institues of Health and the National Sleep Foundation disclose that between 28 and 33 percent of students report falling asleep in class—daily[7]—while 70 percent of teens have trouble waking up in the morning and 64 percent feel tired during class.[8]

Drowsiness and falling asleep at the wheel cause more than one hundred thousand car crashes every year, which accounts for approximately half of auto accidents involving drivers twenty-five and younger (i.e., adolescent drivers).[9] Several studies also confirm reduced scholastic performance in first- and second-period classes, which strongly suggests that sleep deprivation plays a major role in the academic lives of many adolescents.[10]

Teens face several challenges when it comes to sleep. For one, modern society does not encourage healthy sleep habits. Ubiquitous digital displays, buzzing electronics, and electric light keep our minds active long past the time we might naturally fall asleep, but since the majority of us are still required to rise at approximately the same time we were before the technological revolution invaded our homes, almost all of us have lost sleep over the years.

In addition, the teenage life—full of new social drives and opportunities, as well as increased scholastic expectations—is hardly conducive to maintaining adequate levels of sleep. Compounding the problem, teens tend to stay up and sleep in late on the weekends, which negatively affects their internal sleep rhythms and impairs the general quality of sleep they do get.

Finally, research shows that levels of melatonin, the sleep-promoting neurochemical, in adolescents differ from those of younger children and adults. Indeed, puberty changes adolescents' circadian rhythms (i.e., "internal clock"), delaying the time melatonin is naturally released, thereby affecting when teens start feeling drowsy and naturally awaken after sleep. According to researchers, the shift in these circadian rhythms makes it "difficult for teens to go to bed early and be alert first thing in the morning."[11] Shifts in the sleep-wake cycle at puberty mean that most adolescents get their best sleep between 11:00 p.m. and 8:00 a.m., when melatonin levels are highest. The National Sleep Foundation confirms this:

> Scientists have known for a long time now that a person's biological clock shifts forward in adolescence. Instead of feeling drowsy in the evening, teenagers actually tend to become more alert and have a difficult time settling in to sleep (likely because melatonin, which causes sleepiness, is secreted later). In the morning, when people of other ages are awake and primed for the day, teenagers still have elevated melatonin levels and often feel groggy as a result.[12]

This shift in biological sleep patterns, toward later times for both sleeping and waking during adolescence, means it is natural for an adolescent to begin staying up and wanting to sleep in later. Trouble is, the vast majority of schools start earlier as students get older. As you may imagine, the combination of these factors significantly impacts students' minds and behaviors.

Psych 101

Insufficient sleep can cause a variety of struggles for your adolescent, so being aware of both the physiological and psychological dynamics of poor sleep is essential.

According to the American Academy of Pediatrics, adolescents with poor sleep habits exhibit these traits:

- Elevated risk for anxiety and depression
- Increased risk-taking behaviors
- Higher rates of automobile accidents
- Impaired interpretation of social/emotional cues
- Decreased motivation and increased vulnerability to stress
- Lower academic achievement, poor school attendance, and increased dropout rates
- Impairments in attention, memory, organization, and time management[13]

The National Sleep Foundation adds that not getting enough sleep can lead to aggressive or inappropriate behavior such as yelling at friends or being impatient with teachers and family members. It can also cause one to eat too much or crave unhealthy foods like sweets and fried foods that lead to weight gain and can contribute to acne and other skin problems.[14]

Dr. Helene A. Emsellem, author of *Snooze or Lose!*, notes that going without enough sleep can make a teen more likely to get sick because the number of T-cells—cells that help us stay healthy—in their bodies falls by 30 to 40 percent. And sleep-deprived teens are more likely to use alcohol and drugs than those who don't.[15]

Insufficient sleep in adolescents is also associated with higher risk of sports-related injuries, lower standardized test scores,[16] stimulant abuse (caffeine and/or narcotic), and increased crime.[17]

In order to help adolescents understand the importance of sleep, share the facts with them. To truly make an impact on their sleep schedules, however, you need to make specific changes. Start by evaluating what you believe about sleep.

Faith 101

Many Americans may believe early risers are more successful and that people can learn to live on little sleep, but according to Harvard researcher Dr. Steven Lockley, that notion is neither true nor healthy.[18] Lockley points to a deep and pervasive lie that people, including adolescents, believe—that they can overcome the body's needs.

The Bible is clear: sleep is a gift from God and should be received with gratitude. Psalm 127:2 says, "It is useless for you to work so hard from early morning until late at night, anxiously working for food to eat; for God gives rest to his loved ones" (NLT).

With their lifestyle, parents too often communicate that sleep is a luxury and that to get ahead or enjoy life, you have to sacrifice rest. This simply isn't true. We appreciate how the NET renders Psalm 127:2: "He can provide for those whom he loves even when they sleep."

Do you believe this? Do you believe that God's provision is enough for you, or does rising early and staying up late, toiling for money, success, a clean house, or simply the freedom to watch or play more define your life? Is technology robbing you of the rest you need? If it is, you can be certain your teen will struggle with the same issue. Dr. David Greenfield notes, "The phone's never off, so we're never off. . . . You sleep with it next to your pillow [but] we're not designed to be vigilant 24/7."[19]

We're not designed to be vigilant around the clock. God created sleep for us because he loves us. Learning to implement better sleep habits yourself and helping your teen do the same may be an issue of obedience and trust for you. As we obey God's commands to rest and trust that he can and will provide for us, we can enjoy the gift of sleep and all its benefits.

Try It Today

Some adolescent sleep habits may be the result of bad lifestyle choices and stubbornness; parents should address these behavior issues. When erratic sleep patterns are the result of changing biology and natural circadian rhythms, however, simple changes in sleep hygiene can make profound differences. Just as proper oral hygiene help prevents tooth decay, healthy sleep hygiene forestalls the nasty side effects of sleep deprivation. Here are some quick tips to get you and your teen started:

- **Make your adolescent's room "sleep friendly."** It should be cool, quiet, and dark.
- **Increase exposure to natural light in the morning.** This signals the body to wake up.
- **Stick to a schedule.** Consistency promotes natural sleep rhythms, enabling everyone to fall asleep and wake up easier. Also, staying within two hours of your schedule on the weekend will help.
- **Keep a notepad nearby.** Jotting down to-do lists or journaling a few thoughts before bedtime helps address worries that keep people awake.
- **Establish a bedtime ritual.** Doing the same relaxing activities (e.g., taking a warm shower or bath, reading, praying, etc.) trains your body to recognize when the time for sleep approaches.
- **Evaluate "essential activities."** You may need to reprioritize what you do and when. The number of uninterrupted hours of sleep you get matters, so plan accordingly.

- **Limit caffeine intake.** And always keep in mind that no pill, vitamin, or drink substitutes for sound sleep. Most people recognize that consuming caffeine close to bedtime can negatively impact sleep, but high caffeine consumption early in the day can influence sleep habits as well. Nicotine and alcohol also interfere with sleep.
- **Eat and drink wisely.** A heavy nighttime meal or snack impacts sleep cycles. And while no one wants to wake up as a result of drinking too much before bed, going to bed dehydrated may also cause sleep disturbances. Research shows that warm beverages, especially those containing calcium, can promote sleep. Grandma's advice to drink warm milk doesn't seem so quaint in light of scientific research.
- **Exercise.** Physical activity throughout the day increases the likelihood of sound sleep. Exercising too close to bedtime, however, can interfere with sleep, so finish your workout early.
- **Don't try to force it.** Attempting to "make yourself fall asleep" can be pointless and frustrating. Teach your adolescent that if they cannot sleep after twenty minutes, reading or listening to relaxing music until they feel drowsy is a good option.
- **Avoid nighttime stress.** When the body releases the stress hormone cortisol, alertness increases. Wrestling with difficult discussions, tackling large and demanding projects, even "watching the clock" before bed can cause the body to produce sleep-inhibiting levels of cortisol.
- **Limit work hours for adolescents.** Studies show that teens who work part-time sleep less than their peers. Those who work more than twenty hours per week are the most negatively impacted, so limit work hours when possible.
- **Nap early or not at all.** A thirty-minute or less nap can rejuvenate a flagging body and mind. Sleeping longer than that, or napping after dusk, however, can negatively impact your sleep.
- **Look for the warning signs of sleep disorders.** If your adolescent implements healthy sleep hygiene habits and still struggles

with insomnia, consider having him or her evaluated for narcolepsy, restless leg syndrome, sleep apnea, or other chronic sleep-disrupting conditions.

We'd like to leave you with one final tip, which deserves special attention for adolescents:

• **Power down one hour prior to bedtime.** Electronic devices emit a form of light—blue light—particularly effective at inhibiting the release of melatonin. For this to happen, a person doesn't even have to be staring directly at a screen. If enough blue light hits the eye, even indirectly, the brain halts the release of melatonin. Climbing into bed with a tablet or a laptop, or leaving a glowing screen on in an adolescent's room, makes it especially difficult to sleep soundly. For sleep-deprived teenagers, this is a recipe for disaster.[20] An added benefit of the whole family powering down before bed is that other activities—reading, prayer, conversation—may occur in the quiet space created in an electronics-off-before-bed home.

21

I'm Starving

Anyone wanting to stir up mommy guilt needs use only two words: healthy eating. With this ostensibly positive phrase—Isn't healthy eating a good goal?—anxiety, shame, and defensiveness can descend on even the most conscientious of moms. After all, you can always *do more*: nix sugar, cut back on processed foods, add more whole grains and omega-3s, and on and on.

Years ago, I (Jerusha) burst into a tearful rage after Jeramy mentioned—without any ill intent—that it would be nice to have more fresh fruits and vegetables around the house. Sitting there with both girls under the age of two, barely capable of getting through the grocery store once a week, I felt angry and ashamed.

Guilt over our family not eating healthy enough has lurked in the background most of my mommy life, and I have to be honest: my five years as a part-time homeschooler were the worst. "Supermoms" sent their kids to enrichment classes with thermoses of seaweed soup and freshly-squeezed carrot juice (true, "it-happens-in-California" story!). I went home and beat myself up for having Goldfish crackers as the number one item on my shopping list.

Like most of you reading this book, I want my kids to eat well. I know the health risks of a poor diet. I see the difference in my adolescent daughters after a slumber-party junk food binge. But also like most of you, I struggle to make healthy eating a reality. When you consider an adolescent's natural drive to resist what parents suggest combined with biochemical urges prompting anything-but-healthy dietary choices, the phrase impending doom comes to mind.

It doesn't have to, though. Our family has discovered that even small changes in our eating habits make a big difference. We all feel better eating well, and feeling great makes it easier to continue adjusting and sticking with resolutions.

This chapter certainly isn't meant to leave you feeling uptight about every bite that goes into your mouth. Perhaps the most helpful idea I've encountered about healthy eating can be summed up as "the 80/20 rule." If you eat well 80 percent of the time, you can relax about the 20 percent of the time when healthy options aren't available or when you're celebrating something special.[1] Eating 80/20 *is* possible. You can do it, and so can your teen.

One of the worst things we can model for teenagers is anxiety about food and healthy eating, so before we jump into this chapter, let's agree to leave the guilt here. Unburdened, we can take a look at how the food adolescents eat and the choices they make impact the body, mind, and spirit.[2]

Bio 101

Because teens make many decisions about food on their own, tend to have additional resources and opportunities to buy food outside the home, and are often heavily influenced by peer choices and media exposure, helping them establish healthy eating patterns is an important goal. Adolescents need more energy (in the form of food) than both children and adults, and rapid growth spurts occurring during adolescence often drive teens to consume large amounts of food. Many of you—perhaps even today—have heard your teenager moan, "I'm *starving*."

Left to their own devices, most adolescents have notoriously poor eating habits. The vast majority of adolescents don't consume enough nutrient-rich foods (fruits, vegetables, whole grains, and lean proteins) to optimize the incredibly important growth and development happening in their body and brain. Throughout this book, we've discussed the remarkable process of neural remodeling occurring in your adolescent's brain; try running that on Yoo-hoo and Funyuns.

Unfortunately for adolescents in the United States, the typical diet is high in all the wrong things—sugar, calories, saturated fat, and trans fats. Consuming what's readily available may leave teenagers in worse health, with lower overall energy and decreased satisfaction.

Renowned neuroscientist Dr. Daniel Amen puts it succinctly: "What you consume on a daily basis directly affects the health of your brain and body, and proper nutrition is the key. I often say if you have a fast-food diet, you will have a fast-food brain and an overweight body. To be your best self, get optimal nutrition from the food you put in your mouth."[3]

In his book, *Change Your Brain, Change Your Body*, Dr. Amen outlines important general facts about nutrition and the body. We've adapted and applied them to teenagers here:

- **Food affects your teen's attitude and energy level.** Eating well gives people energy that lasts all day and can significantly decrease mood swings.
- **Your adolescent's eating habits influence overall health.** Nutrient-rich foods lead to a stronger immune system, cardiovascular and digestive health, as well as peak brain functioning.
- **Eating well impacts your adolescent's academic performance.** The ability to think quickly and clearly is tied to your diet. Brain-friendly foods enhance mental sharpness, helping adolescents stay focused and remain attentive.
- **Good nutrition leads to better physical and athletic performance.** Greater stamina and strength, as well as a reduced incidence of injury, result from quality nutrient intake.

- **Your adolescent's appearance and eating habits are closely tied.** People who have healthy diets tend to look healthier. The food we consume affects not only the size of our bodies (i.e., weight and shape) but also our skin, hair, nails, and overall physique.[4]

Today's adolescents are surrounded by food options. In 2012, the US Census Bureau listed 662,487 food-service establishments,[5] and a recent report from the National Restaurant Association indicates the number now exceeds 990,000.[6] In 1975, an average American grocery store stocked just over 8,900 items. Today's supermarkets carry in excess of 43,000 items,[7] and less-expensive, high-calorie, packaged foods account for a significant portion of the increase.

Teenagers are not merely exposed to far more food options, they're also subject to the constant suggestion that more equals better value. Portions offered by restaurants and fast-food chains usually outstrip the recommended USDA serving sizes, often registering double the amount of calories, fat, and sodium than considered healthy for single-meal intake.[8]

Neurologically, there are two major problems with the current state of affairs. One, teenagers' undeveloped self-restraint makes it more difficult for them to resist temptations, particularly when they're overly tired, hungry, or emotional. A less-than-mature ability to control one's desires combined with the ever-present ability to eat more than the body needs is certainly an issue. The other concern is that the kinds of foods that harm rather than help the brain are more

Fast Facts

Total percentage of empty calories that make up a typical diet: 40 percent

Daily intake of calories recommended (for an active teenager): 2,000

Average number of calories Americans consume daily: 3,800

readily available at the places teens eat when on their own: fast-food venues, the mall, even many schools.

All this to say, one of the most important things we as parents can teach our adolescents about eating involves good old self-control. Easier said than done for many adults who struggle with that very issue. Why should we exercise self-restraint when we're eating? The reasons are manifold.

Most people already know that poor eating can lead to a slew of health problems: obesity, diabetes, cardiovascular and digestive disorders, mental health issues, as well as increased risk of lung, esophageal, stomach, colorectal, and prostate cancers.[9] Maybe you've heard that eating a healthy breakfast—something many sleepy-headed teens skip on a daily basis—improves cognitive function (especially memory), reduces absenteeism, and improves mood.[10] Most of us know a few basic facts about nutrition, but a good number of parents feel paralyzed when it comes to developing their own healthy eating habits and helping their adolescents.

What if we could take some of the stress out of healthy eating by reducing the fundamentals to a few simple principles?

Psych 101

Very few people are emotionally balanced when it comes to food. Think about how many people you know who eat or drink for emotional reasons (when they're happy, they celebrate with food, and when they're down, they drown their sorrows in Häagen-Dazs). Consider how many people are freaked out about what they eat, and when, and how. Then think how many people "couldn't care less," eating what they want, when they want, but also suffering the consequences.

In order to avoid these extremes, we'd like to give you some guiding principles for healthy eating that aren't about counting grams or calories, restricting everything, or giving yourself license. Once you've started to implement these things, you can help your adolescent do so too.

- **Eat from the rainbow.** Aside from applying the 80/20 (or, if you're feeling great, the 90/10) rule, learning to eat from the rainbow has been the best advice we've received about healthy eating. If you're consistently choosing foods with a variety of colors, you'll get far more nutrients than you have been previously. Throw some red bell peppers on your sandwich, slather on the avocado, go for that juicy peach in the summer. Look for bright pink salmon, deep blueberries, and lean red meats. Having a Caesar salad is great, but branch out, adding some snap peas to a bed of mixed greens, chopping up some roasted broccoli, and topping it with grilled chicken and your favorite cheese. Think variety. Think color. Healthy choices will happen.

- **Get back to the farm.** The healthiest diet our country ever had revolved around what could be grown or gathered on the family farm. Fresh lean meats, natural dairy products and eggs, and veggies and fruits galore are the best staples of a healthy diet. Whenever possible, choose fresh, not packaged or processed. I like how the authors of *The Daniel Plan* put it: "If it was grown on a plant, eat it. If it was made in a plant, leave it on the shelf."[11]

- **Boost your brain.** Everyone benefits from eating brain-smart foods, and adolescents are no exception. Indeed, because of the radical changes occurring in their brains, choosing brain-friendly foods over other options is a great place to make small adjustments. (See the endnotes for a handy list from the Amen Clinics.[12]) Some of these brain-friendly foods you'll find you already love. Great! Add more of those things. If you think you "hate vegetables," you've probably never had them prepared well. Grilling almost any veggie adds fantastic flavor. Our girls actually started to ask for more zucchini and onions once we started grilling them with olive oil, garlic, and sesame seeds. You can also slow roast veggies with garlic, olive oil, herbs or spices (we like Himalayan pink salt), and lemon. For unfamiliar items, try finding a recipe that sounds palatable or a restaurant that specializes in preparing tasty dishes and give them a try. What do you have to lose?

- **Love the food you're eating.** Both you and your adolescent will eat healthier if the healthy food you prepare tastes great. If you're trying to force a boiled, sauceless chicken breast with a side of wilted broccoli and a wafer-thin slice of sprouted grain toast down your teenager's throat, you won't get anywhere. For most teens, making the conversation about "right" and "wrong" ways to eat or "healthy" vs. "unhealthy" choices leads to teenage tune-out. But if you make the issue enjoying food and enjoying what a healthy body, nourished by good food, can do and look like, you'll have a better shot at adolescent buy-in.

Faith 101

Some people mistakenly believe that God doesn't really care about the body and that what we eat doesn't impact our spiritual life. To be perfectly blunt, these are lies. The Bible talks frequently about eating, both the process of it and the ways in which food and eating impact our relationships with others, him, and ourselves.

Both you and your adolescent will benefit from keeping two essential spiritual principles in mind:

- **Eating and drinking is a matter of glorifying God.** In 1 Corinthians 10:31 we encounter the clear command: "Whether you eat or drink, or whatever you do, do it all for the glory of God" (NLT). What you choose to do with your body and the food choices you make either bring glory to God or they don't. Making poor choices—including the bad decision to simply not care—wasting the potential of the body and energy he's given, or subjecting ourselves to disease does not glorify God. On the other hand, he receives great glory when you wisely enjoy the good gifts he's given (see Ps. 145:16; 1 Tim. 6:17).

- **The stomach makes a very poor god.** The book of Philippians speaks candidly about those for whom "their god is their
  stomach, and their glory is in their shame. Their mind is set on
  earthly things" (3:19). Both extremely healthy and extremely unhealthy eaters can make food the focus of their lives. Their minds
  are set on earthly things (whether Snickers bars or smoothies).
  The true and living God, who created food and our bodies,
  is the only one worthy of our service. When our focus is on
  him, eating healthy becomes a natural outgrowth of a vibrant
  relationship. If you listen for the voice of God, you'll find that
  eating wisely becomes not only possible but also desirable for
  you and your teen.

Try It Today

Involve your adolescent in the process of preparing foods, especially
making his or her own favorites but also trying new recipes and talking
about what that day or week's menu might be. We agree with celeb-
rity chef Marcus Samuelsson, who claims, "I cannot stress a greater
importance than to teach the young generation about the risks of
unhealthy eating. A great way to pique their interest in nutrition is to
involve them more in the cooking process. They not only will learn to
cook for themselves, but also develop a lifetime of healthy habits."[13]

Including your son or daughter in the process of meal planning,
preparing, and *enjoying* will benefit them in a number of ways, including but not limited to helping them develop healthy eating habits.
At a time in life when making conversation may be difficult, having
a shared project (cooking a tasty meal) can be a great way to spend
time together. Your fifteen-year-old son might not be talking in more
than single syllables, but he probably does like to eat! It also prepares
teens for the "adult world," and perhaps even marriage and family,
where their food choices will impact others as well.

22

What's Wrong with Me?

Parents of adolescent girls consistently use one word to describe their daughters' lives: *drama.*

When our oldest daughter turned twelve and our youngest was ten, Jerusha realized that an unexpected apprehension about the adolescent years had descended on her. She began to joke with other parents about "getting ready for the battle" of the teenage years, particularly considering we had two girls who soon would experience the hormonal highs and lows of being a woman. One quiet morning, God reminded Jerusha, "Fear is not my plan for you. Look for the joys, not the troubles, and greet trials as they come. My strength and peace are enough for you and for them."

As our girls have grown into their teenage years, this has been something Jerusha has clung to, and it's something we pass on to you today. God is well acquainted with both the beauty and the drama of femininity. We hope this chapter will equip and empower you in his complete sufficiency.

Bio 101

Puberty. What memories does that word spark in your mind? Embarrassing elementary school assemblies? An even more humiliating middle school health class? Stuffing an odd book or pamphlet in your backpack? For moms of Jerusha's generation, perhaps it's a Judy Blume book or "the talk" about hormones and (insert theatrical music here) "*it.*"

Many if not most people believe that puberty starts with the development of sexuality and increased production of sex hormones. While this is not untrue, the reality is that all of this originates in the brain.

As a young woman matures and neural remodeling begins, her brain becomes more "plastic" (remember, by that word we mean malleable, adaptable, and sensitive). The chemical makeup of her neurological system changes as well, particularly in the emotional limbic system. Because her limbic system becomes more readily aroused in the time before and throughout her adolescent years, teenage girls experience a figurative roller coaster of emotions that may (or perhaps we should say probably *will*) soar to previously unexperienced highs and plummet to undesirable lows.

For these reasons, puberty alters the female brain and body in a manner that stretches far beyond the development of sexuality. As levels of sex hormones like estrogen and progesterone dramatically increase during puberty, the very structure of neurocircuits is chemically altered.

In addition, as Dr. Laurence Steinberg notes, "Sex hormones promote myelination, stimulate the development of new neurons, and facilitate synaptic pruning. Puberty makes the brain more sensitive to all sorts of environmental influences, both good and bad. And it stimulates a dramatic increase in brain plasticity, making us not only more attentive to the world, but more easily influenced by it in potentially enduring ways."[1] Truly, puberty is a remarkable time of radical brain transformation.

For many parents and their daughters, puberty also feels like an emotional tsunami hitting the family. During this season, elevated and fluctuating hormonal levels "influence a multitude of functions and emotions, including anger, sorrow, joy, memory, aggression, thirst, appetite, weight, fat distribution, the development of secondary sex characteristics . . . and higher intellectual functioning. In short, they bring about a makeover of the body and personality."[2]

Scientists once believed that genes played the primary role in determining when puberty would begin. The argument went that if your parents matured early, you likely would too. Today we understand a broader picture of how pubescence begins, which includes a complex interplay of genetic, environmental, and even familial dynamics.

For instance, weight gain, the distribution of fat throughout the body, and the presence of the protein leptin—which stimulates production of the puberty-inducing neurochemical kisspeptin—influence the onset of puberty. The presence of "endocrine disruptors" in the environment also impacts pubescent development (we'll discuss these later in the chapter). Even melatonin, the hormone that regulates our sleep, plays a role in puberty. Research shows that girls with higher melatonin levels go through puberty later.

Some of the most fascinating studies about puberty demonstrate that family dynamics play a powerful role in its onset. Undue family stress can spark early pubescent development, as can the presence of non–biologically related, sexually mature males. On the other hand, girls with an active and supportive father tend to experience puberty at average and healthy ages.

Researchers behind one study, which tracked young women over eight years, reported that a father's presence in the home and a greater level of father-daughter affection predicted later pubertal timing. Healthy mother-father relationships also contributed strongly. "In summary, the quality of fathers' investment in the family was the most important feature of the family environment relative to daughters' pubertal timing."[3]

Independent clinicians have replicated these findings in other studies. Researchers who followed 762 girls concluded that a supportive father delayed puberty, and a strong relationship between parents slowed it additionally. "In contrast, the biological father's absence, or friction between parents, is associated with earlier puberty, sexual activity and pregnancy."[4]

Bottom line: the closer the emotional connection between a father and daughter, the later she will start developing. This is fascinating in light of the fact that as girls age, fathers sometimes struggle to relate to them. It's easy to cuddle and kiss a toddler or a six-year-old who climbs up onto Daddy's lap. A moody thirteen-year-old can be a different story.

It's absolutely essential, however, that dads recognize their daughters *need* them. This isn't pop psychology or a guilt-inducing parenting tip. As puberty approaches, a dad's natural tendency may be to pull back, but this is precisely the opposite of what your daughter needs. In fact, as Dr. James Dobson so aptly notes, "Girls can read that discomfort with the accuracy of a laser."[5] Dads: affection is a gift you can give to your growing girl. Offer it freely.

Daughters also need a general understanding of their menstrual cycle, and by that we don't merely mean the kind offered by sterile booklets handed out to horrified sixth-graders, some (perhaps many) of whom have already started their periods. Most women don't actually know what happens in their bodies every month. Jerusha discovered many important dynamics while reading Lorraine Pintus's wonderfully wise, excellently researched, and compassionately written book *Jump Off the Hormone Swing.*[6]

We can understand a woman's monthly drama in terms of a four-act drama or the seasons of the year. During the "spring" week, the "world looks bright, and the mood is upbeat. Neurotransmitters in the brain, including serotonin, dopamine, and norepinephrine, are more active, facilitating thought, memory, and intellectual capability."[7]

Pintus describes what a woman (young or more mature) may feel during this week: optimistic, confident, productive, social. She may think, "I can conquer the world!" "I'll take care of that," or "Let's have a party." Here's why: during this season of the month, the ovaries release estrogen, the sex hormone responsible for most feminine sexual traits. Estrogen also plays a role in keeping "our minds sharp, our energy high, and our emotions cheerful. Estrogen causes cells to grow and multiply. . . . When you see the word *estrogen*, think 'energy.'"[8]

Your daughter can learn to harness the extra energy and creativity that estrogen brings during this portion of her cycle. This is also a time to watch carefully, however, as the extra estrogen and the energy that comes with it can make it easy for young women unaccustomed to reining themselves in to overdo.

During the following week, the "summer" of the menstrual cycle, estrogen levels reach their peak and then level off. Though the dynamics of her cycle differ as a woman ages, for pubescent or adolescent girls, energy during this week is also elevated, though typically not quite as high. In all likelihood, her mood is more stable—it's more difficult during this time to upset or worry her. Alas, it can't always be spring or summer. Estrogen is about to take a fall.

As ovulation in a young woman occurs, fluctuating levels of progesterone and testosterone play a significant role. Pintus notes that mood shifts come on the scene here: a girl may be "confident then conflicted, calm then anxious—as hormones rise and fall." She may think, "'I'm confused.' 'I can do this; no I can't,' 'Why am I doing this?' 'Why am I doing anything?'"[9] This is the time for a girl to listen to her body (difficult even for adult women to learn, so it's great to start this training early) and anticipate changes.

During the "fall" week, estrogen continues to plummet, as do progesterone and endorphins. As a result, a girl's mood may darken; she may draw "within herself." These hormonal changes act like toxins in the brain and can create feelings of low self-esteem, hypersensitivity, sadness, and anger, symptoms we typically associate with PMS (premenstrual syndrome).

Finally, during the "winter" week, her period begins. She may feel exhausted, sensitive, and highly emotional. It's time to rest and to expend less energy, allowing the body to do what God so masterfully designed it to do.

Helping our daughters understand this drama equips them for a fuller life of wise and winsome femininity, as does a basic grasp of PMS. Humorous definitions of PMS proliferate—including Pardon My Screaming, Puffy Mid Section, Psychotic Mood Swings, or Pass My Shotgun—but according to the *Mayo Clinic Internal Medicine Concise Textbook*, "pre-menstrual syndrome (PMS) is the cyclic occurrence of symptoms that are sufficiently severe to interfere with some aspects of life, and that appear with consistent and predictable relationship to the menses [monthly period]."[10] Physical cramps; head, stomach, and/or backaches; bloating; weight fluctuations; lethargy; food cravings; acne; and breast tenderness plague many. Emotional symptoms like quick-temperedness, nervousness, crying spells, mental cloudiness, and general moodiness also occur. Spiritual symptoms, including shame, guilt, and feelings of low-self worth, also plague many young women. It ain't easy being a girl!

Being aware of her own cycle and the "seasons" of her month is important for a girl and her parents. It's also essential to evaluate the level of stress, exposure to substances that impact hormonal levels, and relationship dynamics that will influence your daughter. Let's wade into that complexity now.

Psych 101

We've already alluded to the significant role of family stability in a young woman's puberty journey. The onset of menstruation is not the only thing influenced by a strong, supportive family, however. Parental steadiness (or lack thereof) impacts a girl's entire emotional and hormonal landscape. If Mom and Dad are able to take adolescent ups and downs in stride, a teenage girl will fare far better than her peers in anxiety-heavy or explosive homes. For this reason, parents should embrace—note, we didn't say enjoy—that emotions will fluctuate during this time, often dramatically so, and determine ahead of time to keep their cool.

Parents also benefit from refusing to take everything personally. If your daughter expresses doubts about her worth and identity, don't automatically see this as a referendum on your parenting. If any of her criticisms or concerns are valid, address them. But remember, as Dr. Dobson shrewdly observes, "Through adolescence, there will be recurring times of moodiness, anxiety, anger, self-pity, and depression. There will also be periods of giddiness, elation, and happiness. Emotions are on a roller coaster from . . . one day—or one hour—to the next."[11] If you take every one of your daughter's tirades or tears personally, the drama will drag all of you under.

Physician and author of *The Female Brain* Dr. Louann Brizendine offers further insight. In an adolescent girl's "new estrogen-driven reality, aggression also plays a big role. The teen girl brain will make her feel powerful, always right, and blind to consequences. Without that drive, she'll never be able to grow up, but getting through it, especially for the teen girl, isn't easy. As she begins to experience her full 'girl power,' which includes premenstrual syndrome, sexual competition, and controlling girl groups, her brain states can often make her reality, well, a little hellish."[12]

Mom, Dad, don't try to convince your wailing daughter this is "no big deal." *Everything* feels like a big deal. Patiently listen if your daughter wants to talk, give her the space to feel (though you certainly can ask her to express her moodiness in her bedroom), and know that this too shall pass.

In addition, keep in mind that puberty often causes girls to pull away from the people they love. It's a very confusing time. Simultaneously, strong physical forces—most significantly rising estrogen levels—increase a young woman's longing for connectedness.[13] Don't leave your daughter to receive attention and affection only from peers (even if she tells you that's what she wants). A deficit of connectedness can create vulnerability in girls whose parents withdraw during this tumultuous time.

Particularly tense moments arise when a mom and daughter(s) experience hormonal fluctuations at the same time. Whether a mom is fighting PMS, perimenopause, or menopause, her daughter's puberty journey may clash with her own hormonal cycle, creating an emotional bomb waiting to detonate. Fathers, you can help mitigate the potential stresses and "run interference" between the generations. Moms, you can learn to control your own emotions by understanding your body better and making wise choices. But if either parent goes berserk, you can plan on your adolescent doing the same.

It may help you to understand and plan that "once stressed, teens require a more lengthy recovery time than adults. Teenage girls are particularly at risk. Progesterone, which is released in larger amounts with puberty, lets cortisol run rampant. Once a teenage girl becomes stressed, it is very difficult to get her physically and mentally under control."[14] Remember, too much cortisol is toxic for the brain. We can help our teen girls by compassionately giving them time and space to simmer down (again, you may kindly suggest she do this in her own room).

Parents can also encourage healthy choices, which lead to healthy emotions:

- It's tempting for women of all ages to "treat" their hormonal surges with food (aka "Ben & Jerry's therapy"). We can help our daughters resist this. Weight gain and the unhealthy distribution of fat in a woman's body significantly influence the hormonal levels in her body. Imbalanced hormones lead to imbalanced emotional and spiritual reactions.

   Moms, model for your daughter wise ways to approach your monthly cycle. Expel tension in vigorous exercise. Eat smaller, protein-rich meals to keep your blood sugars level. Avoid rather than indulge in excess sugar. If you want some chocolate, choose dark chocolate over heavily processed varieties. Drinking water and eating fiber flushes toxins from your system that contribute to uncomfortable symptoms connected to your period.

- Stress plays a huge role in the monthly drama as well. As far as is possible, delay your own important appointments and decisions during more emotional seasons of the month; help your daughter do the same. Of course you can't organize your life around your period or your daughter's. You can operate, however, with a clear awareness of how stress impacts everyone.

- With stress, cortisol floods the brain and reduces the natural stores of progesterone, which helps maintain a woman's peace and well-being. As adrenaline levels increase, restoring balance becomes harder. Teaching your daughter to lessen the impact of unavoidable stress and eliminate unnecessary stress is a priceless gift.

- Another healthy choice you can make is to limit your daughter's (and your) exposure to endocrine disruptors, chemicals that cause the body's natural hormones to fluctuate unhealthily. Endocrine disruptors can be found in many processed plastics, pesticides, cosmetics, personal hygiene products, meat, and dairy items.[15] You can use the TEDX[16] list to determine if products you use contain these harmful chemicals.

- Finally, as your daughter matures physically, watch out for any disturbances in her overall mental health. Between 3 and 8 percent of women suffer from PMDD (premenstrual dysphoric disorder), a severe, sometimes debilitating condition related to PMS. Medical treatment is advisable.

Symptoms of a broader struggle with mental health, present apart from a girl's menstrual cycle, also should be monitored carefully. The National Institutes of Health cites a connection between the progression of puberty and increase in depression. Progesterone puts girls at a higher risk for mood disorders, so know the signs and seek help sooner rather than later.[17] For more information on depression, refer to chapter 25.

Faith 101

If you and your daughter deliberately choose to be physically, emotionally, and spiritually prepared for puberty and for the ongoing drama of the female cycle, you will reap many benefits. Preparation leads to greater peace. Our friend Lorraine encourages women to apply Proverbs 22:3 to their monthly cycle. The NLT version reads, "A prudent person foresees danger and takes precautions. The simpleton goes blindly on and suffers the consequences."

So, moms, ask yourself: What challenges do I often face with my cycle? What does my daughter seem to battle most often? Jerusha suffers from terrible headaches at ovulation and a couple days before her period. She also knows that beyond the normal "irritability and emotional ups and downs" that lots of women face, she struggles to let things go when she's feeling "hormonal." Knowing this actually empowers her to make a choice that may "feel" wrong but is actually very *right* (like walking away from a conversation that could easily turn into a fight).

If you live in a hurricane state and there's a tropical storm warning, you take precautions. You can learn to do likewise when it comes to your monthly cycle. Some women find increasing their exercise during the week before their period helps reduce tension. Limiting (or cutting out) caffeine can do the same. Planning *not* to have tough conversations about money, grades, friends, and so on is also a very good idea, as is encouraging extra sleep and quiet "alone time."

In addition, parents can help their adolescent daughters stay strong spiritually by debunking myths about being a woman, particularly that menstruation is a curse. God created your daughter and gave her the potential to carry life within her. She probably won't be able to fully embrace the joy of that now, but you can slowly build her confidence in that truth by talking about femininity positively.

Another important spiritual myth to dispel is "PMS made me do it." As women, we need to take responsibility for our choices, even during the seasons of our monthly cycle. Teach your daughter the power of confession, repentance, and forgiveness by modeling these things for her, not only during her period but certainly with an added measure of grace in that time.

Try It Today

Help your teenage girl to track her period (a simple way is to put a dot or icon on the calendar on the date her period begins each month) and recognize the patterns of any PMS symptoms. Try specifically targeted tactics to relieve symptoms (aromatherapy for headaches, for instance, or vigorous exercise to combat irritability). Encourage her not to fight against the body God gave her or push herself beyond her God-given limits but rather to embrace the beauty of her feminine brain and form. Your daughter is God's priceless masterpiece; remind her of that as often as possible!

23

It's Not All I Think About!

Once testosterone started flooding my (Jeramy's) body, surges of anger, defiance, aggression, untamed desire, or all of the above would periodically explode within me, often unbidden and without obvious provocation. I was a fuse itching to be lit. In fact, if you ask my pastor from those days, he'll tell you I was the most hotheaded punk to darken the door of Valley Bible Church.

I'm probably not the only guy who's been tossed out of a church baseball game, but I'm ashamed to admit that I'm one of the few who responded by kicking church property in an uncontrolled outburst of frustration. Not one of my finer moments.

As a teenager, I distinctly recall trying to stare down my dad—my six-foot-four, 225-pound father—who was patiently explaining something I didn't want to hear. As I attempted to glare my resistance into him, he cracked a half smile and said, "Son, you aren't gonna win this one." That did it. Not knowing what else to do, but keenly aware that any physical display would get me in serious trouble, I grabbed a pillow and literally held it in front of my face to block him from view.

After a nasty relationship breakdown, I sat behind the steering wheel of my Chevy stepside truck and punched the windshield in a fit of hurt and anger. Watching it spiderweb crack in front of me, one thought raced through my head: "You idiot." Later, a police officer issued me a fix-it ticket, and I had to shell out hard-earned cash to replace the windshield.

I never thought, "Wow. I have a lot of emotions that I don't know what to do with." During adolescence, I was too confused for a moment of clarity like that, but I really didn't know the best way to express my thoughts and feelings. Rage seemed manlier than tears, but it didn't get me anywhere. And I haven't even touched on the crazy way puberty impacted my thoughts about girls.

Being a teenage guy twenty-some years ago, dealing with the storm and stress constantly brewing inside me, was tough. It's every bit as tough—and uniquely difficult in many ways—for today's adolescent males. Fortunately, we know more about their brains than ever before.

Bio 101

Way back when you first heard the sordid tale of "how your body will change during puberty," you probably learned that a major contributor to male development is the sex hormone testosterone. When you consider that adolescent boys have *thirty times* more testosterone by their early twenties than they did at age ten, you can imagine the challenge of adjusting to this new chemical profile. Scientists have discovered even more about testosterone over the last two decades, however, so hang on to your hats and glasses.

We now know that the amygdala and the hypothalamus—areas of the brain that help mediate the body's response to fear and danger—are particularly sensitive to testosterone, which causes these neural structures to grow larger in young men. While all teenagers experience heightened activity in the brain's limbic system, and particularly the amygdala, adolescent males have even bigger and busier amygdalae than girls. The results: assertiveness, aggression, shorter attention span, and increased sex drive.

Researchers also recently discovered that unlike children or adults, adolescent males show "enhanced activity in the part of the brain that controls emotions when confronted with a threat."[1] And fMRI studies reveal that even if study participants were directly instructed *not* to acknowledge a perceived threat, the automatic neural responses in adolescent males were so strong that they blew reaction results for adult men out of the water. Teenage boy brains, in many ways, operate on high alert, always anticipating threats and awaiting offensive orders.

Another team of scientists, evaluating measurements of brain activity, discovered that "teenage boys were mostly immune to the threat of punishment but hypersensitive to the possibility of large gains."[2] For many adolescent males, instead of deterring deviant behavior, the threat of punishment incites what resembles a cognitive game of chicken. Parents who hold potential consequences over teenage boys may inadvertently ignite their son's large-and-in-charge amygdala, growing each day of adolescence under the influence of testosterone and other hormones.

On top of all this, brain-derived neurotrophic factor (BDNF), a molecule crucial for evaluating danger, is *less active* in adolescent male brains. This means that while teenage boys are emotionally volatile and on "high alert," they are also *less able* to accurately assess threats. It's no wonder they seek emotionally charged experiences! According to neuroscientist Dr. Frances Jensen, "This double whammy—a jacked-up, stimulus-seeking brain not yet fully capable of making mature decisions—hits teens pretty hard, and the consequences to them, and their families, can sometimes be catastrophic."[3]

Let's put all of this together: Puberty starts. Testosterone and other hormones flood the male body. The limbic system revs up, and teenage boys develop large and highly active amygdalae, intensifying emotions. At the same time, the typical teenage male brain is less effective at calculating risk and reacts to the threat of punishment as an invitation to push the limits. In the midst of all this, sexual desire awakens with ferocity. Do you think our teenage guys could use our compassion and help? It doesn't take a neuroscience degree to answer that question. It does take, however, a significant amount of patience and discernment to live wisely in response.

Psych 101

When we were younger, people often quipped that teenage guys have "one thing on their minds." Everyone knew what that "one thing" was, and people either shook their heads in a resigned, "boys will be boys" sort of way or vehemently warned of the dangers of untamed sexual desire. Neither approach has proven particularly effective.

We want you to know, right from the outset, that there's *a lot* more going on in the mind of an adolescent male than thoughts about sex. Don't believe the lie that adolescent males can be reduced to their sexual urges. If you do, you'll miss the opportunity to cultivate true masculinity in the teenage guys with whom you interact. We all benefit from remembering that:

- **An instant and disposable mindset infects teenage guys.**[4] In a world where everything happens quickly and everything's made to be broken, adolescent males struggle to develop characteristics like patience and perseverance. As any parent knows, both forbearance and resilience are necessary for adult life. Part of the reason we have more toddler men than mature males in media, business, and other arenas is because teenage boys never grow out of their "I want what I want, now" attitude. They dispose of phones, water bottles, and relationships with equal flippancy.

  As a parent of a teenage son, you have a unique call to teach your emerging man about sticking with commitments, even when it's inconvenient (for him and maybe for you too!), honoring others (basic manners are never out of style), and delaying gratification (e.g., *not* getting the latest technology simply because it's available) while practicing contentment and gratitude.

Be on the lookout for opportunities to encourage patience and perseverance in your adolescent boy.

- **Allowing your son to teach you something makes you an ally.** There are plenty of times your son will view you as an "enemy," so capitalizing on every moment of shared purpose and pleasure is crucial. Your son may not be able to express it, but he needs to feel competent in some arena. When you allow an adolescent guy to teach you something, he gains confidence and feels a sense of accomplishment. Trust us; you want him to experience this around you whenever possible, as he will often struggle with feelings of inferiority outside your home. Since parental humility ranks high on the list of traits teens esteem, when you allow your son to help you with technology or show you a skill he's recently mastered, you also earn his respect.

- **You can expand that vocabulary.** Parents of teenage boys frequently complain that they can't get anything more than a word (or a measly grunt) out of their sons during the adolescent years. Of course, this isn't true of every young man; our friends have twin teenage sons who could give the chattiest of girls a verbal run for their money! That said, most boys lag behind their female counterparts when it comes to a working vocabulary for emotions. For an adolescent guy, "I'm bored" can mean anything from "I'm restless" to "I'm hurting or angry and I want to be distracted so I don't have to feel it."

  Neurologically, teenage boys have strong emotional reactions (remember, large-and-in-charge amygdalae) but less sophisticated vocabularies and relational intuition. Parents, stop expecting your teen boy to know how to verbalize his experiences and emotions; instead, *teach* him to do these things. For some, this will feel like retreading worn ground; you may have exerted concerted effort during your son's childhood, helping him "use his words" rather than express himself physically or stew internally. Take heart! The lessons you spent time teaching in childhood will come back.

Using words to identify your own experiences and emotions gives your son a vocabulary to do the same. Dads, it's especially helpful for you to model this. Teach your son the difference between emotions: frustration, regret, passion, anger, fear, wariness, lethargy, apathy, and so on. He needs to know that each of these feelings impacts him, and the world around him, in unique ways. Having words to articulate his experience helps your son make sense of a time of life often riddled with nonsense.

- **Beating the odds may not be easy, but it is possible.** Roughly 68 percent of adolescent males view pornography on a regular (at least weekly) basis.[5] At the time of this writing, the average adolescent male is exposed to porn first at age eleven.[6] We have no doubt that age will continue to drop. And while we included this section in the chapter on adolescent males, it's important that you know porn isn't strictly a "guy's issue." One in three porn-viewers is female.[7]

  While all of this is certainly alarming, our desire in sharing statistics isn't to incite panic but rather to encourage you to plan your attack. Since many adolescents are *unintentionally* exposed to porn, whether at school or at home, monitoring internet usage, installing filters, and engaging openly with your teenagers about this issue is absolutely essential (a one-time "Don't look at porn" talk doesn't cut it here).

  So is evaluating your own habits. Even some television shows and movies could qualify as "soft porn." Setting the bar high for your own purity models self-discipline and accountability to your family. We also highly recommend that you get armed, and then arm your teen, with information about what pornography does to the mind and spirit.

  Unlike other forms of pleasure, porn lights up multiple portions of the brain at once. It incites a frenzy of neural activity that is *highly addictive*. It also damages relational intimacy. Don't be fooled; a little porn isn't harmless. In fact, recent research indicates that many young (even married) men who have regularly viewed pornography struggle with erectile dysfunction, undermining their physical and emotional capacity to enjoy intimacy.[8]

The odds may seem insurmountable, but don't throw up your hands in discouraged defeat; you *can* wage war for your son's success. When people play the odds, they do so because even in the direst of situations, victory can be had. Pray for it. Talk about it. Plan for it, and trust God to bring it about.

Faith 101

Teenage guys crave adventure. In many ways they are neurologically wired for it. The little boy who pretended to slay dragons with a stick in your backyard still wants to be caught up in a story greater than his own, an adventure beyond the scope of his daily life. Part of the reason modern video games appeal to so many young men is that they provide a story line within which guys can play a heroic part. Whether it's a military-style game that allows teenage boys to save the world or a fantasy realm within which he can conquer mythic beasts and win the heart of a ravishingly beautiful princess, the quests and escapades of these alternate realities awaken the natural desire in teenage guys for something more.

In the excellent book he co-authored, *A Parent's Guide to Understanding Teenage Guys*, youth ministry veteran Brock Morgan relates a time during early adolescence when his dad popped into his room to read "something amazing" to him. It happened to be from 2 Corinthians 11, a passage chronicling Paul's sufferings as an apostle: imprisonment, flogging, attempted stoning, shipwreck (times three, no less!), various life-and-death perils at the hands of bandits and false friends, natural disasters, sleeplessness, hunger, exposure, and trumped-up accusations.

Apparently Brock's dad finished regaling him with Paul's tales and asked excitedly, "What adventure Paul had in following Jesus, huh?"

Let's be honest: this isn't the typical response we see to Paul's words. Most parents want their sons to avoid—at all costs—any of those so-called "adventures." For Brock, though, his father's words struck a chord. He observes,

> I had begun to think that following Jesus was about *not* doing certain things. For me the gospel was about sin management, not an adventurously expectant life. But as a kid, I wanted an adventurous, expectant life. Since the time I was little I had imagined myself being chased by bandits and lost at sea and doing dangerous things, all for the mission that I was on. And now my dad read me something that really resonated. For the first time in my life, I thought that maybe God was calling me into a life of adventure.[9]

Teenage boys desperately need a vision for something bigger than their own glory, a life of purpose and vision for something greater. As men, they'll be tempted to measure their value based on their competence, but investing one's identity in work or any other measure of accomplishment (even at church) leads to disaster. As pastor Tim Keller so brilliantly put it, if you succeed, it goes to your head, and if you fail, it goes to your heart.[10]

To become godly men, adolescents need to be invited into a noble adventure, a quest worth pursuing. If you don't believe spreading the life-transforming gospel of Jesus Christ fits that bill, you haven't embarked on the journey yourself. Living for the glory of God is anything but ho-hum, and teenage boys need to be inspired by the truth. Granted, most won't be shipwrecked or battling bandits, but the fight of their lives isn't "against flesh and blood, but against the rulers, against the authorities, against the cosmic powers over this present darkness, against the spiritual forces of evil" (Eph. 6:12 ESV).

Each and every day, voices clamor to tell your son who he is. By the grace of God, and if you are armed with his truth, your voice can rise above the rest. Tell your son over and over that he is a man after God's own heart, a man created for something greater than this earth, a man who will find fulfillment only in surrendering to an adventure far more breathtaking (if also baffling) than any he could compose for himself.

Raising a godly man is no easy task. The dynamics are complex and the commitment is costly; it demands a lifetime investment. You don't have to do it flying solo, though. Indeed, on this journey, you are never alone. The very God who knit your son together in his mother's womb and who determined which genetic traits would express themselves in this unique and remarkable human (currently disguised as a surly teenager) promises to give you insight into your son.

Ask God to give you a vision for your son's true heart. Trust God's Word, not the evidence of a given day. Believe that God can make you creative and quick enough to navigate the sometimes-torrential storm of adolescence, because he not only can, but *he will*—if only you will ask. As the book of James urges, "If you need wisdom, ask our generous God, and he will give it to you. He will not rebuke you for asking" (1:5 NLT). So what are you waiting for? Ask!

Try It Today: "Tell Me More About That"

Next time your son verbally expresses an opinion, use the phrase, "Tell me more about that" to open and extend a dialogue.[11]

Sadly, many parents of teenage boys settle for discussing details: What time do you need to be picked up? Have you done your homework? Who's going to be there? Truth be told, it's tempting to stay on this level, because it's less complicated than traversing the uneven emotional terrain of a teen boy's mind. We *must not* take this path of least resistance when it comes to communicating with adolescent boys.

Ask your son what makes him angry, what makes him laugh, what he daydreams about. If and when he answers, put the "tell me more about that" plan into action. The more you show your son that you're interested in and care about what he thinks, the more likely he'll be to share spontaneously at some point. It's not a guarantee, but your chances of good communication are far greater when you invite your son into an ongoing conversation.

24

I Feel So Ugly

At sixth grade graduation, I (Jerusha) won two awards: Highest Overall Achievement and Ms. Popularity. But Kayla—a *fourth-grader*—got Most Attractive Female. Who thought making these elementary school prizes was a good idea, I have no idea. All I remember is my insides twisting into an ugly knot. Even at eleven, I sensed it didn't matter how successful and popular you were if you weren't pretty.

During my adolescent years, I never felt quite right about my appearance. I was *too this* and *not enough that*, a little more *this* than I "should" be and too much *that* to feel good about myself.

Along with all my girlfriends, I endlessly dissected the imperfections of my body, lamenting the "problems" with my thighs and belly. I drank diet soda for lunch if a big event was coming up. I sometimes rose before dawn to jog, circling our neighborhood in inky darkness, purging guilty calories from the day before or burning calories to "pay for" the day ahead. I recycled negative body thoughts over and over, every day. I tacitly agreed with the lie that people could and would judge me by how I looked. Saddest of all, none of this seemed bizarre to me.

Bio 101

Statistics paint a grim picture regarding our national preoccupation with body image. Apparently, no matter what stage of life or state of fitness we're in, Americans decry their appearance with untamed ferocity.

In a study of three- to six-year-old girls, nearly half were already worried about being fat. Did you catch the age range of that study? We're talking about toddlers and preschoolers here. When surveyed, elementary school children say they'd prefer being handicapped to being overweight. Eighty-one percent of ten-year-olds report being afraid of being fat, and more than half of nine- and ten-year-old girls feel better about themselves if they're on a diet.[1]

While preadolescents often speak of "being fat" in general terms, by the time puberty begins, teens turn inward, focusing specifically and negatively on their particular figures. At age thirteen, 54 percent of American girls are "unhappy with their bodies." By seventeen, 78 percent of girls dislike their size and/or shape. Forty-one percent of teen boys also report overall dissatisfaction with their physical appearance.[2]

In our society, if you don't like what you see, pressure mounts to fix it (or at least try). Teens are not immune to this message. Over 375,000 teenagers are anesthetized for plastic surgery every year.[3]

Most of us can't fathom telling an adolescent that life would be better if they got a nose job, yet how many of us—moms and dads included—communicate *contentment* with our own bodies to our teenagers? Statistics don't present a more positive picture here.

Approximately 91 percent of adult women and 43 percent of adult men are unhappy with their appearance.[4] When one national survey asked, "What would you give up if you could slim down permanently?" 5 percent of respondents were actually willing to give up five years of their life.[5]

According to another nationwide poll, "A whopping 97 *percent* [of women] admitted to having at least one 'I hate my body' moment" every day. "Research found that, on average, women have 13 negative body thoughts daily—nearly one for every waking hour. And a disturbing number of women confess to having 35, 50 or even 100 hateful thoughts about their own shapes each day."[6]

Here's the shocking biological reality behind this situation: we've actually trained ourselves to be this way. Dr. Ann Kearney-Cooke notes, "Neuroscience has shown that whatever you focus on shapes your brain. If you're constantly thinking negative thoughts about your body, that neural pathway becomes stronger—and those thoughts become habitual."[7]

The more adolescents dwell on what they don't like about their bodies, the stronger the neural connections they forge. Moreover, the more prevalent the negative thoughts in a teen's life, the greater the potential for physical problems and emotional strain.

Research indicates that people who obsess about their bodies and diet have chronically elevated levels of the stress hormone cortisol, even when life circumstances aren't otherwise stressed. As a result of increasingly toxic levels of cortisol, those who habitually direct negative attention to their bodies may suffer from elevated blood pressure, lower bone density, increased amounts of unhealthy belly fat, and menstrual problems.[8] Lest you dismiss this with, "I'm sure this is true if you've got an eating disorder," be aware that these symptoms can apply to anyone who has recurrent negative thoughts about their appearance.

Mood swings and emotional outbursts also result from negative body image. Waging an ongoing battle with the mirror or the scale can leave you exhausted and aggravated. What you think about your body directly affects your relationships and your overall life satisfaction, as well as your ability to parent a teen who is vulnerable to the pressures of body dissatisfaction.

If we're going to establish a healthy body image and help our teens do the same, we've got to look beyond the steam—the "I'm so ugly," "I feel so fat" comments—and determine what's making the pot boil: underlying thoughts and beliefs.

Psych 101

As his or her body transforms at record speed, nearly every adolescent's emphasis on body image intensifies. At the same time, the desire to attract the opposite sex increases, and teens almost universally believe the best way to garner attention is through their physical appearance. As if this weren't enough, adolescents also absorb cultural messages about what it means to be attractive and desirable. It's no mystery why teenagers focus so many thoughts—often highly emotional and negative ones—on their bodies!

According to Dr. Nichole Wood-Barcalow, "There are only so many times you can be hit with the message that your body isn't 'right'—whether you see it on TV, hear it from your mom or just feel it in the ether—before you internalize it and start beating yourself up for not being as perfect as you 'should' be."[9]

Many of us have believed the lie that if we could only look a certain way or weigh a certain amount, we'd feel "good enough," be more satisfied with life, and be more acceptable to others. Our teenage sons and daughters have believed the same. But these are *lies*.

For both men and women, body image develops over time and due to a wide variety of factors. Kids teased mercilessly on the playground for being either "weak and skinny" or "fat and slow" often develop an unhealthy self-perspective. A young woman who develops before her peers may receive excessive attention for her blossoming body, causing her to focus inordinately on her physical appearance. Peers and pubescent timing certainly influence body image.

Media also impacts our sons and daughters. Many scientific studies have linked television viewing with increased body dissatisfaction.[10] Printed pictures influence body image as well. One survey found that 70 percent of women felt depressed, guilty, and shameful after looking at a fashion magazine for *only three minutes*.[11] People more readily recognize the negative way women are objectified by the media, but heightened exposure to idealized visions of masculinity—super-lean, strong, and chiseled actors, sports stars, and models—significantly impacts adolescents as well.

Of course, limiting teens' exposure to damaging media images is essential, but you cannot insulate them entirely. You also cannot control what your adolescent hears at school from other students. You can, however, control what *you* say, what you do, and—most importantly—what you think about your body.

Your thoughts are key because no matter what comes out of your mouth (or goes into it), your teen will separate empty talk from what you truly believe. If you're constantly disparaging your body and laughing it off as "just a joke" or with a "but I love myself the way I am" platitude, you're not fooling your adolescent.

Moms, can you stop the "I feel fat," "I just need to lose a few," "I shouldn't have eaten that," "I've got to do something about these wrinkles" commentary? Quit quietly accepting the thought—and subtly transferring it to your teen—that people base their decisions to accept or reject us largely on how we look. Dads, you're not off the hook here. Don't pat your belly and talk about your lack of discipline. Do something!

Teenagers everywhere listen to parents decry their weight, shape, and age, and in their highly emotional adolescent way, they absorb the belief that if they just keep the "right" size, shape, or youthful appearance, they'll feel good enough. Instead of perpetuating this myth that looking a certain way makes you more likable or a better person, let's start communicating the truth: what's on your mind influences your body image even more than how your body looks.

Consider this: You're in the checkout line at Target, and suddenly you think, "My stomach is disgusting." You've had that same belly all day, so why did this thought unexpectedly pop into your head? Is it because you've been staring at nutrition labels or because you're confronted with airbrushed images on magazine covers? Is it because you're sure the clerk looked askance when you went into the dressing room with "that size" pants? Did you have a hard day and feel like eating your way through the take-out food section of the phone book?

If this is the case, no amount of crunches will make you feel better about your stomach. So often what we think about our bodies has very little to do with the reality of what we look like. Our thoughts, and our general satisfaction with life, influence our body image far more than we recognize. We can help adolescents see this.

We can also take these practical steps to establish a healthy body image and communicate it to adolescents:

- **Exercise!** Across the board, "survey respondents who worked out regularly tended to report fewer harsh thoughts than those who didn't. And it's not just that being physically active improves your shape and health; it actually boosts your mind-set, too. . . . Women felt better about themselves after exercising even when their bodies didn't change."[12] Exercise impacts overall neurological health, and its benefits for mind-body health fit right in. Modeling a commitment to exercise—not just talking about it, but actually *doing* it—influences your teen in significant ways.

- **Rewire your brain.** Because you now know that the brain is plastic (able to be changed), focus on strengthening the right brain connections. When your mind starts spinning negatively or when you catch yourself speaking poorly about your body, say, "Stop." Literally say it out loud. This disrupts the flow of your synaptic firing. Share this tip with adolescents who criticize themselves; help them break free and wire their brains well!

- **Evaluate cultural messages with your teen.** Ask your adolescent's opinion about the way advertisements, TV shows, movies, music, magazines, or websites talk about bodies. Point out hypocrisy or inconsistencies. Ask open-ended questions and keep conversations short and interesting. Remember, a comment dropped here or there is often more effective for teens than lengthy discussions.

- **Check the surroundings.** Context powerfully influences body image. If your teen is involved in a sport, activity, or peer group that places emphasis on external appearance, watch carefully for signs of negative body image. Be aware of conversations happening between your adolescent and his or her friends. Some environments, such as college campuses and gyms, are notorious breeding grounds for disordered thinking about food, weight, and overall appearance. Constance Rhodes also observes, "An experience as simple as going to the mall can provoke increased feelings of inadequacy and competition. When you consider that the purpose of retail marketing is to remind consumers that there is something we are lacking, it is no wonder that a brief visit can leave us feeling empty and discouraged."[13] Start watching how you and your adolescent respond in certain situations, and then make adjustments in how and where you spend time.

- **Affirm your body.** Find the things you enjoy about your body and highlight them in front of your teen. For instance, after you finish exercising, you can express how great it feels to be active. You can also verbally thank God for whatever health and strength you have. Gratitude is the ace in your hand against worry and discouragement. You cannot be obsessed with your body and grateful at the same time (more on the mutual exclusivity of thankfulness and worry in chapter 26).

- **Stop commenting on other people's bodies.** Whether you're pointing out positive or negative things, highlighting other people's bodies puts the focus on appearance and, whether you intend to or not, incites comparison and competition. Be honest: there's no *good* reason to evaluate the way someone looks in a bathing suit. Nothing positive comes from you and your teen discussing the appearance of others.

What Every Parent and Teen Should Know

When negative body image escalates, eating disorders may develop. Because "eating disorders are based on the belief that food and eating (or lack of eating) are the key to changing one's entire life," they are about more than just body image.[14] Control, freedom, fear, anger, and painful experiences influence the development of eating disorders.

- Over one-half of teenage girls and nearly one-third of teenage boys use unhealthy weight control behaviors such as skipping meals, fasting, smoking cigarettes, vomiting, and taking laxatives.[15]
- **Bulimia nervosa**—characterized by the excessive consumption and subsequent purging of food through vomiting, laxatives, or obsessive exercise—has been called an adolescent epidemic. An *epidemic*, not a fad or trend. Binging and purging can become addictive because the body releases endorphins after eating, initially calming the brain, sometimes sparking a sense of euphoria. These feelings are short-lived, however, as bulimics later experience guilt, shame, anger, and fear, which drive them to purge the food consumed.
- **Anorexia nervosa** and its pattern of severe food restriction, whether through self-starvation or the consumption of only "safe" foods, deny the body essential nutrients needed to function normally. With prolonged food restriction, the brain's ability

Faith 101

Growing up, I (Jerusha) memorized Ephesians 2:10: "We are God's workmanship, created in Christ Jesus." I love this verse, but the word *workmanship* made me think of something rough and unsophisticated, something that needed, for lack of a better description, a lot of *work*.

In the original Greek, however, the word rendered "workmanship" is actually *poeima*, an ancient term connoting nothing less than an to manufacture and utilize the calming agent serotonin decreases, which—tragically—causes further obsession. Over time, the body begins to shut down. Anorexia nervosa has the highest mortality rate of any psychiatric disorder.[16]

- *Binge eating disorder,* identified by the National Eating Disorders Association as the most common form of dysfunctional eating, involves consistent consumption, over a short period of time, of more food than the body needs. BED is accompanied by distressed emotions and the sense that one is out of control.

- *Sub-threshold eating disorders, or eating disorders not otherwise specified (EDNOS),* silently affect millions of Americans. Because those with EDNOS—men and women who diet chronically, yo-yo between weights, and/or engage in occasional binges, purges, and food restriction—don't usually fit a classic eating disorder diagnosis, they may never seek help for or even be aware of their problem. Between 25 and 40 percent of older adolescents struggle with hazardously unhealthy attitudes toward eating and weight, yet only 6 percent would be diagnosed as clinically anorexic and bulimic, which means a large percentage never get the help they need.[17]

If you suspect negative body image is beginning to control your son's or daughter's life, don't wait. Seek help immediately. Your doctor's office, school, or church may have a list of recommended clinicians.

incomparable work of genius. As God's *poeima*, your teenager is a glorious masterpiece. So are you.

I am particularly fond of Vincent van Gogh's painting *Starry Night*. The vibrant colors, the rich textures, and the subtlety and power of this masterful work simply awe me. I have come to see that God views me as a masterpiece, much like this. In fact, I love to imagine him looking at me as I view that painting—full of passion and vibrant color, depth and complexity.

God sees your teen as a masterpiece, and he or she needs to hear it. God sees you as a masterpiece, and you need to hear it too.

I know some of you are thinking, *Maybe I was God's masterpiece as he originally designed me, but I've ruined my body. If I had my act together, I'd look the way I could and should look.*

This is a lie. There is no "right" appearance, and there is nothing that can *in any way* diminish your heritage as a masterpiece. Believing what God says about you actually enables you, in the healthiest way, to take care of your body with balance, freedom, and joy. Health is important to God—we are, after all, masterpieces and should treat ourselves as such—but it's time to disregard the lie that we'd be happier, accepted, and at peace if we looked a certain way. Your adolescent needs to see that you believe the question of your happiness, acceptability, and lovability was settled forever on the cross, not at the gym.

Let's make it our goal to pray, "Thank you for making me so wonderfully complex! Your workmanship is marvelous—how well I know it" (Ps. 139:14 NLT). If we truly believe what God says about us, our teens will notice.

Try It Today

Starting today, take a two-week break from verbally criticizing your appearance. The less you verbalize things, the less you dwell on them and the less power they have over you. This is true both neurologically and spiritually. We know from science that we strengthen neural pathways with repetition and attention. In the spiritual realm, the enemy tempts us in areas of weakness. Do you think it's possible that when we verbalize things such as "I hate my thighs" or "This makes me look fat," the adversary picks up little ways to attack our hearts and minds? Stop saying negative things about yourself for two weeks and see what happens.

Here's another benefit of not criticizing your body: as you set an example for teens, they'll be attracted to the freedom you're enjoying. At the end of your life, do you think you'll wish that you had been thinner or that you had worried less and enjoyed more? Why live any differently today?

25

I Hate My Life

Lisa knocked on her daughter Avery's door for what seemed like the fiftieth time that day. She knew it was considered normal for teenagers to sleep a lot, especially during summer vacation, but for weeks Avery had been awake less than asleep. It was now 2:00 p.m., and Lisa was concerned. Avery was sixteen. Shouldn't she be out enjoying life, hanging with friends, doing teenager stuff?

Suddenly, the door flew open. Without a word to her mother, Avery walked zombielike to the kitchen, pulled a half gallon of ice cream from the freezer, and headed back toward her room. Lisa honestly didn't know what to do.

"Honey, I'm worried . . ." she began.

Lisa half hoped Avery would fly off the handle and yell; at least that would show some sign of life. Instead, her daughter turned to her and, with a deep, shaking sigh, sank to her knees sobbing.

⦙⦙⦙⦙⦙⦙⦙⦙⦙⦙⦙⦙⦙⦙⦙⦙⦙⦙⦙

Bright, talented, attractive . . . Harrison had it all. Everyone expected great things from him. They'd told him so for as long as he could remember. He'd always had a great relationship with his parents—even after their divorce—and he doted on his three younger half sisters. At school, at church, at the coffee shop where he worked, Harrison was universally loved.

Since his breakup with Julia, though, Harrison was angry inside. He tried to ignore it, but the rage was getting harder to contain. The restlessness Harrison felt from the minute he woke up only intensified throughout the day, and pounding, daily headaches made it almost impossible to concentrate on school. His third-quarter grades slipped, big-time.

Harrison told his parents it was just the stress of working and trying to keep up with homework after practice, but he knew it wasn't just that. He couldn't remember things, even things he'd known for a long time. He'd lost weight, but apparently not enough for anyone else to notice.

Thursday afternoon during sixth period, the dam finally broke. Mr. Gregson was a nice enough guy; Harrison felt bad that he'd done it, but even now, sitting in the vice principal's office, he didn't truly regret punching a hole in the drywall of Mr. Gregson's room. Maybe now they'd see that something was wrong.

Bio 101

Though both Avery and Harrison were battling depression, their struggles were unique. Dealing with similar situations, trying to identify "what's wrong" and "what caused it" leaves many parents bereft. Some would rather chalk concerns up to "teenage nonsense" or dismiss warning signs as a "phase they'll outgrow," but we simply cannot ignore the heartbreaking statistics about adolescent mental health.

According to the National Alliance of Mental Health (NAMH), four million American children and adolescents suffer from a mental health condition that significantly impacts daily life at home, at school, and with peers. Millions more go undiagnosed, suffering yet getting no help.

The NAMH also reports that half of all mental disorders begin by age fourteen. Sadly, despite the presence of effective treatments, *only one in three* people receives help of any kind. Furthermore, long delays between the onset of symptoms in the adolescent years and when (if) treatment begins make conditions more severe and difficult to address.

This is the reality of what teenagers face, but what are the causes? Recent research connects neural remodeling during adolescence to the revelation of underlying neurochemical or structural weakness. Dr. Daniel Siegel observes, "Such vulnerability may have a wide array of causes, from genetics to toxic exposures to adverse childhood experiences such as abuse and neglect. . . . The pruning of childhood circuits that may have been 'at risk' leads to the unmasking of those deficiencies. . . . Even if average pruning occurs, what remains may be insufficient to enable mood to be kept in balance or for thought to be coordinated with reality."[1] Siegel also notes the role of stress in exacerbating the pruning process. When pressure is high, a greater number of "at-risk circuits" may be pruned, diminishing neural effectiveness. Brain functioning suffers and mental health conditions manifest.

Even in otherwise well-functioning people, the adolescent years—full of intense personal change—can introduce challenges with mental health. Transitions in school, friendships, activities, and familial relationships, coupled with the experience of confusing feelings about identity, future plans, and major decisions contribute to adolescent struggles as well.

Avery's and Harrison's stories reveal the complex nature of mental health concerns. Depression doesn't always look one way. Parents sometimes ask us to help them discern whether their teen is really depressed or just experiencing the natural, perhaps even unavoidable, ups and downs of adolescence. This is a difficult question to answer and should be directed to a trusted health care practitioner.

A period of temporarily impaired mood may result from the process of neural remodeling, and neurochemical chaos may correct with age, so the advent of symptoms is "not an 'all-or-none' proposition in which a genetic vulnerability always becomes a psychiatric disorder."[2]

Symptoms of Depression

Symptoms of depression vary widely and may include:

- feelings of sadness, emptiness, helplessness, hopelessness, and/or worthlessness
- anxiety (more details in chapter 26)
- a pervasive sense of guilt and shame
- irritability, bursts of anger or rage
- restlessness
- rigid, inflexible thinking
- uncharacteristic behaviors (lying, sneaking, manipulation, etc.)
- loss of interest in activities once enjoyed
- lack of energy or lethargy
- problems concentrating, remembering information, or making decisions
- insomnia
- hypersomnia (sleeping too much)
- loss of appetite or overeating, leading to weight loss or gain
- talking about death, thoughts of suicide, or suicide attempts
- hallucinations or delusions
- aches, pains, headaches, cramps, or digestive problems that do not go away

Note: Bipolar disorder often develops in adolescence. At least half of all cases start before age twenty-five. With bipolar disorder, symptoms of depression are accompanied by manic behaviors, which may include dramatic mood swings, reckless behaviors, impulsivity, rapid speech, and trouble sleeping. Instead of appearing tired, a person struggling with bipolar may seem hyper or oddly silly. About 10–15 percent of adolescents who battle deep, reoccurring depression develop bipolar disorder,[3] so it's essential to get your teen help. Adolescents at risk for bipolar disorder need a thorough medical examination conducted by a specialist to ensure appropriate treatment is administered.

Other times, however, the onset of symptoms signals the appearance of a serious condition. A medical doctor, qualified counselor, or both should evaluate any teenager consistently and concurrently exhibiting four or more symptoms of depression. Your moody teen might be down for a couple days, but if he or she doesn't bounce back after two weeks, seeking help is extremely important. Remember, the longer the delay between the onset of symptoms and treatment, the more difficult it can be to overcome. As toxic thinking increases, the possibility of feeling better seems more and more remote, which creates a vicious cycle of ever-increasing negativity. Don't leave your teen here!

Neurotransmitters, including serotonin, play a significant role in depression. In healthy brains, serotonin helps people feel relaxed, working in a check-and-balance manner with the emotionally charged amygdala. Certain studies indicate serotonin levels dip during adolescence. For many teenagers, this is no problem; for others, it leads to depression. Clinicians propose that these teens either can't use the serotonin they have effectively or their levels of serotonin are too diminished to be effectual.[4]

Neurotransmitters don't tell us the whole story, however. Most professionals understand that depression results from a complex interplay of genetics, environment, and experience. Be aware of the risks of adolescent depression and intervene quickly. Depression is highly treatable, but help won't come to you. Seek it!

A depressed teen may express, "I've never been happy" or "I don't know why I feel this way," but don't react to these statements. Understand what's behind them. With chronic depression, the hippocampus—which plays an essential role in memory and emotional integration—decreases in size, making it more difficult to recall being happy, process feelings (they really don't understand what they're going through), or learn new things.[5] Imagine if a part of your own brain was progressively shrinking. Wouldn't you hope other people would respond with empathy? Depressed adolescents need compassion first and foremost. Of course, troubling behaviors must also be addressed. But keep in mind: modifying behavior is only effective once we address core issues.

Risk Factors

Your teen is at greater risk for depression if he or she:

- has experienced a stressful life event such as a family death, divorce, bullying, a breakup, or failure in school or in an activity considered personally significant.
- is the victim of abuse or abandonment.
- expresses self-condemnation, perfectionism, or excessive self-criticism.
- is female. Teen girls are twice as likely as boys to develop depression.
- struggles socially.
- suffers from learning disabilities or chronic illness. Both can contribute to the imbalance of neurotransmitters.
- abuses alcohol or drugs. Some recreational drugs, including marijuana, can lead to psychosis, hallucinations, or delusions.
- can trace a family history of mood disorders (remember, however, this is not an "all or nothing" proposition).[6]

Psych 101

Behind the hard realities about depression lies some really good news: with treatment, most adolescents get better, especially if they receive good care early on.

Given the impressionability of teenage brains, early intervention is essential. Your teen's high neuroplasticity can work for or against his or her mental health. Preventing exposure to stresses and substances that cause psychological problems *as well as* addressing problems quickly and courageously are equally important.

Some parents fear treating teens for depression because "overmedicating is such a big problem." This position is certainly understandable, but please don't make a decision about your adolescent's health based on fear of what "could be." Equip yourself with information, pray earnestly, and follow the counsel of trained practitioners you trust.

The human brain, arguably the most complex structure in the known universe, is the one organ that medical professionals rarely look at when considering treatment options. Despite the brain's intricacies, when we think about depression, we tend to view it as a single disorder. Health care practitioners, even well-intentioned ones, often administer a questionnaire, diagnose a problem in twenty minutes, and prescribe the same psychotropic drug for every depressed patient. In some cases, this leads to repercussions that worsen an adolescent's condition or delay healing interminably. Finding a skilled doctor who listens and whom you can trust is nonnegotiable.

Reading about potential problems with treatment increases apprehension in some parents. We like how Dr. Michael Bradley approaches these concerns: "There is no clear bottom line with medication. There are only risks and benefits, which you must weigh. The only truly wrong decision you can make is one based on fear or prejudice. The experts can only offer you their views. The ultimate call must be yours. Wade into the complexity."[7]

Treating depression *is* complex, and medication doesn't take the struggle away. In our experience, both personal and pastoral, medicine simply keeps a person's head above water, enabling him or her to do the hard work of counseling. Sometimes the issues to wade through in therapy are agonizing and specific—abuse, for instance. Other times they are nagging and nebulous: a feeling of never measuring up.

Ultimately, what teens do with the complexity is up to them, not you, not a drug. No antidepressant or therapist can make your teen do, feel, or be anything. They may help a struggler start "getting back to life," however, a simple but profound component in counteracting depression. Treatment gives your adolescent tools to do what he or she needs to do.

While your teen gets treatment, you can focus on the following:

- Talk less, listen more.
- Express love, empathy, and compassion whenever possible.
- Be appropriately affectionate.

Important Facts about Meds

- Studies indicate that a *combination treatment* of medication and counseling works best for most teens with depression.[8]
- Research shows that teens who don't respond to a first antidepressant medication are more likely to get better if they switch to a treatment that includes both medication and therapy.[9]
- Appropriately administered medication won't "make your teen a different person," "turn them into a zombie," or "doom them to a life of taking drugs." On the contrary, it should improve an adolescent's ability to think, engage with life in meaningful ways, and journey toward healing.
- Unfortunately, many well-meaning parents try to play doctor. They may say, "I saw a depression commercial and I think my son needs Cymbalta" or "I read about Paxil online and that seems best for my daughter." Of course it helps to have a basic understanding of a prescribed drug's uses, benefits, and potential side effects. We want you to be discerning, and that involves arming yourself with information, but please leave diagnosis and prescription to trained and knowledgeable medical professionals.
- Getting treatment for your adolescent may be an issue of trust and obedience, not simply "an option." In his book *This Is Your Brain on Joy,* Christian psychologist Dr. Earl Henslin describes this brilliantly: "In almost all cases of a severe depression, we need to use the best, targeted medicines available to get the person out of danger to themselves. There's a point where medicine is simply God's mercy to mankind. Once stabilized, we can look at other alternative therapies that support or perhaps someday will replace medication."[10] For the severely depressed, medication can be God's mercy. Taking it may be a matter of obedience.
- Wherever you stand on the issue of taking psychotropic drugs, judging others will not help. If you believe medicine is a gift from God, arguing defensively with someone who holds a different perspective usually ends rather poorly. The same is true in reverse.
- Although antidepressants are generally safe, all carry a "black box" warning label. In a small percentage of the population, taking psychotropic drugs incites suicidal ideation. For this reason, adolescents should be closely monitored, especially during the initial weeks of treatment.

- Remind your teen that symptoms aren't a sign of personal weakness.
- Encourage your teenager that with time and treatment, they can get better. Patience is important!
- Engage with your adolescent in physical activity of some kind. Exercise is an essential mood improver.
- Help depressed adolescents break large tasks into small chunks. Taking too much on at one time can be exhausting and frustrating.
- Avoid dismissing or minimizing feelings. Don't promise everything will be okay or point out everything that's "right" with life.
- As much as possible, delay making major decisions during seasons of depression.
- Help your adolescent give treatment a fair chance. If a counselor recommends activities between sessions (journaling, exercises, etc.), provide the resources, time, and space to make doing these "assignments" possible.
- Watch out for signs of illicit substance use. Chemical escapes are particularly tempting and dangerous for depressed adolescents.
- Ask teens who talk about death or dying direct questions, including whether they have plans to hurt themselves.
- Never offer to keep conversations about suicidal intentions secret.
- "Pray without ceasing" (1 Thess. 5:17 ESV).

Faith 101

Sadly, a recent nationwide survey revealed that 54 percent of Americans still believe depression is a personal weakness. Despite hundreds of medical studies demonstrating the neurochemical reality of depression, more than half of adults still labor under serious misconceptions about depression. Many Christians assume depressed people just need to trust God more. After reading this chapter, you know that depression powerfully affects—and in many cases debilitates—the body. We can't simply "pray it away."

That said, we cannot ignore that depression is also a spiritual issue. Depression, the physical manifestation of neurochemical chaos, is not a sin, but depression can be connected to bad decisions and toxic thinking in a variety of ways.

Some claim that "thoughts come from your brain as though your brain is generating all aspects of your mental experience." Dr. Caroline Leaf writes,

> People who hold this view are called the *materialists*. They believe that it is the chemicals and neurons that create the mind and that the relationships between your thoughts and what you do can just be ignored.
>
> So essentially, their perspective is that the brain creates what you are doing and what you are thinking. The mind is what the brain does, they believe, and the ramifications are significant. Take, for example, the treatment of depression. In this reductionist view depression is a chemical imbalance problem of a machinelike brain; therefore, the treatment is to add in the missing chemicals [and nothing more].
>
> This view is biblically and scientifically incorrect.[11]

In order to heal, the underlying toxic thinking that sparked, perpetuates, and/or exacerbates depression must be addressed. Depression is the result of blood flow and brain activity; it is also inextricably connected with everyday thinking and beliefs. Being depressed does not make your teenager a bad person any more than having to wear eyeglasses does. Depression can, however, lead to poor choices and the development of unhealthy thinking. Bad decisions and toxic thoughts can also lead to depression.

The spiritual encouragement for this chapter is simple: don't settle for a materialist approach to treatment. Medicine is not enough. Counseling, prayer, and fellowship can be part of the progressive transformation of the mind that God commands in Romans 12:2. Help your adolescent begin this process early. In doing so, you'll equip them for a life of health and hope.

Try It Today

Observe and then write down the food your teens consume, the amount of caffeine they drink, and the number of hours they sleep over the next week. Start today! Ask your adolescents to help in this fact-finding mission if you're unsure what they're eating or whether they're actually sleeping when you think they are. Use any information you gain to determine where changes can be made. Take what goes into your adolescent's body (and your own) seriously! Eating from the rainbow (see chapter 21), establishing healthy sleep habits (see chapter 20), and limiting if not eliminating caffeine will make a huge difference in an adolescent's struggle with depression.

26

What If . . . ?

Jared hadn't felt normal in a long time. He remembered being happy when he was little, but those memories were vague and generic, just a sense that there had been better times. Middle school had changed all that; those years had been marked with ever-increasing worry.

Classes were harder, and he felt anxious about his grades. The kids were meaner, and Jared, who was nicely called a "late bloomer" by adults and cruelly termed lots of unprintable things by other teenagers, had been the subject of some vicious online teasing—not quite cyberbullying, but ugly and hurtful nonetheless.

Now, about to start his freshman year of high school, Jared felt stressed all the time. He hadn't been able to enjoy the summer, even though his parents had done everything they could to make it fun. Even going to a local water park had been worrisome. What if a tube broke open while he was sliding down? What if he got caught in the drain beneath the gigantic wave pool? What if he saw one of the guys from school who hated him for no reason? Jared knew on an intellectual, rational level that these thoughts shouldn't paralyze him with anxiety, but fear gripped him anyway.

At least once a day, something happened, and his breathing became shallow, his heart rate spiked, and his body went on high alert with every muscle tensing, every nerve tingling. He couldn't tell if he wanted to puke, run, scream, or hit something as hard as he could.

Tonight was the fifth night in a row Jared awoke at 2:00 a.m. in a cold sweat. He was sure it had something to do with starting school this morning. *This morning.* How was he going to make it?

Bio 101

Anxiety is one of the most common health concerns experienced by today's adolescents. Depending on the intensity, frequency, and symptoms that characterize it, anxious teens may be described as stressed out, worried, afraid, nervous, freaked out, prone to panic, or throttled by obsession and compulsion. These labels all point to a nearly universal experience for teens: adolescent life is full of uncertainty, and there's always a reason to "flip out."

For many parents, it's difficult to discern between typical stress or worry and the kind of anxiety that needs medical attention. If you're in that position, take a deep breath. (Don't forget, a deep breath really does work to renew brain cells and change your thought processes!) The more anxiety you feel about your son's or daughter's experience, the less able you'll be to see clearly, sort through the facts and fears, and tackle this teenage trial head-on.

Approximately forty million Americans, including 25 percent of the youth population,[1] battle a clinical anxiety disorder, defined by "marked distress and functional impairment in the short-term, [which] can derail the normal developmental trajectory and place youth at risk for a host of poor outcomes over the long term. . . . When left untreated, youth with these conditions are at risk for diminished school performance, compromised family functioning, and increased rates of psychiatric disorder in adulthood."[2]

Using this definition, parents can separate a clinical disorder from relatively normal levels of anxiety. If worry inhibits daily functioning, the development of social skills, and academic advancement, or if fears—like Jared's—are manifesting in physical symptoms, it's time to get help.

Tragically, as is true with depression and other mental health concerns, only a small percentage of sufferers seek treatment. Because adolescents usually aren't proactive in asking for assistance, the numbers are grimmer for this population. We use the word *tragic* to describe this, not to be melodramatic but because anxiety is a highly treatable condition that responds well to a variety of treatments.

Don't dismiss concerns that are impinging on your child's daily life. Assuming "this is just a phase" or hoping "things will get better after . . ." will only delay the important first step of admitting there's a problem. Fearing that the diagnosis of an anxiety disorder condemns your child to a life of mental health struggles or that your teen will have to take medicines that "make him or her a zombie" are unhelpful and untrue suppositions. There's great hope and help available for adolescents with anxiety. If your adolescent has been struggling with anxiety for longer than a couple weeks, be brave; your child needs you to wade into this complexity unafraid and unashamed.

As we've previously noted, the neural remodeling that occurs during adolescence can uncover genetic or chemical vulnerabilities. The teenage brain appears more susceptible to a variety of psychiatric conditions. Knowing this need not increase our worry. Instead, it should inform our awareness and direct our intentions.

In the spirit of these goals, and in order to best confront the anxiety our teenagers face, we must understand a bit about the brain structures that control our experience of fear and worry. Chief among these structures are the left and right basal ganglia. An intricate set of neurological networks, the basal ganglia (BG) play an essential role in the processes of thinking and learning. The BG also help other areas of the brain turn experience and emotion into action.[3]

According to *Change Your Brain, Change Your Life Before 25* author Dr. Jesse Payne, the basal ganglia maintain a healthy body's "idle," integrate feelings and thoughts, make movements smooth by tuning fine motor skills, modulate motivation, and mediate pleasure. When the BG are impaired, either temporarily or for an extended time, the body's "idle" runs too high; hypervigilance, muscle tension, conflict avoidance, and excessive fear of being judged by others result. An adolescent with poor basal ganglia functioning often assumes the worst, "freezes" when nervous, appears shy and timid, engages in self-injurious activities (e.g., biting fingernails or picking skin), and/or complains of headaches and stomachaches. Some teenagers manifest BG problems by exhibiting panic or unhealthy drive, which keeps them from being able to relax or slow down.[4] A variety of anxiety disorders can develop.

In adolescents, *generalized anxiety disorder* (GAD) usually manifests in excessive concern related to family, school, work, extracurricular activities, and social interactions. Those with GAD may be overly anxious about performance, punctuality, or the ability to deal with potential problems.

Social phobia, or *social anxiety disorder*, in teenagers goes beyond normal worries about fitting in. In a battle with this condition, the fear of being judged, rejected, or abandoned, along with an insatiable need to be affirmed, becomes so unbearably weighty that teens may feel physically ill in social situations and lack the skill to "talk themselves down" and "go with the flow." Telling an adolescent fighting this to "just chill" is not only unhelpful, it may in fact increase anxiety, causing a young person to obsess about his or her inability to relax.

Panic disorder is often identified by the dramatic and arresting "attacks" that accompany it. Adolescents experiencing a panic attack may complain of a pounding or racing heart, feeling unable to breathe, tightness in the chest, tingling or numbness in the limbs, excessive sweating, feeling excessively hot or cold, or intense stomach pain. Panic attacks can occur at any point, although many experience them during particularly stressful situations (e.g., a big test at school or participating in a major sporting event) or are awakened by them at night.

Initially identified in soldiers exposed to brutal combat, *post-traumatic stress disorder* is now associated with trauma of many kinds, either experienced or observed. A teenage victim or a witness of physical, sexual, verbal, or emotional abuse may suffer from flashback memories of the trauma. A serious accident, natural disasters, and being threatened physically (e.g., mugging, rape, etc.), can also trigger PTSD. Symptoms associated with PTSD fit into three categories:

- *Re-experiencing the trauma* (through flashbacks, dreams, or frightening thoughts, accompanied by vivid physical sensations)
- *Avoidance symptoms* (staying away from people, places, or things that remind a victim of the trauma; heavy guilt, fear, or depression; memory disturbance; feelings of apathy/numbness)
- *Hyperarousal symptoms* (being easily startled, feeling tense or edgy, angry outbursts/rage, and sleep disorders)

Adolescents—particularly early adolescents—who experience trauma may struggle with problems characteristic of much younger children (e.g., bed-wetting, fear of strangers, excessive clinginess to parents or other "safe" adults). Older adolescents may display disruptive, disrespectful, or destructive behaviors. They may express guilt for not preventing the trauma or the desire to exact revenge against those who have hurt them or those they love.

Obsessive-compulsive disorder (OCD) in adolescents looks very similar to the profile we associate with adults. Sufferers may excessively wash hands to prevent the spread of germs, check and recheck things (e.g., locks, homework answers, or technology) in an effort to self-soothe, or perform tasks in a rigid and ritualistic way because the fear of not doing so is debilitating.

In outlining these forms of anxiety disorder, we hope to empower you with knowledge. For many parents, it's helpful to see in print what their teenager has been doing or expressing for a long time. It may make things more "real," but it also identifies the struggle as something that can be addressed and treated. Once you acknowledge what your teen is facing, you can move toward freedom and wholeness.

Psych 101

If your teenager suffered a serious head injury and doctors told you an area of his or her brain was damaged, I imagine you'd do everything possible to help in the recovery process. Discovering that the neural networks that mediate anxiety in your teen's brain are over- or underactive is no different. Your anxious teenager's brain needs real, tangible help, and you can provide that. Undoubtedly, he or she will also need to make personal decisions to pursue health and continue to do so after the initial healing begins, but as a parent, you are a huge piece in the puzzle. Let's look at some specific ways you can help your teen battle anxiety.

- **Change the statistic.** If only 1 in 3 sufferers pursue help, that means 66 percent get no treatment. Anxiety, like other mental health conditions, is powerfully impacted by lifestyle changes, therapy, medication, or a combination thereof. With treatment, there is great hope for a bright future!
- **You've got to move it.** Intense aerobic exercise combats anxiety in dramatic ways. As Dr. Jesse Payne notes, "When worry or negative thoughts take over, exercise can provide a welcome distraction. Research shows that high-intensity physical activity can even reduce the incidence of panic attacks."[5] If your child is stressing out, activities like going for a run, setting up a punching bag in the garage, or playing a pickup game of basketball can diffuse anxiety. When we recommend this, some parents dismiss the suggestion out of hand: "My kid won't even come out of his room. How am I supposed to get him to exercise?" The answer is, you can't. You cannot control your child any more than you can control the weather. But if you are a person of faith, you know the One who can direct your child's behavior

and motivation. Why not ask God—the blessed controller of all things (see 1 Tim. 6:15)—to help your child get moving? If you move with your teen, the benefits will extend even further.

- **Take what goes in seriously.** The food teens consume matters; the hours they sleep (or don't) and the amount of caffeine they drink do too. Limiting if not eliminating caffeine, eating from the rainbow (see chapter 21), and establishing healthy sleep habits (see chapter 20) will make a huge difference in your adolescent's level of anxiety.

- **Kill your own ANTs, and help your teen do the same.** Dr. Daniel Amen coined this phrase, and coming from Southern California, where hideous, shockingly massive armies of black ants can invade a home at any point, we think it paints a vivid picture. ANTs refer to *automatic negative thoughts*, and they can take numerous forms, from overgeneralizing ("I'll *always* be a loser") to the fortune-telling variety ("I'm going to fail this test and then I'll never get into college") to guilt-beating ANTs ("I should have done this; if I would have done this, I wouldn't be in this stupid situation"). We cannot outline every variety of ANT in this chapter, but for comprehensive help, we refer you to Dr. Amen's excellent books (*Change Your Brain, Change Your Life* is a great place to start). Killing your own ANTs and helping your adolescent do so is a practical way to obey the biblical command to "take every thought captive" (2 Cor. 10:5). Getting serious about killing ANTs reestablishes brain and soul health for you and your adolescent.

- **Mirror healthy reactions to stress.** Your level of worry, fear, and anxiety directly impacts your teenager. If anxiety floods your life or your spouse's, your adolescent may marinate in the same. Learning to control your own anxiety is essential if you want to help your adolescent.

- **Choose to unwind.** I (Jerusha) recently asked a friend what she liked to do. She actually laughed at the question. She couldn't remember the last time she chose to do something just because she liked it. This is a problem, not only because it revealed an undue amount of stress in her life, but also because it's virtually impossible for our teens to learn to relax and unwind if we don't know how to do it ourselves. And I don't mean just flipping on the television. Modeling healthy ways to relax—listening to music, going to a beautiful place, reading a novel, taking a bath or shower—will not only help you process the tensions of the teen years, it will teach your teen as well.

Faith 101

There are over three hundred references to fear in the Bible, which amounts to almost one per day. If you ask us, this is no random coincidence. Life overflows with things that trigger anxiety and worry. Over this reality we have very little control. Whether we live in panic or peace, however, is largely our choice.

In Philippians 4:6–8, the apostle Paul exhorts, "Don't worry about anything; instead, pray about everything. Tell God what you need, and thank him for all he has done. Then you will experience God's peace, which exceeds anything we can understand. His peace will guard your hearts and minds as you live in Christ Jesus" (NLT).

There are several important elements to this passage, but an oft-overlooked one involves the connection between letting go of worry and giving thanks for what God has done. On the surface, it's certainly a nice idea: don't worry; instead, thank God; then you get peace. That sounds great, but is it really practical?

Yes! Brain research clearly shows that anxiety and gratitude are mutually exclusive neural pathways. Physiologically, you *cannot* be anxious and grateful at the same time. In his book *What Happy People Know*, Dr. Dan Baker writes, "During active appreciation, the threatening messages from your amygdala (fear center of the brain) and the anxious instincts of your brainstem are cut off, suddenly and surely, from access to your brain's neocortex, where they can fester, replicate themselves, and turn your stream of thoughts into a cold river of dread. It is a fact of neurology that the brain cannot be in a state of appreciation and a state of fear at the same time. The two states may alternate, but are mutually exclusive."[6]

Don't allow this life-changing truth to pass you by: choosing to give thanks instead of giving in to fear changes more than just your momentary thoughts. It literally changes the structure of your brain! When confronted with worry, you have a choice; so does your teenager. Share this important information with your adolescent.

Also, keep in mind that giving thanks doesn't have to be directly related to your present situation. Right after receiving a cancer diagnosis isn't usually the best time to try thanking God for the way sickness will help you and those around you grow. Instead, try thanking God for something little (salted caramel mochas come to mind). It may sound like a simple step, but it's actually an incredibly powerful one.

Reading the stories of Jesus's life, we see that thanksgiving *always* preceded his miracles.[7] The same is true of the everyday miracle of you and me and our adolescents being released from worry and fear. Our brains literally cannot be grateful and anxious at the same moment. This knowledge is God-given power to be transformed by the renewing of your mind.

Try It Today

Have you ever asked your teenager what he or she fears most? Find a time to ask, and listen carefully. Simply giving your child the space to name his or her fears can be incredibly helpful. Many parents have given up asking their teen straightforward questions. If he or she answers, "I don't know," "Everything," or with an angry, "Why?" don't settle. Another time may be better, but pushing a bit may also be in order.

If you do get a clear response, offer to pray for your child right then. Go back later—perhaps in a couple days—and tell them you'll keep praying. Ask a while later how things are going and whether there's anything specific you can do to help. Again, this may seem simple, but it's actually quite profound. You don't need to be a therapist in order to listen and pray.

Clinicians used to warn parents not to address anxiety for fear of reinforcing it. Current research reveals, however, that gently helping people process the irrationality of their fears can equip them to talk back to their thoughts and move forward. Whatever the concern, let your teen know that he or she can always trust you to empathetically listen, without fear of being rejected or judged.

You can also show understanding by reminding adolescents that anxiety is connected to a highly active brain, a powerful mind which can serve them well, now and in the future. Remind them (and remember yourself) not to give up hope. Overcoming anxiety is not an overnight process, but it is possible.

Appendix A

The Truth about Substance Abuse

Note: This section provides basic information about substance abuse, but it does not outline intervention strategies or enumerate specific treatment approaches. For parents facing crisis situations, we recommend seeking professional help from a pastor, youth worker, or counselor.

For many, adolescence follows a "best of times, worst of times" pattern. Undoubtedly, the teen years are full of stress and strain. Ironically, people also expect high school and college students to have the "time of their lives," to "live it up" before settling into adult life. When you add powerful mood-altering substances like alcohol and drugs to the mix, all of this easily spells disaster.

Because adolescent brains don't naturally tend toward wise decision-making and forethought, teens often struggle to implement healthy coping strategies during stressful times. Those who haven't seen healthy coping skills modeled at home may turn to alcohol, drugs, or other destructive behaviors to deal with problems.

Whether adolescents use a substance because they think that's the only way to have fun or because they are reeling from deep, emotional wounds, it's a myth that a little teenage "partying" never hurt anyone. Let's look at some other prevalent myths about substance abuse, dispelling each in turn.

Myth: Parents can't do much about teenage experimentation.

Truth: Teens report that their parents' attitude toward illicit substance use is a primary determining factor in their own habits. Adolescents are watching; they are listening. What you say, what you model, and how you respond to cultural messages (everything from ads during the Super Bowl to lyrics in music) *matters*. Also, the most basic steps often prove to be highly effective, so don't dismiss obvious solutions. Not stockpiling liquor, thereby making it more accessible, is important. Monitoring where and with whom teens hang out is crucial. Of course your teen may choose to deceive you, but teenage deception is often so poorly planned that it can be exposed with a little prodding; we can thank God for their poor executive functioning here!

Myth: Substance experimentation is no big deal; it's a rite of passage.

Truth: Because teenagers are prone to extremes, adolescent drinking and marijuana use are major concerns. Statistics show that teens don't "party" moderately. The Centers for Disease Control reports that 90 percent of underage alcohol consumption occurs in the form of binge drinking, defined as ingesting large amounts of alcohol in short amounts of time. The vast majority of teenagers drink with the sole purpose of getting drunk. Likewise, they smoke weed with one goal in mind: *getting high* (i.e., plastered, wasted, or any number of synonyms). Why is this so problematic? From a brain development perspective, binge drinking kills neural cells and their connections, especially in regions that control attention and memory.[1] Despite what some media outlets, and many teens, would like you to believe, research also repeatedly illustrates that marijuana use alters the brain, especially during adolescence. According to Dr. Jesse Payne, "Marijuana damages the brain, particularly the memory and learning centers. . . . More recent research has also found that the earlier people start using marijuana, the worse the brain damage is."[2] The teenage brain, already under heavy construction, suffers profoundly from substance abuse. In addition, research indicates that those who drink before age fifteen are *five times more likely* to develop alcohol dependence later in life.[3] As we mentioned earlier, teenagers are particularly vulnerable to addiction because of their highly active reward system and sensitivity to chemicals that act on dopaminergic circuitry. Becoming addicted is a genuine risk for *any* teen who uses substances. Don't risk the future on a "teens will be teens, it'll be okay" wager.

Myth: It's hard to tell when a teen is abusing substances.

Truth: More often than not, the warning signs are clear. Sadly, many parents are too self-involved or stressed out to notice. If your son or daughter consistently breaks curfew, comes home with a fresh piece of gum or wearing different clothes, acts spacey or disconnected, has bloodshot eyes, or gains or loses weight over a short period of time, don't be foolish; address these things head-on. Because symptoms of depression and anxiety can accompany substance abuse, be on the lookout for changes in interests or activities (by choice or being kicked off a team or fired from a job), outbursts of anger (verbal or physical), restlessness or tremors, unexplained absenteeism from school, and digital messages that provoke exaggerated anxiety or ecstasy.

Myth: If I catch my teen experimenting with substances, it's best to crack down hard.

Truth: Firm consequences with lots of empathy produce the greatest results with teenagers. In no way should drug or alcohol abuse be tolerated. You can remain empathetic and caring as you address the situation, however. Try to remember what it was like to be a teenager. In a word: *hard.* It's easy to be confused when the world around you says partying is what adolescent life is all about. If you can remain calm, you'll be able to engage in dialogue. Your son or daughter may not be able to answer "Why?" or "What were you thinking?" but if you ask open-ended questions (e.g., "What did you hope to get out of this?" and "What did you actually get out of this?"), you may uncover some important dynamics. Lecturing, nagging, and threatening are not effective strategies. Don't allow your pride—"How could you do this to us?" or "What did we do wrong?"—to destroy your opportunity to help. Fight fiercely *for* your adolescent, not against him or her.

Appendix B

The Truth about Self-Injury

Note: This section provides basic information about self-injury, but it does not outline intervention strategies or enumerate specific treatment approaches. For parents facing crisis situations, we recommend seeking professional help from a pastor, youth worker, or counselor.

Each and every day, millions of teenagers cut, burn, hit, bite, scratch, or otherwise hurt themselves. Parents fight terror, confusion, and desperation after discovering their child willfully injures him- or herself. According to international research, as many as 24 percent of adolescents have experimented with nonsuicidal self-injury in the past year. Studies also show that between 6 and 8 percent of young adults suffer from "current, chronic self-injury."[1] In order to face this issue with wisdom and compassion, we must debunk myths surrounding self-harm and replace them with solid, hopeful truth.

Myth: Self-harm is a teenage phase that people outgrow.

Truth: While most self-harmers report they started during early adolescence, the frequency and intensity of self-injury actually peaks

in the tumultuous twenties. If you discover self-harming behavior, do *not* ignore it or wait for it to pass. Early intervention and treatment can prevent self-harm from becoming a lifetime struggle.

Myth: Self-injury makes no sense.

Truth: Because self-harm stimulates the release of incredibly powerful and calming neurochemicals, it makes tragic physiological "sense" to those who experience it. When a person self-injures, naturally occurring opiates that are *eight to ten times stronger than morphine* flood the brain, giving self-harmers a potent sense of relief and release. While these are temporary physical sensations, people who self-injure may return to the behavior again and again in an effort to replicate the experience.

Myth: People self-injure because they are violent, like pain, or are mentally ill.

Truth: For the vast majority of sufferers, self-harm is a coping mechanism, not an expression of psychosis. Listen to the reasons self-injurers give for their behavior:

- I feel like I don't have control of anything else.
- It's the only way I can express my pain without hurting people I care for.
- I'm a failed human being.
- To release anger or frustration.
- To punish myself.
- To get relief, to feel something.[2]

Self-harmers aren't crazy; they're hurting and don't know where else to turn. While it's true that some self-injurers struggle with mental health issues or are violent, those who surround self-wounding teenagers must not make assumptions, but rather seek to understand *why* they turn to self-harm. This is the first step toward healing.

Myth: If we can stop the behavior and remove everything dangerous, things will get better.

Truth: Self-harm is an indicator, somewhat like steam escaping from a boiling pot. In order to overcome it, you must address what's making the pot boil. Never forget: people turn to self-injury as a means of relieving emotional pain. Of course it's important to disrupt patterns and remove items that can be used to self-harm. For genuine healing to take place, however, underlying issues must be tackled. Teenage impulses to self-harm start with feelings all of us can understand: rejection, fear, anger, grief, betrayal, sorrow, neglect, disappointment, loss of control. Some people develop healthy ways of addressing emotional turmoil; others overeat, drink, take drugs, or drown themselves in work. You have a coping mechanism; it may or may not be healthy. If we can embrace that teenagers who self-harm are battling feelings we understand, we can set aside misperceptions, deal with the root issues, and help teens develop healthier coping mechanisms. **Important note:** Because high incidences of self-injury occur among those who have been abused and/or struggle with body image issues, it's wise to investigate these possibilities.

Myth: Self-injury is a failed suicide attempt.

Truth: Self-injury is more often a survival technique than an exit strategy. Self-inflicted violence is often a last-ditch effort to grab hold of life, however painful that life may be, rather than a suicide attempt. Indeed, a common refrain among self-harmers is, "I felt I'd die if I didn't cut." Sufferers may entertain thoughts about suicide, and some habitual self-injurers do try to take their own lives, but most self-harmers don't want to kill themselves, but rather something *in* themselves—pain, fear, anger, feelings of worthlessness, and so on.

Myth: The best method for treating self-inflicted violence is medication.

Truth: Self-harm is all at once physical, psychological, and spiritual; a holistic approach is the most effective. Medical and therapeutic treatment is essential, but don't neglect the spiritual dimension of self-injury. Shame plays a major role in self-inflicted violence. Self-harmers often experience shame as a pervasive sense that there is something deeply and irreparably wrong with them. Shame attacks the core of our very selves; it focuses not on a bad thing we've done or said but on who we are. The only antidote is grace, the free gift of God that overcomes shame. In the life-giving words of Lewis Smedes, "We experience grace as power: it provides a spiritual energy to shed the heaviness of shame and, in the lightness of grace, move toward the true self God means us to be."[3] Many self-harmers try to "punish" themselves or "pay for mistakes," but it is by Jesus's wounds that we are healed (see Isa. 53:5). God's grace empowers us to courageously confront what's inside and around us. It then allows us to embrace the Good News that we can be accepted, fully and irreversibly, no matter what our past or present, no matter what unacceptable things we might do in the future. Self-harmers need to hear this.

Recommended resource: Jerusha Clark with Dr. Earl Henslin, *Inside a Cutter's Mind: Understanding and Helping Those Who Self-Injure* (Colorado Springs: NavPress, 2007).

Appendix C

The Truth about Suicide

Suicide is the third leading cause of adolescent death. According to the Centers for Disease Control, however, "deaths from youth suicide are only part of the problem. More young people survive suicide attempts than actually die." Indeed, a nationwide survey of United States high school students found approximately one in every six midadolescents (16 percent) reported seriously considering suicide, 13 percent acknowledged creating a plan, and 8 percent attempted suicide in the twelve months preceding the survey.[1]

Imagine your son or daughter standing with five close friends. Statistics indicate that one of them will seriously contemplate taking his or her own life this year. We cannot ignore these statistics with a "not my child" attitude. A shameful stigma surrounding victims of suicide and their families persists today, shrouding this topic in misperceptions, but suicidal ideation, attempts, and deaths can be prevented when we debunk the myths.

Myth: Only teens with mental health issues are at risk for suicide.

Truth: A wide variety of physical, emotional, and situational factors place adolescents at risk. Teenagers suffering from depression or other mood disorders may battle suicidal thoughts, but other risk factors include stressful life events or losses (e.g., divorce or the death of a close family member or friend), substance use (because alcohol and drugs change the already-delicate chemical balance of the teenage brain), easy access to lethal methods (particularly firearms), exposure to the suicidal behavior of others (usually highlighted by the media), and trouble with the law. Relationship struggles—anger at oppressive authority figures, a romantic breakup, bullying, social isolation—also play a role in the suicidal intentions of adolescents. Statistics are clear: it's not just teenagers with extended histories of mental illness who attempt suicide. In fact, of those who take their own lives, only 15 percent had been diagnosed with a mental health issue.[2] Many people who commit suicide seemed "completely normal" to those around them. Pursue medical and emotional evaluation for a teen if significant changes in mood, circumstances, and/or behavior last longer than two weeks.

Important notes: If a teenager is prescribed psychotropic medication, it can take several weeks for the drug to reach therapeutic levels. Teens should be carefully monitored during this time because antidepressant medications can cause serious, adverse effects in some people. Also, people who have devised a plan for taking their own lives sometimes seem to "get better" right before committing suicide. Cautiously observe and speak openly with teens at risk.

Myth: A lot more teenagers talk about suicide than actually do it.

Truth: Healthy adolescents don't talk about ending their lives. If your son or daughter mentions wanting to die or threatens to take his or her life, act immediately. Statistics reveal that 80 percent of people who commit suicide talked about it before attempting.[3] In verbalizing their thoughts about suicide, teenagers give us the opportunity to help—now. Have your teen's medical doctor evaluate his or her overall health; some problems, such as poor thyroid functioning or anemia, for instance, can cause major mood disruption. Make an appointment with a professional counselor as well, preferably one who has a history of successful work with teenagers. Churches and schools often provide parents with lists of vetted clinicians. Do not wait on these things; your immediate attention is required.

Myth: Talking about suicide with hurting teens "puts the idea in their heads."

Truth: Research clearly shows that teens who have an outlet for their thoughts and feelings are *far less* likely to commit suicide. Directly ask teenagers who have hinted at suicide or wanting to die if they've entertained a plan. This shows that you care and creates a bridge for conversation. "Most teens interviewed after making a suicide attempt say that they did it because they were trying to escape from a situation that seemed impossible to deal with or to get relief from really bad thoughts or feelings."[4] Reaching out openly and listening attentively helps teens see there are other options for facing difficult emotions, circumstances, and thoughts. Also keep in mind that healthy teens benefit from open dialogue about suicide as well. Mentioning to adolescents that people sometimes feel desperate during the tumultuous teenage years normalizes roller-coaster emotions that may otherwise frighten teens and prevent them from speaking out. A teen who knows "crazy" thoughts may occur but don't automatically mean he or she is "mental," needs to be hospitalized, or is destined to commit suicide is much better prepared for potentially unnerving emotional experiences. These teens may become allies to wounded friends as well. Don't ignore this issue; talk with teenagers—your own and their peers—and let them know you are a safe person to whom they can turn in times of trouble.

Important note: Never promise your teen or any other teenager that you will keep secret a confession of suicidal ideation.

Myth: Teens who really want to die will find a way.

Truth: Any small disruption in a suicide plan gives an adolescent another "out. " Every professional counselor can tell stories of kids who *didn't* succeed in taking their own lives simply because they couldn't use a preferred method (usually a gun) that had been removed from the house or locked away. No teenager should have easy access to firearms, by far the number one choice for suicidal adolescents, or poisons, the third most common method. If teens cannot locate these items or have to work "too hard" to find or utilize them, it may provide just enough time for them to be discovered or to reconsider. Don't make it easy for hurting teens to hurt themselves.

Recommended resource: The National Suicide Prevention Lifeline, 1–800–273–TALK (8255), provides a twenty-four-hour, toll-free hotline. Callers are routed to a crisis center to receive immediate counseling and local mental health care referrals. The Lifeline supports people who call for themselves or someone they care about. More resources, including live chat services, are also available at http://www.suicidepreventionlifeline.org/.

Acknowledgments

Together, Jeramy and Jerusha would like to thank . . .

Our Lord and Savior, who wrote his truth into our neurons, hearts, and souls. We love you!

Spencer and Rona Clark, for praying fervently, modeling a life of faith, and staying engaged in our lives—even when Dave and I were wreaking havoc during our teen years. Your investment in and sacrifices for us have shaped our lives in every way.

J. A. C. and LeAnn Redford. You raised four teenagers; that is a marvelous feat in and of itself! Even better, your children became adults who love spending time with you and each other. What wonderful evidence of God's grace and your commitment to him!

Dennis Keating (Pastor Spagootch). Your unwavering support and involvement not only in Jeramy's ministry but also in our entire family is a blessing beyond measure.

Kathy Moratto, for faithfully ministering to our family and church, for cherished friendship, and for merciless teasing.

Tom and Penny Anderson, whose faithful love upholds and blesses us.

Todd Hoyt, for your A+ friendship and crazy linebacker skills on the basketball court (A-).

Jaisen and Lynette Fuson. Your experience in raising teens and your prompting to explore these topics were huge catalysts in the formation of this book. We are grateful to and for you!

Dr. Jay Giedd, who so graciously shared his wisdom (and lemon bars!) with us.

Dr. Daniel Amen, without whom neither of us would understand neuroscience in the slightest. Your personal and professional investment in us has been a tremendous gift from God.

Dr. Earl Henslin, for both walking with us through the raging storms of life and introducing us to an integrated approach to healing the body, mind, and spirit.

Joshua Becker, whose story adds a great deal to this book.

Rebekah Guzman, our beloved editor and friend. There is no one with whom we'd rather work!

Wendy Wetzel, for her incredibly keen editing skills.

Jeramy would like to thank . . .

Roger Lino. Somehow we made it out of our teen years in Rodeo alive. You're a great friend and confidante. Bunk dope!

Brian Aaby. From the day we met, your zeal for God and passion for ministry have spurred me on to greater things for the kingdom.

Dave Hall (Samurai Dave), who encouraged me in the writing and editing process on long flights to Beijing.

The Wednesday Night Guys' Group: Phil Yphantides, Scott Smith, Marcel deNeve, Michael deNeve, and Mitchell deNeve, for faithfully supporting me through the highest highs and lowest lows of my life.

Jerusha would like to thank . . .

Cameron Germann, with whom I never have enough time. Our conversations—whether while hiking or via Skype—always bless and stretch me.

Megan Donovan, for reading chapters and commenting with grace and thoughtfulness. You are a treasure, dear friend.

Jenn Witmondt, who enthusiastically dialogued with me about these issues (on countless occasions!) and whose priceless friendship sharpens me.

Lorraine Pintus. I admire you so much, dear friend. Thank you for spurring me on as a writer and woman of God.

Mary Lockrem, whose invitation to teach a Bible study class on teenage girls first stirred these ideas in me. Still wish I could hire you as my publicist, my friend!

Notes

Introduction

1. Interview with Dr. Jay Giedd, "Inside the Teenage Brain: The Teen Brain Is a Work in Progress," *Frontline*, PBS, produced by Sarah Spinks, 2002, accessed September 23, 2015, at http://www.pbs.org/wgbh/pages/frontline/shows/teenbrain/interviews/giedd.html.

Chapter 1 You Don't Understand

1. Paul David Tripp, *Age of Opportunity: A Biblical Guide to Parenting Teens*, 2d ed. (Phillipsburg, NJ: P & R Publishing, 2001), 30. Thoughts in the following paragraphs were developed in response to his writing.
2. Michael Bradley, *Yes, Your Teen Is Crazy!* (Gig Harbor, WA: Harbor Press, 2002), 112.
3. Adele Faber and Elaine Mazlish, *How to Talk So Teens Will Listen and Listen So Teens Will Talk* (New York: Harper Collins, 2005), xvi.

Chapter 2 Leave Me Alone

1. Sheryl Feinstein, *Inside the Teenage Brain: Parenting a Work in Progress* (Lanham, MD: Rowman & Littlefield Education, 2009), 8.
2. Jim Burns, *Teenology* (Grand Rapids: Bethany House, 2011), 19.
3. See Daniel Siegel, *Brainstorm: The Power and Purpose of the Teenage Brain* (New York: Jeremy P. Tarcher/Penguin, 2013), 33–34.
4. Laurence Steinberg, *Age of Opportunity: Lessons from the New Science of Adolescence* (New York: Houghton Mifflin Harcourt, 2014), 133.
5. Bradley, *Yes, Your Teen Is Crazy!*, 201.
6. John Santrock, *Adolescence*, 8th ed. (New York: McGraw-Hill, 2001), 28–29.
7. Steinberg, *Age of Opportunity*, 135.

Chapter 3 But *Why?*

1. Mark Oestreicher, *A Parent's Guide to Understanding Teenage Brains* (Loveland, CO: Simply Youth Ministry/Group, 2012), 37.
2. Ibid., 39.
3. Adapted from James Marcia, "Life Transitions and Stress in the Context of Psychosocial Development," in T. W. Miller (ed.), *Handbook of Stressful Transitions Across the Lifespan* (New York: Springer, 2010), 22.
4. Ric Garland, quoted in ibid., 22.
5. Oestreicher, *A Parent's Guide to Understanding Teenage Brains*, 45.

Chapter 4 I'm So Bored

1. For an excellent review of the scientific evidence and research in this field, see Dr. Adriana Galván, "The Teenage Brain: Sensitivity to Rewards," *Current Directions in Psychological Science* 22, no. 2 (April 2013): 88–93. Full text available online at http://cdp.sagepub.com/content/22/2/88.full#cited-by. Accessed February 18, 2015.
2. Dopamine serves other important purposes in the body, but for the purposes of this book, we will focus on its role in the reward system.
3. Siegel, *Brainstorm*, 67.
4. Daniel Siegel, "Dopamine and Teenage Logic," *The Atlantic*, January 24, 2014, http://www.theatlantic.com/health/archive/2014/01/dopamine-and-teenage-logic/282895/. Accessed February 18, 2015.
5. Andrea Solarz, "Developing Adolescents: A Reference for Professionals," American Psychological Association pamphlet, 2002. Accessed October 19, 2015, at http://www.apa.org/pi/families/resources/develop.pdf, 3.
6. Feinstein, 12.

Chapter 5 That Could Be *Epic*

1. See Lee Bowman, "New Research Shows Stark Differences in Teen Brains: An Interview with Dr. Ruben Gur," Scripps Howard News Service, May 11, 2004, accessed February 10, 2015, at http://www.teach-the-brain.org/forums/archive/index.php/t-48.html, and Ruben C. Gur, "Brain Maturation and the Execution of Juveniles," *The Pennsylvania Gazette*, January/February 2005, accessed February 10, 2015, at http://www.upenn.edu/gazette/0105/0105expert.html.
2. Siegel, *Brainstorm*, 69.
3. Ibid., 66.
4. Steinberg, 92.
5. Kim Fischer, "Study Finds Presence of Peers Heightens Teen Sensitivity to Rewards of a Risk," Temple University News Center, April 4, 2011, accessed February 10, 2015, at http://news.temple.edu/news/study-finds-presence-peers-heightens-teen-sensitivity-rewards-risk.
6. Steinberg, 76–77.
7. See Bradley, 212.
8. Steinberg, 77.
9. Dallas Willard, *The Divine Conspiracy* (New York: HarperCollins, 1998), 12.

10. Iraneus of Lyons's quote, "*Gloria enim Dei vivens homo*," is found in his *A Treatise against the Heresies* (originally published in Latin as *Adversus Haereses*). Full Latin text available at https://archive.org/stream/adversushaerese00irengoog#page/n6/mode/2up, accessed October 19, 2015. See book 3, chapter 20.

Chapter 6 But Nothing Happened

1. See Steinberg, 15.

2. If you're looking for a solid resource on discipline techniques for teens, we recommend Jim Fay and Cline Foster, *Parenting Teens with Love and Logic* (Colorado Springs: NavPress, 2006), which helps parents establish firm boundaries with empathy.

3. Quoted in Shannon Brownlee, "Inside the Teen Brain" *U.S. News & World Report*, August 9, 1999, 48. Available online at http://sitemaker.umich.edu/sw633.articles/files/usnews1999.pdf. Accessed February 24, 2015.

4. See M. Linkletter, K. Gordon and J. Dooley, "The Choking Game and YouTube: A Dangerous Combination," *Clinical Pediatrics* 49, no. 3 (March 2010): 274–279, accessed February 24, 2015, at http://cpj.sagepub.com/content/49/3/274; A. Wang, A. Cohen, and S. Robinson, "Neurological Injuries from Car Surfing," Journal of Neurosurgery: Pediatrics 4 (November 2009): 408–13, accessed February 24, 2015, at http://thejns.org/doi/pdf/10.3171/2009.4.PEDS08474 and Michael Strangelove, "Vodka in Your Eye: Attempts to Dismiss 'Vodka Eye Shots' as a 'Faux Trend' Misunderstand How the Copycat Dynamic of YouTube Works," *The Mark*, June 10, 2010. Accessed February 24, 2015, at http://pioneers.themarknews.com/articles/1678-vodka-in-your-eye/#.VOzxckJvmGM.

5. See Jesse Payne, *Change Your Brain, Change Your Life Before 25* (Ontario, Canada: Harlequin, 2014), 95.

6. Ibid., 93.

7. Adapted from Bradley, *Yes, Your Teen Is Crazy!*, 236.

Chapter 7 What Do You Want Me to Say?

1. Angela Oswalt, MSW, ed., and C. E. Zupanick, PsyD, "The Maturing Adolescent Brain," accessed October 19, 2015, at http://gracepointwellness.org/1310-child-development-theory-adolescence-12-24/article/41158-the-maturing-adolescent-brain.

2. Mary Bauer, "Language Development in Teenagers," LiveStrong, February 17, 2015, http://www.livestrong.com/article/226031-language-development-in-teenagers/. Accessed March 3, 2015.

3. P. Thompson, J. Giedd, R. Woods, et al., "Growth Patterns in the Developing Brain Detected by Using Continuum Mechanical Tensor Maps," *Nature* 404 (March 9, 2000): 190–93.

4. Feinstein, 67.

5. Aislinn Laing, "Teenagers 'Only Use 800 Different Words a Day,'" *The Telegraph*, January 11, 2010, http://www.telegraph.co.uk/education/educationnews/6960745/Teenagers-only-use-800-different-words-a-day.html. Accessed March 3, 2015.

6. Fay and Cline, 212.

7. Dr. Michael Bradley gives excellent advice regarding this in his book, *Yes, Your Teen is Crazy*, page 174.

8. Bradley, 178.

Chapter 8 Why Are You Freaking Out?

1. Payne, 28.
2. Andrew Coleman, *A Dictionary of Psychology*, 3rd ed. (London: Oxford University Press, 2008), 248.
3. See Fay and Cline, 66–67.

Chapter 9 Why Are You Looking at Me Like That?

1. Based on the research of Dr. Albert Mehrabian, professor emeritus of UCLA's School of Psychology, recorded in his books *Silent Messages: Implicit Communication of Emotions and Attitudes* (Belmont, CA: Wadsworth Publishing, 1981), 76, and *Nonverbal Communication* (New Brunswick, NJ: Aldine Transaction, 2007), 182.
2. Especially portions of the temporal lobes and limbic system.
3. Yurgelun-Todd and her colleagues' first studies were performed at Harvard's McLean Hospital Cognitive Neuroimaging and Neuropsychology Laboratory and reported in "Functional Magnetic Resonance Imaging of Facial Affect Recognition in Children and Adolescents," *Journal of the American Academy of Child & Adolescent Psychiatry* 38, no. 2 (1999): 195–99, accessed October 20, 2015, at http://www.jaacap.com/article/S0890-8567(09)62897-5/abstract. Further studies were recorded in "Social Anxiety Predicts Amygdala Activation in Adolescents Viewing Fearful Faces," *Developmental Neuroscience: Neuroreport* 16, no. 15 (October 2005): 1671–75; "Fear-Related Activity in the Prefrontal Cortex Increases with Age During Adolescence: A Preliminary fMRI Study," *Neuroscience Letters* 406, no. 3 (November 2006): 194–99; and "Cerebral Correlates of Amygdala Responses During Non-Conscious Perception of Facial Affect in Adolescent and Pre-Adolescent Children," *Cognitive Neuroscience* 1, no. 1 (March 2010): 33–43.
4. Dr. Yolanda van Beek and Dr. Judith Semon Dubas, "Age and Gender Differences in Decoding Basic and Non-Basic Facial Expressions in Late Childhood and Early Adolescence," *Journal of Nonverbal Behavior* 32 no. 1 (March 2008): 37–52.
5. Adolescents displayed increased activity in the limbic system when attempting to interpret facial expressions they were shown, particularly in the amygdala, a small almond-shaped region in the medial and temporal lobes that processes memory and emotions, particularly in the case of strong emotions like fear.
6. See Dr. Catherine Sebastian et. al "The Social Brain in Adolescence: Evidence from Functional Magnetic Resonance Imaging and Behavioural Studies," *Neuroscience Biobehavioral Reviews* (2010), doi: 10.1016/j.neubiorev.2010.10.011.
7. Jennifer Wells, "The Brain: For Adolescents, a Scary Path to Full Development," *The Toronto Star*, June 24, 2010, http://www.thestar.com/life/health_wellness/2010/07/24/the_brain_for_adolescents_a_scary_path_to_full_development.html. Accessed June 25, 2014.
8. Between 370 and 390, depending on translation.
9. According to research conducted at Echnische Universität in Munich, Germany. See Andreas Hennenlotter et. al, "The Link between Facial Feedback and Neural Activity within Central Circuitries of Emotion—New Insights from Botulinum Toxin–Induced Denervation of Frown Muscles," *Cerebral Cortex* 19, no. 3 (2009): 537–42; doi: 10.1093/cercor/bhn104.
10. Quote attributed to Thich Nhat Hanh in Ron Gutman, *Smile: The Astonishing Powers of a Simple Act*, TED talk transcript (New York: Ted Conferences LLC, 2011).

11. "The Therapeutic Effects of Smiling," in *An Empirical Reflection on the Smile*, ed. Millicent H. Abel (Wales, UK: Edwin Mellen Press, 2002), 218–55.

12. Alicia A. Grandey et. al, "Is Service with a Smile Enough? Authenticity of Positive Displays during Service Encounters," *Organizational Behavior and Human Decision Processes* 96, no. 1 (January 2005): 38–55.

13. "One Smile Can Make You Feel [Like] a Million Dollars," *The Scotsman*, March 4, 2005, accessed June 25, 2014 at http://www.scotsman.com/news/health/one-smile-can-make-you-feel-a-million-dollars-1-738272.

Chapter 10 Aren't You Sorry?

1. R. Cunnington Molenberghs and J. Mattingley, "Brain Regions with Mirror Properties: A Meta-Analysis of 125 Human fMRI Studies," *Neuroscience and Biobehavioral Reviews* 36, no. 1 (January 2012):341–49, accessed October 19, 2015, at http://www.ncbi.nlm.nih.gov/pubmed/21782846.

2. R. Mukamel, A. Ekstrom, J. Kaplan, M. Iacoboni, and I. Fried, "Single-Neuron Responses in Humans during Execution and Observation of Actions," *Current Biology* 20, no. 8 (April 2010): 750–56, http://www.sciencedirect.com/science/article/pii/S0960982210002332. Accessed March 9, 2015.

3. See V. Gallese, "The 'Shared Manifold' Hypothesis: From Mirror Neurons to Empathy," *Journal of Consciousness Studies* 8, no. 5–7 (May 2001): 33–50, http://www.ingentaconnect.com/content/imp/jcs/2001/00000008/F0030005/1208. Accessed March 9, 2015.

4. Dr. Caroline Leaf, *Switch On Your Brain: The Key to Peak Happiness, Thinking, and Health* (Grand Rapids: Baker, 2013), 112.

5. See Giacomo Rizzolatti and Leonardo Fogassi, "The Mirror Mechanism: Recent Findings and Perspectives," *Philosophical Transactions B* of the Royal Society of London, vol. 369, no. 1644 (April 28, 2014):1–12, accessed October 20, 2015, at http://rstb.royalsocietypublishing.org/content/royptb/369/1644/20130420.full.pdf.

6. Adapted in part from Jim Burns, *Teenology*, 106.

7. Bradley, 131–32.

8. For a fascinating read on this, try neurosurgeon David I. Levy's book *Gray Matter* (Carol Stream, IL: Tyndale, 2011).

9. Ellen Michaud, "Discover the Power of Forgiveness," *Prevention*, January 1999, 110–15.

10. We recommend Lewis Smedes's books on forgiveness, *Forgive and Forget: Healing the Hurts We Don't Deserve* (New York: HarperSanFrancisco, 1997) and *The Art of Forgiving: When You Need to Forgive and Don't Know How* (New York: Ballantine Books, 1996). Jerusha also included a chapter on forgiveness in her book, *Every Thought Captive: Battling the Toxic Beliefs that Separate Us from the Life We Crave* (Colorado Springs: NavPress, 2006).

Chapter 11 What's Wrong with My Friends?

1. We're speaking generally here, assuming that a teen's home is a safe place. Development in abusive situations often follows a different course.

2. Steinberg, 95.

3. Thanks to Arlene Pellicane and Gary Chapman for the ideas in this paragraph.

4. Steinberg, 100.

5. Kevin Leman, *Have a New Teenager by Friday* (Grand Rapids: Revell, 2011), 96.

Chapter 12 It's Not Like We're Getting Married

1. Drs. Beverly and Thomas Alan Rodgers, *The Singlehood Phenomenon* (Colorado Springs: NavPress, 2006), 121–22.

2. Feinstein, 27.

3. Burns, 89–90.

4. Thoughts for this section adapted in part from Thomas Umstattd Jr.'s blog post, "Why Courtship Is Fundamentally Flawed," at ThomasUmstattd.com, August 12, 2014, accessed March 12, 2015, at http://www.thomasumstattd.com/2014/08/courtship-fundamentally-flawed/. Accessed March 12, 2015.

5. Timothy Keller, *The Meaning of Marriage* (New York: Riverhead Books, 2011), 44.

6. Adapted from Sally Lloyd-Jones, *The Jesus Storybook Bible* (Grand Rapids: Zonderkidz, 2007), 200.

Chapter 13 This Is Sooooo Awkward

1. Burns, 82.

2. In this section we will focus narrowly on oxytocin. Male and female sex hormones will be discussed in chapters 22 and 23.

3. H. Lee, A. Macbeth, J. Pagani, and W. Scott Young III, "Oxytocin: The Great Facilitator of Life," *Progress in Neurobiology* 88, no. 2 (June 2009): 127–51. Accessed October 19, 2015, at http://www.sciencedirect.com/science/article/pii/S030100820900046X.

4. Siegel, *Brainstorm*, 239.

5. Jerry Large, "Shedding Light on the Teen Brain," *The Seattle Times*, June 8, 2009. Accessed October 19, 2015, at http://seattletimes.com/html/jerrylarge/2009312466_jdl08.html.

6. See Steinberg, 47.

7. Jennifer Aubrey, "Sex and Punishment: An Examination of Sexual Consequences and the Sexual Double Standard in Teen Programming," *Sex Roles* 50 (7–8): 505–514, doi:10.1023/B:SERS.0000023070.87195.07.

8. J. Brown et al., "Sexy Media Matter: Exposure to Sexual Content in Music, Movies, Television, and Magazines Predicts Black and White Adolescents' Sexual Behavior," *Pediatrics* 117 (April 2006):, 1018–27.

9. The Kaiser Foundation, "Gender Roles: A Series of National Surveys of Teens about Sex," December 2002, http://wayback.archive.org/web/20060308172558/http://www.kff.org/entpartnerships/upload/Gender-Rolls-Summary.pdf. Accessed February 9, 2015.

10. D. Hallfors, M. Waller, C. Ford, C. Halpern, P. Brodish, and B. Iritani, "Adolescent Depression and Suicide Risk: Association with Sex and Drug Behavior," *American Journal of Preventive Medicine* 27, no. 3(2004): 224–31.

11. Joseph J Sabiaa, and Daniel I. Rees, "The Effect of Adolescent Virginity Status on Psychological Well-Being," *Journal of Health Economics* 27, no. 5 (2008): 1368–81; and R. Rector, K. Johnson and L. Noyes, "Sexually Active Teenagers Are More Likely to Be Depressed and to Attempt Suicide," The Heritage Foundation,

2003, http://www.heritage.org/research/reports/2003/06/sexually-active-teenagers-are-more-likely-to-be-depressed. Accessed February 9, 2015.

12. Ilene Lelchuk, "UCSF Explores Teens' Post-Sex Emotions," *San Francisco Chronicle*, November 16, 2007, http://www.sfgate.com/bayarea/article/SAN-FRAN CISCO-UCSF-explores-teens-post-sex-2617439.php. Accessed February 9, 2015.

13. L. Bogart, R. Collins, P. Ellickson, and D. Klein, "Association of Sexual Abstinence in Adolescence with Mental Health in Adulthood," *Journal of Sex Research* 44, no. 3 (2007): 290–98, http://www.tandfonline.com/doi/abs/10.1080/00224490701444005#. VNkdCEJvmGM, accessed February 9, 2015; and R. Finger, T. Thelen, J. Vessey, J. Mohm, and J. Mann, "Association of Virginity at Age 18 with Educational, Economic, Social, and Health Outcomes in Middle Adulthood," *Adolescent and Family Health* 3, no. 4 (2004): 164–70.

14. Bradley, 25.

15. Chap Clark, *Hurt 2.0: Inside the World of Today's Teenagers* (Grand Rapids: Baker Academic, 2011), 125–26.

16. Solarz, "Developing Adolescents," 8.

17. Tripp, 87.

Chapter 14 But It's Mine

1. You can find Joshua Becker at www.becomingminimalist.com. He is the author of *Simplify: 7 Guiding Principles to Help Anyone Declutter Their Home and Life* and *Living with Less: An Unexpected Key to Happiness*.

2. This and the following quotes come from a personal interview with Joshua Becker, March 19, 2015.

3. B. Knutson et al, "Neural Predictors of Purchases," *Neuron* 53, no. 1 (January 2007), 147–56, http://ac.els-cdn.com/S0896627306009044/1-s2.0-S0896627306009044-main.pdf?_tid=f907716e-ce65–11e4-b500–00000aab0f02&acdnat=1426789989_004 9a7fec74d684f3ee77d11cfd8461e. Accessed March 20, 2015.

4. Marsha L. Richins, "When Wanting Is Better Than Having: Materialism, Transformation Expectations, and Product-Evoked Emotions in the Purchase Process," *Journal of Consumer Research* 40 (June 2013), 1–18. Emphasis added.

5. Martin Lindstrom, *Buyology: Truth and Lies about Why We Buy* (New York: Crown Business, 2008), 124–26.

6. Martin Lindstrom, *Brand Sense: Sensory Secrets Behind the Stuff We Buy* (New York: Free Press, 2010), 5.

7. Ibid., 134–35.

8. Tim Kasser, *The High Price of Materialism* (Cambridge, MA: MIT Press, 2002), 22.

9. Thorin Klosowski, "Why We're So Materialistic, Even Though It Doesn't Make Us Happy," December 19, 2013, accessed March 20, 2015, at http://lifehacker.com/why-were-so-materialistic-even-though-it-doesnt-make-1486081424.

10. M. Bauer, J. Wilkie, J. Kim, and G. Bodenhausen, "Cuing Consumerism: Situational Materialism Undermines Personal and Social Well-Being," *Psychological Science* 23, no. 5 (2012): 517–23, http://faculty.wcas.northwestern.edu/bodenhausen/BWKB2012.pdf. Accessed March 20, 2015.

11. Results of market research firm OnePoll.com's survey of 2,000 shoppers, summarized by Dayana Yochim, "Women Spend 399 Hours a Year Shopping," The

Motley Fool, February 28, 2011, http://www.fool.com/how-to-invest/personal-finance/savings/2011/02/28/women-spend-399-hours-a-year-shopping.aspx. Accessed March 20, 2015.

    12. Melinda Beck, "Thank You. No, Thank You: Grateful People Are Happier, Healthier Long after the Leftovers Are Gobbled Up," *Wall Street Journal*, November 23, 2010.

    13. C. Nathal DeWall et al., "A Grateful Heart Is a Nonviolent Heart: Cross-Sectional Experience Sampling, Longitudinal, and Experimental Evidence," *Social Psychological & Personality Science* 3, no. 2 (March 2012): 232–40.

    14. Richard Swenson, *In Search of Balance* (Colorado Springs: NavPress, 2010), 40.

    15. G. K. Chesterton, *The Crimes of England* (1915; A Word to the Wise ebook version, 2013), frontmatter.

    16. See Augustine, *City of God*, Book IV, 33, trans. Marcus Dods (Peabody, MA: Hendrickson, 2009), 125–126.

Chapter 15 Hold On, I Just Have to Send This

    1. M. Becker, R. Alzahabi, and C. Hopwood, "Media Multitasking Is Associated with Symptoms of Depression and Social Anxiety," *Cyberpsychology, Behavior, and Social Networking* 16, no. 2 (February 2013): 132–35, http://www.ncbi.nlm.nih.gov/pubmed/23126438, accessed March 23, 2015; and V. Rideout, U. Foehr, and D. Roberts, "Generation M2: Media in the Lives of 8- to 18-Year Olds," Kaiser Family Foundation, January 2010, accessed March 23, 2015, at https://kaiserfamilyfoundation.files.wordpress.com/2013/04/8010.pdf, accessed March 23, 2015.

    2. Frances E. Jensen with Amy Ellis Nutt, *The Teenage Brain: A Neuroscientist's Survival Guide to Raising Adolescents and Young Adults* (London, UK: Thorsons, 2015), 207–11.

    3. Personal interview with Dr. Jay Giedd, March 1, 2015.

    4. Amanda Lenhart, "Teens, Smartphones & Texting," Pew Research Center Report, March 19, 2012, http://www.pewinternet.org/2012/03/19/teens-smartphones-texting/, accessed March 23, 2015; "Share of teenagers who owned a cell phone or smartphone in the United States in 2012, by race/ethnicity," Statista.com, http://www.statista.com/statistics/256542/teen-cell-phone-and-smartphone-ownership-in-the-us-by-ethnicity/, accessed October 12, 2015.

    5. Alex Cocotas, "Kids Send a Mind Boggling Number of Texts Every Month," *Business Insider*, March 22, 2013, http://www.businessinsider.com/chart-of-the-day-number-of-texts-sent-2013-3. Accessed March 23, 2015.

    6. L. Rosen, K. Whaling, L. Carrier, N. Cheever, and J. Rokkum, "The Media and Technology Usage and Attitudes Scale: An Empirical Investigation," *Computer in Human Behavior* 29, no. 6 (November 2013): 2501–11, http://www.ncbi.nlm.nih.gov/pmc/articles/PMC4338964/. Accessed March 23, 2015.

    7. S. Lemola, N. Perkinson-Gloor, S. Brand, J. Dewald-Kaufmann, and A. Grob, "Adolescents' Electronic Media Use at Night, Sleep Disturbance, and Depressive Symptoms in the Smartphone Age," *Journal of Youth and Adolescence* 44, no. 2 (February 2015):405–18, http://link.springer.com/article/10.1007%2Fs10964–014–0176-x#page-1. Accessed March 23, 2015.

    8. Payne, 104, 112.

9. Todd Wilms, "It Is Time for a 'Parental Control, No Texting While Driving' Phone," Forbes.com, September 18, 2012. Accessed October 19, 2015, at http://www.forbes.com/sites/sap/2012/09/18/it-is-time-for-a-parental-control-no-texting-while-driving-phone.

10. Dr. Gary Chapman and Arlene Pellicane, *Growing Up Social: Raising Relational Kids in a Screen-Driven World* (Chicago: Northfield Publishing, 2014), 44.

11. E. Tandoc, P. Ferrucci, and M. Duffy, "Facebook Use, Envy, and Depression among College Students: Is Facebooking Depressing?" *Computers in Human Behavior* 43 (February 2015): 139–46.

12. Keith Wilcox and Andrew T. Stephen, "Are Close Friends the Enemy? Online Social Networks, Self-Esteem, and Self-Control," *Social Science Research Network*, September 22, 2012.

13. University of Edinburgh Business School, "More Facebook Friends Means More Stress, Says Report," *Science Daily*, November 26, 2012, http://www.sciencedaily.com/releases/2012/11/121126131218.htm. Accessed March 23, 2015.

14. We recommend Chapman and Pellicane's discussion of this in *Growing Up Social*, 80–82.

15. "Statistics: Product," Youtube.com, https://www.youtube.com/yt/press/statistics.html. Accessed March 23, 2015.

16. Susanne Ault, "Survey: YouTube Stars More Popular Than Mainstream Celebs Among US Teens," *Variety Digital News*, August 5, 2014, https://variety.com/2014/digital/news/survey-youtube-stars-more-popular-than-mainstream-celebs-among-u-s-teens-1201275245/. Accessed March 23, 2015.

17. Katie Marsal, "Apple's iOS App Store reaches record 7.8M daily downloads," Apple Insider, http://appleinsider.com/articles/14/11/24/apples-ios-app-store-reaches-record-78m-daily-downloads. Accessed March 23, 2015.

18. "Google Search Statistics," available live at Internet Live Stats, http://www.internetlivestats.com/google-search-statistics/. Accessed March 23, 2015.

19. "Total Number of Websites," statistics available live at *Internet Live Stats*, http://www.internetlivestats.com/total-number-of-websites/. Accessed March 23, 2015.

20. Nicholas Carr, *The Shallows: What the Internet Is Doing to Our Brains* (New York: W. W. Norton, 2011), 125 and 116.

21. Kathy Koch, *Screens and Teens: Connecting with Our Kids in a Wireless World* (Chicago: Moody, 2015), 83.

22. Ibid.

23. Swenson, 205.

24. Andy Henion and Mark Becker, "Multiple Media Use Tied To Depression, Anxiety," *Michigan State University Today*, December 4, 2012, http://msutoday.msu.edu/news/2012/multiple-media-use-tied-to-depression-anxiety/. Accessed March 23, 2015.

25. Leaf, *Switch On Your Brain*, 102.

26. Gaëlle Desbordes et al., "Effects of Mindful-Attention and Compassion Meditation Training on Amygdala Response to Emotional Stimuli in an Ordinary, Non-Meditative State," *Frontiers in Human Neuroscience*, November 1, 2012, http://www.ncbi.nlm.nih.gov/pmc/articles/PMC3485650/. Accessed March 23, 2015.

27. Maria Konnikova, "The Power of Concentration," *New York Times Sunday Review*, December 15, 2012, http://www.nytimes.com/2012/12/16/opinion/sunday/the-power-of-concentration.html?_r=0. Accessed March 23, 2015.

28. Robert Siciliano, "Teens' Online Behavior Can Get Them in Trouble," McAfee, June 3, 2014, https://blogs.mcafee.com/consumer/teens-and-screens. Accessed March 24, 2015.

Chapter 16 It's Not That Bad

1. Siegel, *Brainstorm*, 90–91.
2. Steinberg, 17.
3. Adapted from Chapman and Pellicane, 21–22, and Tripp, 155.
4. Fay and Cline, 73.
5. Tripp, 155.
6. Burns, 157.
7. Eric Stice and Heather Shaw, "Adverse Effects of the Media Portrayed Thin-Ideal on Women and Linkages to Bulimic Symptomatology," *Journal of Social and Clinical Psychology* 13, no. 3 (1994): 288–308, https://www.deepdyve.com/lp/guilford-press/adverse-effects-of-the-media-portrayed-thin-ideal-on-women-and-Zfe0lnCqiO. Accessed March 26, 2015.
8. Wendy Spettigue and Katherine A. Henderson, "Eating Disorders and the Role of the Media," *Journal of the Canadian Academy of Child and Adolescent Psychiatry* 13, no. 1 (February 2004): 16–19, http://www.ncbi.nlm.nih.gov/pmc/articles/PMC2533817/. Accessed March 26, 2015.
9. "The Body Project: Facilitator Fact Sheet," The Body Project, http://www.bodyprojectsupport.org/assets/pdf/materials/facilitator_fact_sheet.pdf. Accessed March 26, 2015.
10. Allison Field, et al., "Prospective Associations of Concerns about Physique and the Development of Obesity, Binge Drinking, and Drug Use Among Adolescent Boys and Young Adult Men," *The Journal of the American Medical Association Pediatrics* 168, no. 1 (January 2014): 34–39, http://archpedi.jamanetwork.com/article.aspx?articleid=1766495. Accessed March 26, 2015.
11. Feinstein, 89 and 91.
12. Ibid.
13. Zaheer Hussain and Mark Griffiths, "Excessive Use of Massively Multi-Player Online Role-Playing Games: A Pilot Study," *International Journal of Mental Health and Addiction* 7, no. 4 (October 2009): 563–71, http://link.springer.com/article/10.1007%2Fs11469–009–9202–8. Accessed March 26, 2015.
14. The American Academy of Pediatrics, "Policy Statement—Media Education," http://pediatrics.aappublications.org/content/early/2010/09/27/peds.2010–1636.full.pdf+html. Accessed March 27, 2015.
15. Chapman and Pellicane, 76.
16. *Random House Dictionary*, s.v. "pop culture" (New York: Random House, 2015).
17. Walt Mueller, "5 Truths About Pop Culture," Center for Parent/Youth Understanding, 2004, http://www.cpyu.org/resource/5-truths-about-pop-culture/. Accessed March 27, 2015.
18. Leaf, *Switch On Your Brain*, 85.
19. Francois Fénelon, *Fénelon: Talking with God*, modern English version, trans. Hal M. Helms (Brewster, MA: Paraclete Press, 1997), 76.

Chapter 17: How Do I Know That's True?

1. Kara E. Powell and Chap Clark, *Sticky Faith: Everyday Ideas to Build Lasting Faith in Your Kids* (Grand Rapids: Zondervan, 2011), 15–16.

2. Dr. Andrew Newberg, quoted in Robert Crosby, "Faith and the Brain: An interview with Dr. Andrew Newberg," *Leadership Journal*, Summer 2014, 29, emphasis added.

3. Ibid., 28.

4. Ibid., 28.

5. Ibid., 29.

6. Fuller Search Institute, *Effective Christian Education: A National Study of Protestant Congregations* (Minneapolis: Search Institute, 1990), quoted in Powell and Clark, 64.

7. Powell and Clark, 77.

8. Ibid., 73.

9. Ibid., 46.

10. The thoughts in this paragraph were inspired by Paul David Tripp's teaching.

11. Steinberg, 34.

12. Ibid.

13. Daniel Kahneman, *Thinking, Fast and Slow* (New York: Farrar, Straus and Giroux, 2011), 24.

Chapter 18 It's Not My Fault

1. Francis Collins, Lowell Weiss, and Kathy Hudson, "The Heredity and Humanity: Have No Fear. Genes Aren't Everything," *The New Republic*, June 25, 2001, http://www.arn.org/docs2/news/heredityandhumanity0711.htm. Accessed April 7, 2015.

2. Tripp, 112.

3. Fay and Cline, 14.

Chapter 19 I Can't Take This!

1. Lisa Eiland and Russell D. Romeo, "Stress and the Developing Adolescent Brain," *Neuroscience* 249 (2013), 162–71.

2. Jensen, 22.

3. Research conducted by the American Psychological Association, referenced in Swenson, 160. See also Dr. Caroline Leaf, *Who Switched Off My Brain: Controlling Toxic Thoughts and Emotions* (Southlake, TX: Switch On Your Brain International, 2007), 9.

4. Feinstein, 58, and Jensen, 172–73.

5. John C. Ortberg, "Taking Care of Busyness," *Leadership Journal*, Fall 1998, http://www.christianitytoday.com/le/1998/fall/8l4028.html; and Bill Gaultiere, "Ruthlessly Eliminate Hurry," February 20, 2013, http://www.soulshepherding.org/2013/02/ruthlessly-eliminate-hurry/. Accessed April 9, 2015.

6. Swenson, 85.

7. This idea adapted from Richard Swenson's thoughts. See Swenson, 71.

8. Thanks to Dr. Daniel Siegel for this fantastic phrase!

9. Siegel, 291.

Chapter 20 I'm So Tired

1. Valerie Strauss, "Checking It Out: Why Teens Stay Up Late—and School Starts Early," *The Washington Post*, October 6, 2009, http://voices.washingtonpost.com/answer-sheet/sleep/checking-it-out-why-do-teens-g.html. Accessed January 5, 2015.

2. "Sleep, Learning, and Memory," Division of Sleep Medicine, Harvard Medical School, http://healthysleep.med.harvard.edu/healthy/matters/benefits-of-sleep/learning-memory. Accessed on January 7, 2015.

3. "Benefits of Sleep," Division of Sleep Medicine, Harvard Medical School, http://healthysleep.med.harvard.edu/healthy/matters/benefits-of-sleep. Accessed on January 5, 2015.

4. "Consequences of Insufficient Sleep," Division of Sleep Medicine, Harvard Medical School, http://healthysleep.med.harvard.edu/healthy/matters/consequences. Accessed on January 7, 2015.

5. Payne, 110.

6. Siegel, *Brainstorm*, 256.

7. C. Calamaro, T Mason, and S. Ratcliffe, "Adolescents Living the 24/7 Lifestyle: Effects of Caffeine and Technology on Sleep Duration and Daytime Functioning," *Pediatrics* 123, no. 6 (June 2009): 1005–10, http://www.ncbi.nlm.nih.gov/pubmed/19482732. Accessed January 7, 2015.

8. Feinstein, 72.

9. "Teens and Sleep," National Sleep Foundation, http://sleepfoundation.org/sleep-topics/teens-and-sleep. Accessed January 7, 2015.

10. See Amy Wolfson and Mary Carskadon, "Understanding Adolescents' Sleep Patterns and School Performance: A Critical Appraisal," *Sleep Medicine Reviews* 7, no. 6 (2003): 491–506; and Scott E. Carrell, Teny Maghakian, and James E. West, "A's from Zzzz's? The Causal Effect of School Start Time on the Academic Achievement of Adolescents," American Economic Journal: Economic Policy 3, no. 3: 62–81, accessed November 5, 2015, at http://pubs.aeaweb.org/doi/pdfplus/10.1257/pol.3.3.62.

11. Sarah McKibben, "Wake-Up Call," *The Association for Supervision and Curriculum Development Newsletter* 56, no. 4 (April 2014), http://www.ascd.org/publications/newsletters/education_update/apr14/vol56/num04/Wake-Up_Call.aspx. Accessed January 5, 2015.

12. "Teens, School and Sleep: A Complex Relationship," The National Sleep Foundation, http://sleepfoundation.org/sleep-news/teens-school-and-sleep-complex-relationship. Accessed January 5, 2015.

13. "Let Them Sleep: AAP Recommends Delaying Start Times of Middle and High Schools to Combat Teen Sleep Deprivation," American Academy of Pediatrics, August 25, 2014, http://www.aap.org/en-us/about-the-aap/aap-press-room/Pages/Let-Them-Sleep-AAP-Recommends-Delaying-Start-Times-of-Middle-and-High-Schools-to-Combat-Teen-Sleep-Deprivation.aspx#sthash.gXXwmkJO.dpuf. Accessed January 7, 2015.

14. "Teens and Sleep," 1.

15. Dr. Helene A. Emsellem, with Carol Whiteley, *Snooze or Lose: 10 "No-War" Ways to Improve Your Teen's Sleep Habits* (Washington, DC: Joseph Henry Press, 2006), 25, 44.

16. Editorial board, "A Smarter Way to Start High-Schoolers' Days," *The Washington Post*, August 18, 2013, https://www.washingtonpost.com/opinions/a-smarter

-way-to-start-high-schoolers-days/2013/08/18/e2d24276-f49f-11e2-9434-60440856fa
df_story.html. Accessed January 7, 2015.

17. McKibben, "Wake-Up Call."

18. Meeri Kim, "Blue Light from Electronics Disturbs Sleep, Especially for Teen-agers," *The Washington Post*, September 1, 2014, https://www.washingtonpost.com/national/health-science/blue-light-from-electronics-disturbs-sleep-especially-for-te enagers/2014/08/29/3edd2726-27a7-11e4-958c-268a320a60ce_story.html. Accessed January 7, 2015.

19. Beth Kassab, "Are You Addicted to Your Smartphone?" *Orlando Sentinel*, November 25, 2013.

20. Michelle Healy, "Docs Urge Delayed School Start Times for Teens," *USA Today*, August 25, 2014, http://www.usatoday.com/story/news/nation/2014/08/25/pediatricians-late-school-start-time-good-for-teens/14338565/. Accessed January 7, 2015.

Chapter 21 I'm Starving

1. Some recommend following a 90/10 rule, and we can attest that the healthier you and your teen eat, the better you'll both feel.

2. Note: This chapter will cover topics of nutrition. For information on body image and the interplay during adolescence, turn to chapter 24, "I Feel So Ugly."

3. Dr. Daniel Amen, *Change Your Brain, Change Your Body* (New York: Three Rivers Press, 2010), 83.

4. Adapted from Amen, 83–84.

5. "Economic Census: Industry Snapshots, Accommodation and Food Services (NAICS 72)," US Census Bureau, 2012, http://thedataweb.rm.census.gov/TheDataWeb_HotReport2/econsnapshot/2012/snapshot.hrml?NAICS=72. Accessed January 8, 2015.

6. See "2014 Restaurant Industry Forecast," National Restaurant Association, http://www.restaurant.org/News-Research/Research/Facts-at-a-Glance. Accessed January 8, 2015.

7. "What to Do When There Are Too Many Product Choices on the Store Shelves?" *Consumer Reports*, January 2014, http://www.consumerreports.org/cro/magazine/2014/03/too-many-product-choices-in-supermarkets/index.htm. Accessed January 8, 2015.

8. J. Savage, J. Fisher, L. Birch. "Parental Influence on Eating Behavior: Conception to Adolescence," *The Journal of Law, Medicine & Ethics* 35, no. 1 (2007): 22–34, accessed October 22, 2015, at http://www.ncbi.nlm.nih.gov/pmc/articles/PMC2531152/#R3.

9. Centers for Disease Control, "Nutrition and the Health of Young People," updated August 28, 2015, and accessed October 22, 2015, at http://www.cdc.gov/healthyschools/nutrition/facts.htm.

10. A. Hoyland, L. Dye, C. L. Lawton, "A Systematic Review of the Effect of Breakfast on the Cognitive Performance of Children and Adolescents," *Nutrition Research Reviews* 22 (2009): 220–43.

11. Rick Warren, Dr. Daniel Amen, Dr. Mark Hyman, *The Daniel Plan: 40 Days to a Healthier Life* (Grand Rapids: Zondervan, 2013), 38.

12. You can find a list of the top fifty brain foods on the Amen Clinics website at http://www.amenclinics.com/cybcyb/50-best-brain-foods/.

13. Marcus Samuelsson, "Cooking for Huffington Post's Oasis and Teaching Healthy Eating Habits," *Huffington Post Food*, October 6, 2011, http://www.huffingtonpost.com/marcus-samuelsson/cooking-for-huffington-po_b_998255.html. Accessed May 20, 2015.

Chapter 22 What's Wrong with Me?

1. Steinberg, *Age of Opportunity*, 42–43.
2. Ibid.
3. B. Ellis, S. McFayden-Ketchum, K. Dodge, G. Pettit, and J. Bates, "Quality of Early Family Relationships and Individual Differences in the Timing of Pubertal Maturation in Girls: A Longitudinal Test of an Evolutionary Model," *Journal of Personality and Social Psychology* 77, no. 2 (August 1999): 387–401, http://www.ncbi.nlm.nih.gov/pmc/articles/PMC2791962/. Accessed December 24, 2014.
4. B. Ellis, J. Bates, K. Dodge, D. Ferguson, J. Horwood, G. Pettit, and L. Woodward, "Does Father Absence Place Daughters at Special Risk for Early Sexual Activity and Teenage Pregnancy?" *Child Development* 74 (2003): 801–821.
5. Dobson, *Bringing Up Girls* (Wheaton: Tyndale, 2010), 94.
6. See Lorraine Pintus, *Jump Off the Hormone Swing* (Chicago: Moody Press, 2011), 39–42.
7. Dobson, 204.
8. Pintus, 30.
9. Ibid., 41.
10. Thomas Haberman and Amit K. Ghosh, eds., *Mayo Clinic Internal Medicine Concise Textbook* (Rochester, MN: Mayo Clinic Scientific Press and Informa Health Care, 2008), 879.
11. Dobson, 201.
12. Dr. Louann Brizendine, *The Female Brain* (New York: Broadway Books, 2007), 30.
13. Fascinatingly, high levels of estrogen in infancy are similarly linked with the desire for closeness.
14. Feinstein, 58.
15. Amy LaRue, ND, "Xenoestrogens—What Are They? How to Avoid Them," originally posted in the October 2012 newsletter of the Women in Balance Institute, http://womeninbalance.org/2012/10/26/xenoestrogens-what-are-they-how-to-avoid-them/. Accessed December 24, 2014.
16. "TEDX List of Potential Endocrine Disruptors," TEDX—The Endocrine Disruption Exchange, http://endocrinedisruption.org/endocrine-disruption/tedx-list-of-potential-endocrine-disruptors/overview. Accessed May 22, 2015.
17. Feinstein, 107.

Chapter 23 It's Not All I Think About!

1. Doug Carlson, "Teenage Brain: Studies Explain Risky Behavior," Florida State University Press Release, August 28, 2014, https://www.fsu.edu/indexTOFStory.html?lead.bhide. Accessed April 14, 2015.
2. Ibid.
3. Jensen, 21.

4. Portions of this paragraph adapted from Mark Oestreicher and Brock Morgan, *A Parent's Guide to Understanding Teenage Guys: Remembering Who He Was, Celebrating Who He's Becoming* (Loveland, CO: Group Publishing, 2012).

5. "Pornography Statistics: Annual Report 2015," Covenant Eyes, http://www.covenant eyes.com/pornstats/. Accessed April 14, 2015.

6. "The Stats on Internet Pornography," Daily Infographic, January 4, 2013, http://www.dailyinfographic.com/the-stats-on-internet-pornography-infographic. Accessed April 14, 2015.

7. Ibid.

8. See Valerie Voon et al., "Neural Correlates of Sexual Cue Reactivity in Individuals with and without Compulsive Sexual Behaviours," *PLOS One Journal*, July 11, 2014; Simone Kühn and Jürgen Gallinat, "Brain Structure and Functional Connectivity Associated with Pornography Consumption," *JAMA Psychiatry* 71, no. 7 (2014): 827–34; and see *Your Brain on Porn* at http://www.yourbrainonporn.com/porn-induced-ed-media for an extensive list of articles and videos on the topic.

9. Oestreicher and Morgan, Kindle location, 448–51.

10. Keller made this statement during a lecture on the topic "Redefining Work," given at the Gospel Coalition's 2013 National Conference. Accessed October 24, 2015, at *The Acton Institute Power Blog*, http://blog.acton.org/archives/55225-tim-keller-on-how-the-bible-shapes-the-way-we-work.html.

11. Thanks to Mark Oestreicher and Brock Morgan for this stellar suggestion.

Chapter 24 I Feel So Ugly

1. Constance Rhodes, *Life Inside the Thin Cage* (Colorado Springs: Shaw Books, 2003), 71.

2. Ibid.

3. See Dr. Naomi Weinshenker, "Teenagers and Body Image," May 1, 2014, http://www.education.com/reference/article/Ref_Adolescents_Body/. Accessed February 4, 2015.

4. See National Eating Disorders Association, "A Silent Epidemic," 2012, http://www.nationaleatingdisorders.org/silent-epidemic, accessed February 5, 2015; "11 Facts about Body Image," DoSomething.org, https://www.dosomething.org/facts/11-facts-about-body-image; and Carolyn Costin, *The Eating Disorder Sourcebook* (Los Angeles, CA: Lowell House, 1999), 83.

5. Dana Hudepohl, "How Much Would You Risk to Lose Weight?" *Glamour*, July 2002, 81.

6. Shaun Dreisbach, "Shocking Body-Image News: 97% of Women Will Be Cruel to Their Bodies Today," *Glamour*, February 3, 2011, http://www.glamour.com/health-fitness/2011/02/shocking-body-image-news-97-percent-of-women-will-be-cruel-to-their-bodies-today. Accessed February 4, 2015.

7. Ibid.

8. Jennifer L. Bedford and Susan Barr, "The Relationship between 24-Hr Urinary Cortisol and Bone in Healthy Young Women," *International Journal of Behavioral Medicine* 17, no. 3 (September 2010): 207–215.

9. Dreisbach, 1.

10. For a scientific review of 77 studies that link media exposure to negative body image, see S. Grabe, L. Ward, and J. Hyde, "The Role of the Media in Body Image

Concerns Among Women: A Meta-Analysis of Experimental and Correlational Studies," *Psychological Bulletin* 134 (2008): 460–76.

11. B. J. Gallagher, *Everything I Need to Know I Learned from Other Women* (York Beach, ME: Cohari, 2002), 109.

12. Dreisbach, 1.

13. Rhodes, 135.

14. Michelle Graham, *Wanting to Be Her* (Downer's Grove, IL: InterVarsity Press, 2005), 159.

15. Ibid.

16. J. Arcelus, A. Mitchell, J. Wales, and S. Nielsen, "Mortality Rates in Patients with Anorexia Nervosa and Other Eating Disorders," *Archives of General Psychiatry* 68, no. 7 (2011): 724–31.

17. Dr. Alan Schwitzer, quoted in Rhodes, *Life Inside the "Thin" Cage*, 22.

Chapter 25 I Hate My Life

1. Siegel, *Brainstorm*, 97–98.

2. Ibid., 99.

3. Ibid.

4. Feinstein, 107.

5. "Shrinkage, Not the Shrinks," *BrainWise*, Johns Hopkins Department of Psychiatry and Behavioral Sciences (Winter 2008), http://www.hopkinsmedicine.org/psychiatry/about/publications/newsletter/archive/08_winter/shrinkage.html. Accessed December 23, 2014.

6. Adapted from "Recognizing Teen Depression," MedlinePlus, National Institutes of Mental Health, http://www.nlm.nih.gov/medlineplus/ency/patientinstructions/000648.htm. Accessed December 15, 2014.

7. Bradley, 326.

8. "Treatment for Adolescents with Depression Study (TADS)," National Institute of Mental Health, 2009, http://www.nimh.nih.gov/funding/clinical-trials-for-researchers/practical/tads/index.shtml. Accessed December 23, 2014.

9. "Treatment of SSRI-resistant Depression in Adolescents (TORDIA)," National Institute of Mental Health, updated March 11, 2014, https://www.clinicaltrials.gov/ct2/show/NCT00018902, accessed October 24, 2015.

10. Dr. Earl Henslin, *This Is Your Brain on Joy* (Nashville: Thomas Nelson, 2009), 145.

11. Leaf, *Switch on Your Brain*, 31–32.

Chapter 26 What If . . . ?

1. E. J. Costello, S. Mustillo, A. Erkanli, G. Keeler, and A. Angold, "Prevalence and Development of Psychiatric Disorders in Childhood and Adolescence," *Archives of General Psychiatry* 60 (2003): 837–844.

2. Tara S. Peris and Adriana Galván, "Contextual Modulation of Medial Prefrontal Cortex to Neutral Faces in Anxious Adolescents," *Biology of Mood & Anxiety Disorders* 3 (2013): 18, http://www.biolmoodanxietydisord.com/content/3/1/18#B2. Accessed December 22, 2014.

3. These areas include the hippocampus, frontal lobe, and corpus callosum. See Leaf, 181–82.

4. See Payne, 80.

5. Ibid., 208.

6. Dan Baker, PhD, and Cameron Stauth, *What Happy People Know: How the New Science of Happiness Can Change Your Life for the Better* (New York: St. Martin's Press, 2003), 81.

7. Ann Voskamp, *One Thousand Gifts: A Dare to Live Fully Right Where You Are* (Grand Rapids: Zondervan, 2010), 72.

Appendix A The Truth about Substance Abuse

1. See Siegel, *Brainstorm*, 264.

2. Payne, 89.

3. Statistics in this section from the US Centers for Disease Control and Prevention, "Alcohol and Public Health: Frequently Asked Questions," http://www.cdc.gov/alcohol/faqs.htm#young. Accessed April 16, 2015.

Appendix B The Truth about Self-Injury

1. "Fast Facts: Overview," International Society for the Study of Self-Injury, http://itriples.org/self-injury/fast-facts/. Accessed April 16, 2015.

2. Quotes taken from a self-injury forum, "PRO_SI," LiveJournal forum, http://pro-si.livejournal.com. Accessed April 16, 2015. Caution: this journal can be explicit and is not recommended for teens.

3. Lewis Smedes, *Shame and Grace: Healing the Shame We Don't Deserve* (New York: HarperCollins, 1993), 108.

Appendix C The Truth about Suicide

1. Statistics from the US Centers for Disease Control, "Suicide Prevention: Youth Suicide," updated March 10, 2015, http://www.cdc.gov/ViolencePrevention/suicide/youth_suicide.html. Accessed April 16, 2015.

2. Burns, 209.

3. Ibid.

4. "Suicide," *TeensHealth*, reviewed by D'Arcy Lyness, PhD, July 2014, http://kidshealth.org/teen/your_mind/feeling_sad/suicide.html. Accessed April 17, 2015.

Dr. Jeramy Clark received his Masters of Divinity and Doctorate of Ministry from Talbot Theological Seminary. He served as a youth pastor for seventeen years before becoming the pastor of discipleship at Emmanuel Faith Community Church. His role includes overseeing men's and women's ministries, care and counseling, and small groups. Jeramy roasts, brews, and savors coffee of all varieties, plays pickup basketball, is a drummer, and enjoys surfing.

Jerusha Clark coauthored four books with Jeramy, including three bestsellers, prior to launching a writing and speaking ministry focused on helping others glorify and enjoy God, one thought at a time. Her books include *Every Thought Captive*, *The Life You Crave*, and *When I Get Married*. Jerusha has also written on depression, self-injury, and other mental health concerns. On quiet days, you can find Jerusha bodyboarding or reading at the beach, her absolute favorite place. Jeramy and Jerusha have two amazing teenage daughters and love ministering together at churches, retreats, schools, and conferences. The Clarks live in Escondido, California.